The Judicial Imagination

Arendt in Orin? Jute la...
p. 130

when a person
becomes human
in general."

#p.29 the collapse
of the morally
sacred

p.24 - any event that
doesn't become
took or it become
an expedient in

p.2 → Nazi lawlessness

p.3: today: attention to
the power of memory, of survival

p.24 to restore ethical
meaning

must also despair...

P.10 ✓ ethic of justice for the...

P.16 ***
p.32 justice is a memory of
victims

The Judicial Imagination

Writing After Nuremberg

Lyndsey Stonebridge

Edinburgh University Press

© Lyndsey Stonebridge, 2011, 2014

Edinburgh University Press Ltd
The Tun – Holyrood Road
12(2f) Jackson's Entry
Edinburgh EH8 8PJ

First published in hardback by Edinburgh University Press 2011

www.euppublishing.com

Typeset in 10.5/13 pt Sabon
by Servis Filmsetting Ltd, Stockport, Cheshire, and
printed and bound in the United States of America

A CIP record for this book is available from the British Library

ISBN 978 0 7486 4235 9 (hardback)
ISBN 978 0 7486 9125 8 (paperback)
ISBN 978 0 7486 8891 3 (epub)

The right of Lyndsey Stonebridge
to be identified as author of this work
has been asserted in accordance with the
Copyright, Designs and Patents Act 1988,
and the Copyright and Related Rights
Regulations 2003 (SI No. 2498).

Contents

Acknowledgements   vii
Illustrations   ix

Introduction
Gathering Ashes:
The Judicial Imagination in the Age of Trauma   1

Part I: Writing After Nuremberg

1. 'An event that did not become an experience':
    Rebecca West's Nuremberg   23

2. The Man in the Glass Booth:
    Hannah Arendt's Irony   47

3. Fiction in Jerusalem:
    Muriel Spark's Idiom of Judgement   73

Part II: Territorial Rights

4. 'We Refugees':
    Hannah Arendt and the Perplexities of Human Rights   101

5. 'Creatures of an Impossible Time':
    Late Modernism, Human Rights and Elizabeth Bowen   118

6. The 'Dark Background of Difference':
    Love and the Refugee in Iris Murdoch   141

Bibliography   166
Index   173

Acknowledgements

My first thanks are to those gracious and generous colleagues in the Faculty of Arts and Humanities at the University of East Anglia who covered for me while I completed this book on leave; special thanks are due to Mark Jancovich, Stephen Benson and Karen Schaller. A travel grant from the British Academy made possible my work in the Muriel Spark and Rebecca West archives at the McFarlin Library, Special Collections, University of Tulsa, where I benefited from the kind assistance of Marc Carlson and his colleagues. Thanks too to the Cogut and Pembroke Centers at Brown University for inviting me to speak on West and Hannah Arendt. Earlier versions of Chapter 2 and Chapter 4 were published in *New Formations* and *Textual Practice* and I am grateful for permission to reproduce some of that work here. The Department of Gender and Cultural Studies at the University of Sydney was a wonderful place to visit while I was writing this book; warm thanks to Natalya Lusty and the members of my Arendt and Freud masterclass (and Ross Jones and Gordon Bey). In Cenne Monesties, France, I thank my mother, Jean McCaig (for the pop-up maternelle), Dennis Kennedy (*mon lecteur*) and Christa Lutter (for Mulisch and Montauban). The following friends and colleagues have also enriched this project with their generous sharing of thoughts and work: Mary Jacobus, Marina MacKay, Dirk Moses, Patricia Owens, Adam Piette, Rachel Potter, Debra Rae Cohen, Denise Riley, Michael Rothberg, Eyal Sivan, Suzanne Stewart Steinberg and Rebecca Stott. Andy Carpenter and Joe Kennedy gave invaluable assistance in putting the manuscript together. Jackie Jones at Edinburgh University Press understood and supported this project from the beginning. My children, those fierce advocates of natural justice, Joe and Mizzy, were brilliant at fighting off the Sontarans so I could write in peace. Their father and my partner, Shaun Hargreaves Heap, carried our home on his back, sometimes quite literally, as we zigzagged across continents; I thank and salute him.

Illustrations

Figure 1   Rebecca West's Visitor Pass for the International Military Tribunal at Nuremberg. Reproduced by kind permission of the Special Collections, McFarlin Library, University of Tulsa.

Figure 2   From *The Specialist* (1999), Rony Brauman and Eyal Sivan. Reproduced by kind permission of Eyal Sivan.

For my mother, with thanks

Gathering Ashes: The Judicial Imagination in the Age of Trauma

She thought: there will have to be a terrible justice blowing
all over the world to avenge all the needless suffering [. . .]
It will take a long time to change this, she thought, we learn
very little, we learn very slowly. She was afraid she would be
reporting disaster and defeat her whole life.

    I'm not getting anywhere, she thought. What I need is an
opening sentence, not a conclusion.

Martha Gellhorn, A Stricken Field (1940)[1]

Justice requires us to calculate with the incalculable.

Jacques Derrida, 'Force of Law'[2]

Witness to the first convulsions of the Nazi occupation of Europe
in Czechoslovakia, journalist Mary Douglas, in Martha Gellhorn's
extraordinarily prescient 1940 novel, *A Stricken Field*, imagines a future
justice: a terrible justice, she thinks it will have to be, to avenge all this
senseless, needless suffering. But even as the demand for justice lies
everywhere around her – in the arbitrary arrests, capricious violence,
lines of desperate refugees, and lost and starving children that the novel
describes with such immediacy – Mary has doubts. What if we take so
long to understand the nature of this crime that it simply keeps on per-
petrating itself? What if we can never catch up with justice? On the other
hand, if we arrive at justice too soon, do we not risk falsely concluding
an event we have only begun to comprehend? I need a beginning, not a
conclusion, she thinks.

    It is not just because she is pressed too close to the moment that
Mary cannot find her beginning. You do not form a sense from
Gellhorn's novel that, given time, history will eventually unravel itself
into a moral narrative. Something about what Mary witnesses resists

being put into writing. Gellhorn knew this; in fact, it was why she wrote the novel in the first place. Much of *A Stricken Field* incorporates passages from the reports she filed at the same time, as if she had to be in Czechoslovakia twice in 1938, once in fact and once in fiction, to capture what she is seeing. Even the novel's fictional retelling is a belated form of historical witness. Gellhorn later claimed that she wrote about Czechoslovakia because she could not bear to write about the suffering she had seen in the Spanish Civil War. ('The enemy was the same; the people were equally abandoned, alone, and related by pain.'[3]) Desiring a future justice, a conclusion before the end, Gellhorn, like her fictional self-portrait, is instead pulled back to a present of ever-heaping atrocity.

After the war, the law and politics set about furnishing the sort of conclusion desired by Mary Douglas and so many others. As the Nuremberg trial and the Paris Peace Conference in 1946, the drafting of the Universal Declaration of Human Rights in 1948 and, thirteen years later, the trial of Adolf Eichmann in Jerusalem all demonstrated, the law was at its most audacious and creative in the immediate postwar period. This, we are often told, was the dawn of the new era of human rights: a conclusion to the worst that could have happened that would give the world a new moral and political beginning. However much a newly chilly political postwar reality meant that this beginning never really got started, the imaginative pull of that juridical moment was – and remains – considerable. It was a fiercely engaged passion for the future of justice that drew many of the writers discussed in the pages that follow to those events: Rebecca West to Nuremberg, Hannah Arendt and Muriel Spark to the Eichmann trial, Elizabeth Bowen to the Paris Peace Conference, and Martha Gellhorn to all three. But as these concerned and complicated women all also understood, just because the law was at work again, it did not necessarily follow that justice was finally happening. It was not simply a return to the law that was so desperately needed in the wake of Nazi lawlessness, but a way of imagining how what had happened profoundly changed the ways in which it was possible to think about justice and judgement in the first place. Before the world could conclude, it needed to begin again.

Hannah Arendt was one of the first to grasp the political and historical magnitude of this task, which is why her work is the seam that runs straight through this book. The real monstrosity of Nazi totalitarianism, she observed during the Nuremberg trial, was that by making anything possible its crimes exploded 'the limits of the law'. That is why the Nazis on trial at Nuremberg look so smug, she complained in a much-quoted letter to Karl Jaspers; they know that their guilt, in contrast to all criminal guilt, oversteps and shatters any and all systems [. . .] We are simply not equipped to deal, on a human, political with a guilt that is beyond crime and an innocence that is beyond goodn or virtue. This is the abyss that opened up before us as early as 1933 (muc earlier, actually, with onset of imperialistic politics) and into which we have finally stumbled. I don't know how we will ever get out of it.[4]

It is possibly because Gellhorn's Mary Douglas senses the law-shattering potential of what she was witnessing in Europe that she imagines a 'terrible' and avenging postwar justice: as if only an apocalyptic whirlwind – divine justice – could reach down into the abyss. But in his reply, Jaspers cautions Arendt against bestowing Nazi crime with a streak of Biblical 'greatness'. Once you are at the limits of legal reason, it is all too easy to spiral away from the political sense of human justice Arendt so anxiously wants to revive. 'The way you do express it', he writes, 'you've almost taken the path of poetry.'[5] For the rest of her life, Arendt will attempt to arrive at an idiom of judgement that neither normalises the law-shattering nature of Nazi crime, nor turns it into poetry; to find a way of writing, as well as a political philosophy – the tight entwining of the two will prove crucial – capable of rescuing political and juridical life from the abyss into which it had been thrown. Her and others' effort to imagine justice from within the stricken fields of Nazi atrocity is at the heart of the project of this book.

Traumatised law

If the legal system did not shatter, as Arendt first feared, then it continually encountered its own limits in the second half of the twentieth century. Nowhere in the history of postwar justice was this more evident than in the overwhelming testimonies of the survivors who, after years of silence, finally took the stand during the Eichmann trial in 1961. If, today, attending to the traumatic memories of the survivor has become our contemporary judicial paradigm, this, in part, is because of the decision to place witness testimony at the heart of the trial in Jerusalem. The stories told on the witness stand, however, no more fitted into a narrative of beginnings and endings than did the experience Gellhorn struggled to put in writing in 1938. To give a much-cited instance, when the writer and survivor, Ka-Zetnik, finally collapsed in the courtroom, unable to speak any longer, what he testified to was not the story of Auschwitz but the sheer difficulty, some would say impossibility, of putting the experience of the camps into the language demanded by the law. Eichmann may have been the one on trial, but it was the survivors who made their appeal to the court – an appeal to the reality of the camps.

Ka-Zetnik's breakdown in Jerusalem is key to Shoshana Felman's *The Juridical Unconscious: Trials and Traumas in the Twentieth Century* (2002), the first study to disclose the connections between trauma and the law, the trial and literature, legal and poetic justice, also central to my concerns here. For Felman, Ka-Zetnik's collapse embodies the psychic lacuna at the heart of the historical experience of trauma.[6] 'It was', Martha Gellhorn wrote similarly of the trial's testimonies in an article for *The Atlantic*, 'visible torture for all the witnesses to speak; one wandered in his head, screamed something wordless but terrifying to hear, fainted, remembering Auschwitz.'[7] Often, tortured speech erupts in the middle of testimony, as though the abyss into which not only the victims, but the world, had been thrown opens up in the middle of the courtroom. Gellhorn again: 'The old man cried out suddenly, "A planet without a visa!"' The man, a lawyer himself, had been describing carefully, and with a legislator's eye for detail and evidence, what life had been like for Jews in Germany before the war.[8]

Witnessing the testimonies of survivors in the Jerusalem courtroom in 1961, Gellhorn finally discovers the objective and ethical correlative for the justice she had begun to seek in the refugee fields of Czechoslovakia. Neither was she alone in recognising that the outpouring of grief in Jerusalem signalled the beginnings of a new kind of justice. Many see the traumatic testimonies of the Eichmann trial, and those that have followed in more recent trials, as part of a crucial turn from cold universalising reason towards the more contingent hazards of ethical witnessing in postwar legal history. The narrative that leads from silence to witness, from the calculations of the law to recognising the incalculable nature of what was on trial, has today become standard in understandings of postwar law and justice.[9]

In this book, I track a parallel path through the same history. However, rather than taking traumatic testimony as the end point for a more ethical justice, in the chapters that follow I linger with the blocks, political as well as ethical, that Nazi crime put (and continues to put) on historical and judicial understanding. The crime which nobody was meant to see, I argue, left a truly blinding legacy. Not only, as the Nuremberg legislators worried, would seeing not necessarily mean believing (the court made the calculated decision to minimise witness testimony on this basis), but also one of the most pernicious legacies of the camps was the way they set endless demands on comprehension itself. Those demands do not always lead to clarity (which was why Hannah Arendt was critical of the prosecution's promotion of witness testimony during the Eichmann trial). How to judge in a world still fog-bound by Nazi crime is a question that preoccupies most of the writers drawn to the question of justice in this period; the answers they give are not always easy.

Gellhorn, for example, gives an uncomfortable measure of the difficulty of thinking through the fog when she crosses through Jerusalem's Mandelbaum Gate (the no-man's-land that separated Israel and Jordan) in 1961, a passage she describes as a entering into 'world of dream'. (Later Muriel Spark will graft Gellhorn's description of this journey into her novel of the same name.) While her report on the Eichmann trial brilliantly invokes the force of the trauma she witnessed in the courtroom, and is itself an act of ethical witness, the tone for her companion report for *The Atlantic*, 'The Arabs of Palestine', is very different. Measured, precise, descriptive: one might be tempted to describe it as trauma-free, were it not for the sense that the invocation of the trauma of Eichmann's victims makes itself felt in the absolutism with which Gellhorn denies the possibility that the trauma can translate across historical experience. 'None of these Arabs has suffered anything comparable to what survivors of modern war know,' she writes, and then, with breathtaking certainty, 'none can imagine such catastrophe.'[10] There is a deeply felt politics here. Gellhorn was absolutely unwavering in her support for Israel; that was one lesson she said she took from Dachau and she never forgot it. (Gellhorn was one of the first journalists to enter the camp.)[11] More troubling, perhaps, for the ethical turn in some contemporary trauma theory, is the way she grounds that politics on empathy – on imagining the catastrophe.

The Palestinian refugees lack 'empathy', Gellhorn writes (she has been asking them about the Eichmann trial); and it is because they lack the capacity for 'entering into the emotions of others', for hearing and responding to testimony, that Gellhorn in turn feels no empathy for them. 'It is hard to feel sorrow for those who only sorrow over themselves.' Indeed it is. But on what grounds does lacking empathy disqualify one from the entitlement of justice? If justice is to be tied to an empathetic imperative – an imperative to witness and absorb the suffering of the other – how soon before it falters before the fantasy of deserving or undeserving victims? How virtuous does one need to be before one's cries for justice are answered? Absolutely, it seems: 'To wring the heart past all doubt, those who cry aloud for justice must be innocent,' Gellhorn concludes. Empathy, then, becomes the pivot upon which political judgement turns. It is as though the work of 'imagining the catastrophe' (a formulation also evoked in some current trauma theory) can only begin by circumscribing the catastrophe's experiential and imaginative limits.

The point of this example is not to condemn piously the narrowness of Gellhorn's ethical range, as though she should have passed through the Mandelbaum Gate bearing witness to the suffering of all who she encountered, like some kind of saint. The politics of that moment then, as now, are far too bleak. (The intransigence of the political is partly my point here.) It is rather to emphasise how the blinding nature of the Nazi crime can perpetuate itself in the very discourses that are intended to put it on trial. This was a paradox of which Hannah Arendt was keenly aware. As much as historical and judicial comprehension can be transformed by trauma (which is the argument of Felman's *The Juridical Unconscious*), it can also be thwarted or blocked by the effort to contain it, which is my argument here.

Returning to Arendt

'*Beyond the capacities of human comprehension*' (italics in original) is how Arendt once described a world that has rendered the categories of guilt and innocence immobile with its insouciant reduction of human life to mere matter. From Arendt's perspective, to claim, like Gellhorn, that only the absolutely innocent are entitled to justice would be to miss totally the true monstrosity of a crime that attacks not only guiltless victims, but the very basis of comprehension, and hence justice, narrative and history too. 'Human history has known no story more difficult to tell,' she wrote in a 1946 review essay of *The Black Book: The Nazi Crime Against the Jewish People*, one of the first attempts to document the genocide for a disbelieving world. Innocence beyond virtue, and guilt beyond crime, are no longer categories by which to judge, for Arendt, not least because such distinctions have been corrupted irretrievably by the very absolutism that condemned all Jewish people, saints and sinners, small children and those old enough to have good cause for regret, to the 'status of possible corpses' in the first place. Absolute innocence does not wring the heart of all doubt, as in Gellhorn's disturbing formulation; it sets impossible terms on historical judgement itself. This 'monstrous equality in innocence . . . destroys the very basis on which history is produced – which is, namely, our capacity to comprehend an event no matter how distant we are from it.'[12] For Arendt, there can be no future, no new insights, no new memories, unless the 'real story of the Nazi-constructed Hell is told' with this profound rupture in thought and memory firmly in mind.[13]

In what follows I read Arendt as a judicial historiographer of that constructed Hell. In this I take my cue from Seyla Benhabib's *The*

Reluctant Modernism of Hannah Arendt (2000). Reading sometimes with, sometimes against Arendt, Benhabib's study reveals the extent to which she is (like her friend Walter Benjamin) as much a late modernist historiographer of fragmentation, dislocation, displacement and rupture as she is (like her former lover and tutor Martin Heidegger) an early modernist caught in a nostalgic search for 'the lost and concealed essence of phenomena'.[14] While Benhabib's work (like that of Richard Bernstein, Dana Villa, Mary Dietz and Patricia Owens, among others) has done much to retrieve Arendt's work from the cliché of the 'anti-modernist lover of the Greek polis' for political theory, by contrast Anglo-American literary history (unlike comparative literary studies) has been slow to return to her work with a similar curiosity and rigour.[15] This seems strange, to put it mildly, considering just how steeped in literary culture Arendt's work is. Not only does she write, and brilliantly so, on writers such as Schelling, Lessing and Heine, and their heirs, Kafka, Benjamin, Brecht and Isak Dinesen; it takes a peculiarly cloth-like ear not to appreciate the extent to which Arendt understood the close proximity between her thinking and writing. Crystalline structures shatter and re-form in her prose, treasures are lost and found in the art of the essay, as Arendt pursues the foundations of her own thought in a language both stylised and unmistakably edgy. Only now is this aspect of her work coming into critical view.[16]

One suspects, however, that this relative neglect is not just because Arendt's European literary archive is mistaken for a nostalgic evocation of a time before tradition was irretrievably broken (as though she herself had not noticed), but more tellingly because she writes so emphatically outside of the framework of traumatic testimony that has come to dominate discussion of postwar justice. It was, after all, her own cloth ears to the testimony of survivors in *Eichmann in Jerusalem* (1963) which made the book offensive to so many when it was first published. As early as her 1946 review of *The Black Book,* Arendt was clear that, while the real story of the camps must be told, she had doubts about the political–juridical value of such testimony by itself: 'Those who one day may feel strong enough to tell the whole story will have to realize . . . that the story *in itself* [italics in original] can yield nothing but sorrow and despair – least of all, arguments for any specific political purpose.'[17]

Many have read this as a failure of empathy on Arendt's part. (Note how ethics, again, turns on the presence or absence of an empathetic imagination.) But, as I suggest in Chapter 2, this repudiation has less to do with the depth of Arendt's feelings for suffering (which, in any case, we can never know) and more with her sense that the trauma of the camps must be pushed into thinking and judgement. Accusations that Arendt thereby locks suffering out of the political world, thus condemning the victims of the crime she sought to understand all her life to voicelessness, overlook the extent to which the politics of the voice traumatised by Nazi crime is at the very heart of her project. As Benhabib has shown, Arendt's affirmation of the political realm is driven (some might say haunted) by her earlier engagement with the homelessness at the heart of being (*Dasein*) uncovered by existential philosophy. To act in the political world, for Arendt, is to speak that homelessness. Her famous critique of totalitarianism, in this respect, is an attempt to rescue Heidegger's phenomenological subject from a politics of nostalgic despair, for a future politics of plurality.

This shifting between ontology and politics, and correspondingly between trauma and speech, matters for the project of this book because it opens up a different set of connections between trauma, language, and legal and literary justice, from those exposed by theorists of traumatic testimony. When Arendt writes about Eichmann she does so with a biting irony that does not so much (or at least not only) repudiate suffering, as dramatise what it means to think and act in the wake of the catastrophic collapse of distinctions – the making anything possible – of the camps. Irony is not the kind of literary justice that Felman finds disclosed in the mute body of Ka-Zetnik, but it starts from a very similar acknowledgement of the limits of legal reason.[18] It is, indeed, precisely this refusal to abandon political judgement from within, as it were, an abyssal collapse of conceptual categories that gives the texture of Arendt's writing its extraordinary historical charge.

While Arendt's turn to the question of judgement in the wake of the Eichmann trial is well documented in the scholarship on her work (often as a source of political and philosophical trouble), identifying her idiom of judgement as a kind of irony here gives me a starting point from which to reconstruct the development of another tradition of literary justice in the postwar period. Running parallel to the struggle for the victims to have the reality of the camps acknowledged by the law – and the slow and difficult ascent of that reality into the world's juridical consciousness is part of the story I tell here – is the writing of a generation of writers who, having cut their intellectual teeth on the cosmopolitan ambitions of an earlier modernism, forge new literary idioms of judgement in their postwar encounters with the law. These are secondary witnesses to Nazi crime: public intellectuals who inhabit courtrooms, diplomatic meetings, public committees, refugee camps, newspapers and magazines, as well as write novels, reviews and essays; and who voice the dilemmas of their time, not only in their commitment to justice, but in the riskiness of their prose.

'Judging without banisters' was how Arendt described the challenge of the Eichmann trial to Jaspers.[19] Writing without banisters well describes the responses to the Nuremberg International Military Tribunal and the Eichmann trial discussed in the first three chapters of this book. Running through this writing is a sense of a world unable to imagine a justice big enough for the crime which those courts attempted to try. In Rebecca West's reports on Nuremberg and Muriel Spark's novel of Jerusalem in 1961, *The Mandelbaum Gate* (1965), for example, both first published, like Arendt's reports on the Eichmann trial, in William Shawn's *New Yorker*, the sense of there being a moral void at the heart of legal reason is fleshed out through the creative deployment of melodrama. With its overdrawn villains and victims and moral absolutism, melodrama enacts the same discrepancy between legal and literary justice that Felman identifies as exposed by traumatic testimony. With melodrama, however, it is the absence of the experience of justice itself, not, as in testimony, the trauma to which it has to answer, which is pushed into the foreground. When West later complained that Nuremberg was an event 'that did not become an experience', what she meant was that it failed to deliver an aesthetics of judgement adequate to the crime.[20]

An experientially meaningful sense of justice is not only mourned at mid-century (as, for example, in the lost certainties performed in melodrama); its absence is also angrily and bitterly decried. Whence Arendt's biting irony in her report on the Eichmann trial: a repudiation of the pathos of suffering that was echoed by her fellow *New Yorker* contributor in Jerusalem, Muriel Spark. If, for this generation, the time had not yet come for the ethics of memory to put the world to rights, and if imagining the suffering at the heart of the catastrophe seemed to miss the moral mark, this was not least because these writers felt that they were still very much living within the crime itself. Indeed, it is because, as Spark will put it in her account of the Eichmann trial, the 'massacre is still living', that a furiously ironic voice also frequently marks the distance that justice has yet to travel in this writing.[21]

The calamity of the stateless

'The massacre is still living.' 'The real story of the Nazi-constructed hell is desperately needed for the future,' Arendt wrote in her *Black Book* review, not least because its facts 'have become the basic experience and the basic misery of our times.'[22] Arendt does not only mean that the camps have 'poisoned the very air we breathe' and 'inhabit our dreams at night and permeate our thoughts during the day'.[23] The massacre does not only live on in our minds. What she means is that totalitarianism's rendering superfluous of human life has insinuated itself into the world at a fundamental level; the misery is not over, because the conditions for that basic misery are still in place. The death camps (Arendt is clear on this) were absolutely and traumatically unprecedented in their radically non-utilitarian senselessness. But key among the constellation of different strands that made them possible was the creation of what she called the 'calamity of the stateless'. The second reason why Arendt's writing runs through this book is her acute political, historical and linguistic understanding of how that calamity became the basic misery of our times.

If the law struggled to catch up with justice in the postwar period, this was not least because the trauma was still being lived not only in the memories of survivors (often in a silent hell imposed by a disbelieving or indifferent world), but also by new categories of stateless persons that emerged in Europe, Asia and the Middle East. Before the Eichmann trial finally legitimised the memory of the camps (and before, we could say, the intractability of trauma appeared on the political horizon), the continuities between the refugee and the death camps were visible to many observers; few, however, would have gone so far as Giorgio Agamben in claiming a 'perfectly real filiation' between the unspeakably cruel, but at least nominally utilitarian, herding of the stateless into camps, and the absolute lawlessness of the death factories.[24] Indeed, cast within a history of political statelessness, Gellhorn's later repudiation of the Palestinian refugees' claims to justice also begins to look like a disavowal of an unwelcome historical and political proximity. (Neither will this be the last time when an ethics of empathy and identification disguises the role that the politics of nationalism plays in the creation of suffering.)

The question of the political and moral power of the nation state was a matter of much late-modernist anxiety; indeed, one can track the move from high to late modernism through the catastrophic decline of cosmopolitan horizons from the 1930s through to the Cold War.[25] Rebecca West's concern with the small states of Yugoslavia in the mid-1930s, for example, is the crucial background to her attendance at the Nuremberg trial. Those small states, like Czechoslovakia, came into being as the result of the treaties that concluded World War One. At the same time, the Minority Treaties were drafted to protect those minorities who suddenly found themselves stateless and unprotected by their host countries. Charging, as Arendt put it, a rather pathetic 'League of Nations with safeguarding the rights of those who, for reasons of territorial settlement, had been left without national states of their own', the

Treaties threw into sharp relief the paradox of human rights. The claim that human rights were inalienable had been in tension with the fact that only the positive workings of state sovereignty could grant rights to citizens ever since the eighteenth century. As countries pushed their stateless minorities across their borders with an ever more audacious impunity, by 1938 no fiction of natural rights could fuzz the fact that to be stateless was to be rightless. Arendt's account of this moment in her famous chapter, 'The Decline of the Nation-State and the End of the Rights of Man' in *The Origins of Totalitarianism* (1951) is as remarkable for its clarity as it is for its prescience:

> man had hardly appeared as a completely emancipated being who carried his dignity within himself without reference to some larger encompassing order, when he disappeared again into a member of a people. From the beginning the paradox involved in the declaration of inalienable human rights was that it reckoned with an 'abstract' human being who seemed to exist nowhere, for even savages lived in some kind of social order . . . The full implication of this identification of the rights of man with the rights of peoples in the European nation-state system came to light only when a growing number of people and peoples suddenly appeared whose elementary rights were as little safeguarded by the ordinary functioning of nation-states in the middle of Europe as they would have been in the heart of Africa.[26]

As European imperialism began to gorge on itself, the continent found a new *leitmotif* in the figure of the refugee.

Arendt's critique of human rights has found a second life in contemporary critical refugee studies, particularly since Agamben's appropriation of her work for his vision of a biopolitical life without rights.[27] My interest in the second half of this book, however, is with what happens when this new extra-juridical category of being – a 'new kind of human beings', in Arendt's evocative hybrid translation – gets into writing. Arendt gave her own brilliant answer to this question in an early essay, 'We Refugees' (1943), in which she stakes out a vanguard for the refugee in a political speech which is powerfully charged with its own homelessness (the subject of Chapter 4). For Arendt, to speak 'as' a refugee is not simply to claim missing rights; it is to enact that deprivation in language. The irony that marked Arendt's response to Eichmann's crime turns out to have its origins in the dislocation of statelessness. To judge after the camps, I claim, for Arendt at least, is to also to speak from within the very homelessness that made them possible.

When the refugee inmates of the Woomera detention camp in Southern Australia sewed their mouths together some sixty years later, in 2002, they, too, enacted the political deprivation of the stateless in an eloquent and ironic performance of speechlessness.[28] This is a totally

different kind of speechlessness from Ka-Zetnik's. Lip-sewing is a willed political repetition of rightlessness from within a refugee camp, not the awful still-living nightmare of the death camp inhabiting the body of a survivor. But that speechlessness has a shared history. To point out that continuity is emphatically not to claim equivalence between different traumas. It is, however, to insist, with Arendt, that as much as justice requires an ethics of remembrance, we also urgently need a historiography capable of destroying what still exists. '[W]e learn very little, we learn very slowly': recall Mary Douglas's despairing but prophetic words in the refugee fields of Czechoslovakia in 1938. Our inability to negotiate the tensions between so-called natural rights and the brute realities of national politics continues to produce catastrophes.

Tracking how statelessness occupies (or fails to occupy) postwar literary culture, I suggest in these pages, is one way of beginning to understand how that failure is imaginative, as well as political. The connection between postwar discourses of human rights and literary culture is far from trivial. When the drafters of the Universal Declaration of Human Rights (UDHR) set about trying to stop people leaking out of juridical and political categories in 1948, as Joseph Slaughter has demonstrated, they turned to the novel, particularly the European *Bildungsroman*, for a model of rights-bearing personhood.[29] In the final two chapters of this book I pursue the connection between political rights and literary ethics in the writing of Elizabeth Bowen and Iris Murdoch, two writers who, between them, track the passage of homelessness from the haunted beings of the modernist novel to the lived reality of the refugees, exiles and displaced persons who changed the moral and political landscape of postwar Europe.

Bowen's postwar writing is a devastating late-modernist riposte to the idea that the self-legitimising national subjects of the *Bildungsroman* could ever hope to provide a model for human rights. The political displacements of mid-century are so extreme, she suggests, that they have pushed the novel form to its epistemological and aesthetic limits. In the world of the displaced person, fictional sovereignty turns out to be as elusive as a glimpse of a tear splashing down a diamond brooch (the scene which concludes her 1968 novel, *Eva Trout, or Changing Scenes*). By contrast, writing from within the twilight world of the refugee, Murdoch attempts to resuscitate the novel form as a genre fit for the 'new kinds of human beings' Arendt had identified in 1943. If, as I claim, she fails in this moral project, this is because the novel (at least as it emerges from the European tradition) proves no longer capable of grounding an ethics large enough to accommodate what Arendt describes as a world where 'the loss of home and political status' has become 'identical with expulsion from humanity altogether' (*OT* 377). If we now look to testimony to give full voice to that expulsion from humanity, this is not least because, in the end, the novel failed to be what Murdoch wanted it to be: a refuge for the missing persons of the mid-twentieth century. To this extent, the end of this book takes us to the point where a literary history that tracks the rise of testimony in twentieth-century literary and legal culture begins.

Gathering ashes

Iris Murdoch began her career in the same place as Martha Gellhorn: in the refugee camps of Europe – in her case, on the postwar Austrian–Yugoslav border. From camps to courtrooms, from the hot offices of the *New Yorker* by the East River, overlooked by the United Nations building, to the dusty taxis of 1961 Jerusalem, from Paris, Rome and London to the writing and philosophy classes of the Ivy League: to track the itineraries of this set of writers is to find oneself in one of the final constellations of Anglo-American cosmopolitanism. Many knew one another. Arendt did not care for Rebecca West, whereas Gellhorn admired her very much. West reviewed both Spark and Murdoch on at least one occasion. Murdoch saw herself as Bowen's literary heir, and the two were friends. Endearingly, Lionel Trilling has a footnote in just about everybody's biography. Bowen, Murdoch, Spark and West would have been irritated to find themselves in the relative backwater of British Fiction Studies in today's literary and academic catalogues. For all four, any putative Britishness was frequently beside the point. As for Arendt, whose *Eichmann in Jerusalem* led to accusations that she had betrayed the Jewish people, so half-Jewish Scot turned Catholic convert Spark also discovered that to go to Jerusalem in 1961 was to find one's relation to one's race put on trial. Writing out of their Anglo-Irish heritage, West and Bowen keenly appreciated the perplexities that emerge in the chasm between rights and national citizenship (both claimed Burke as an intellectual ancestor). Murdoch imagined an Anglo-Irish origin for herself and, like many mid-century British intellectuals, tended to wish, rather, that she had been Jewish, actually. I give the last words of this book to her lover, Franz Baermann Steiner, the Jewish anthropologist, poet and aphorist.

Being ill at ease in categories of national and racial identity, as well as their commitment to political justice, gave all these writers a unique vantage point from which to look at the abyss into which their century had been thrown. There is a sense too, of course, that gender already gave them a purchase on the experience of, if not being entirely expelled from, then being put to one side or submerged under political and juridical conceptions of supposedly universal humanity. All understood the difficult middle between *les droits de la femme* and *les droits de la citoyenne*. It is a mistake, however, to assume that it follows that their critiques of the law therefore entail any straightforward shift from politics to ethics (a slippage I have been resisting throughout this introductory chapter). Ravit Reichman, whose recent book, *The Affective Life of Law* (2009), moves across a similar terrain to the one I cross here, by contrast, suggests that a shared emphasis on the 'ethical care' of the other ties West and Arendt's writing together. (Her other example is Virginia Woolf's writing in the wake of World War One.) This is not a characterisation in which either would have recognised themselves with ease. Notwithstanding their joint fascination with Augustinian love (on whom each wrote an early study), both were too concerned with the political consequences of brute history to think that an ethics of care alone was – or should be – capable of grounding the law.[30]

Rather the direction of travel tends to be back to a juridical politics not, to be sure, undisturbed by the demand for a new kind of justice in the wake of Nazi crime, but not completely shattered by it either. In a powerful reading of Poussin's *Gathering the Ashes of Phocion*, given as part of a lecture in 1993, the philosopher Gillian Rose excavated a space for a politics of the judicial imagination that many of the writers I read here seem to move in. Poussin's painting shows Phocion's wife and her servant outside the gates of Athens, gathering up his ashes, prior to taking them home and, in the wife's case, eating them. A good political citizen, Phocion was condemned to death (like Socrates by drinking hemlock) in a capricious demonstration of state power. The mistake, Rose argues, is to think that the gathering of his ashes represents a new Jerusalem. We should not be too quick to assume that the incorporation of the dead into the private body of the mourner outside the walls of the *polis* opens up an alternative ethical space for justice. Rose argues:

> The gathering of the ashes is a protest against arbitrary power, it is not a protest against power and law as such. To oppose anarchic, individual love or good to civil or public ill is to deny the third which gives meaning to both – this is the other meaning of *the third city* – the just city and just act, the just man and the just woman. In Poussin's painting, this transcendent but mournful justice is configured, its absence given presence, in the architectural perspective which frames and focuses the enacted justice of the two women.
>
> To see the built forms themselves as ciphers of the unjust city has political consequences: it perpetuates endless dying and endless tyranny and it ruins the possibility of political action.[31]

The immediate context for this example is the politics of architecture after Auschwitz (Rose was a consultant for the Polish Commission for the Future of Auschwitz in the 1990s), but elsewhere Rose also describes how the building of that third city is intrinsic to the writing of three German Jewish women, Rahel Varnhagen (the subject of Arendt's first book), Rosa Luxemburg (about whom she wrote extensively) and Arendt herself.[32] Each of these women 'exposed the inequality and insufficiency of the universal political community of her day,' Rose writes, 'but without retreating to any phantasy of the local or exclusive community: each stakes the risks of identity without any security of identity.'[33]

I want to start this book, however, by evoking another painting about the framing and spaces of legal, historical and political justice. Sitting in the same press gallery at Nuremberg as Rebecca West was the British artist, Laura Knight, perhaps better known for her innovative interiors of domestic life than her war art. In her painting of the trial (reproduced on the cover of this book), Knight splits her canvas both spatially, between interior and exterior, and temporally, between the present and the immediate, and as yet not at all distant, past. On the right side, inside the dark red interior of the Nuremberg courtroom, sit the Nazi defendants in the dock, already posed in the insouciant banality that will become their historical trademark. This interior is framed on two sides by the grey-blanched landscape of the recent war; at the top of the painting a city still burns; sweeping down and away from the city are more ruins, rubble and, just in front of the unseeing men on the defence's benches, are piled the naked limbs of the victims of Nazi power. On the very front bench, the thin white arm of a victim (survivor or living corpse?) attempts to pull his or her body into the courtroom.

On one interpretation, we could say that the painting stakes out the need for the law to witness the catastrophe against which it now attempts to legislate. We can read Knight, in other words, as criticising the law's blindness to trauma. From this perspective, the history of postwar justice as it develops across the twentieth century could also possibly be traced by watching that arm pull the body of the victim into the courtroom and begin to testify. With that move, we might imagine, the spaces of the painting would gradually reconfigure: a witness stand instead of a defence bench, a voice from across the divide of law and trauma beginning to speak. 'A planet without a visa . . .'

In writing this book, however, I have become wary of trying to push Knight's painting into an ethical future tense too soon. Now I think that it is perhaps only in retrospect, after the transformation of the war crime trial into the trauma trial, that we can say that the painting only anticipates a need for traumatic experience to be felt within the interior the courtroom. In fact, Knight's perspective firmly guides the eye not :ross the canvas from the ruins into the courtroom, but vertically, from ↼ue depths of the court up, through the benches, and back to the city on the hill where, in fact, the fires might just be about – not to raze the city entirely – but to burn themselves out. The two areas of contrast in the painting are joined in a third space: we are meant to look up and see the city. Ciphering the meanings of Knight's painting once again, then, we could now say that the tension between trauma and the law can be resolved neither by the law itself, nor by the full force of trauma being allowed to resonate across the courtroom, but only by keeping in view that third space, the city on top of the hill, which, if the fires are indeed beginning to burn themselves out, will need to be rebuilt. This, at least, is the lesson I take from Laura Knight, Gillian Rose and Hannah Arendt: in the end, justice will be neither subsumed under an incalculable trauma, nor calculated only from within the law, but imagined in the just city, and through a politics which makes both law and ethics meaningful.

It perhaps goes without saying that the need to find a political mediation between the law and ethics seems as pressing today as it did in 1945. Perhaps even more so. Shoshana Felman's *The Juridical Unconscious* was completed under the shadow of 9/11. Quoting George Bush's typically rhetorically vacant 'Whether we bring our enemies to justice or bring justice to enemies, justice will be done,' Felman commented then:

> As a pattern inherited from the great catastrophes and the collective traumas of the twentieth century, the promised exercise of *legal* justice – of justice by trial and law – has become civilization's most appropriate and essential, and most ultimately meaningful response to the violence that wounds it.[34]

From within the catastrophe of that moment, few could have predicted that Bush's call to 'legal justice' was in fact the prelude to a breathtaking contempt of the law. The promised civilised exercise of such a justice, the fantasy, we might now say, that trauma could be tried through the law, turned out to be meaningless. This book was written under the shadows of the Iraq and Afghan wars, Guantánamo and Bagram Airbase. As truly frightening as the violence of recent times, has been the blatant opening up of new pockets of state-sponsored lawlessness. Arendt's generation would have been dismayed, but perhaps not surprised. 'They were to be disregarded, just as though they did not exist. The next step, to conduct them from virtual to non-existence, then became easy.'[35] This is not Arendt describing the camps, but her friend, Mary McCarthy, in 1971 reporting on the trial of Charles Medina, one of the American soldiers accused of the massacre of villagers in My Lai, Vietnam. As the writers in this book testify, that disappearing trick was no random atrocity, but the product of the abyss into which the world was thrown in the last century – where we still linger.

Notes

1. Martha Gellhorn, *A Stricken Field* (1940; London: Virago, 1986), pp. 119–20.
2. Jacques Derrida, 'Force of Law: The "Mystical Foundation of Authority" ', trans. Mary Quaintance, *Cardozo Law Review*, vol. 11, 5/6, 1990, p. 947.
3. Gellhorn, *A Stricken Field*, p. 306.
4. Hannah Arendt, letter to Karl Jaspers, 17 August 1946, 43, in *Hannah Arendt, Karl Jaspers Correspondence 1926–1969*, ed. Lotte Kohler and Hans Saner (New York: Harcourt Brace, 1992), p. 54.
5. Karl Jaspers, letter to Hannah Arendt, 19 October 1946, 46, in *Hannah Arendt, Karl Jaspers Correspondence*, p. 62.
6. Shoshana Felman, *The Juridical Unconscious: Trials and Traumas in the Twentieth Century* (Cambridge, MA: Harvard University Press, 2002).
7. Gellhorn, 'Eichmann and the Private Conscience', *Atlantic Monthly*, February 1962, p. 4.
8. Ibid., p. 6.
9. See Felman, *The Juridical Unconscious* and Lawrence Douglas, *The Memory of Judgment: Making Law and History in the Trials of the Holocaust* (New Haven, CT: Yale University Press, 2001).
10. Gellhorn, 'The Arabs of Palestine', *Atlantic Monthly*, October 1961, p. 59.
11. Gellhorn, 'Dachau', *The Face of War* (1945; London: Granta, 1999), pp. 195–204. Gellhorn was a loyal supporter of Israel in the 1967 war, and went so far as to suggest withdrawing United Nations support for the Palestinian refugee camps on the grounds that their presence continued to feed anti-Israel propaganda. See 'Casualties and Propaganda', 'Why the Refugees Ran' and 'Thoughts on a Sacred Cow', also in *The Face of War*, pp. 298–312.
12. Arendt, 'The Image of Hell', in *Essays in Understanding, 1930–1954: Formation, Exile, and Totalitarianism*, ed. Jerome Kohn (New York: Schocken, 1994), p. 199.
13. Ibid., p. 200.
14. Seyla Benhabib, *The Reluctant Modernism of Hannah Arendt* (2000; Lanham: Rowman & Littlefield, 2003), p. xi.
15. See Richard Bernstein, *Hannah Arendt and the Jewish Question* (Cambridge, MA: MIT Press, 1997); Mary Dietz, 'Arendt and the Holocaust', in *The Cambridge Companion to Hannah Arendt*, ed. Dana Villa (Cambridge: Cambridge University Press, 2000), pp. 86–112; Patricia Owens, *Between War and Politics: International Relations and the Thought of Hannah Arendt* (Oxford: Oxford University Press, 2007); and Dana Villa, *Arendt and Heidegger: The Fate of the Political* (Princeton: Princeton University Press, 1996). Two key studies of Arendt from Comparative

Literature are Dagmar Barnouw's *Visible Spaces: Hannah Arendt and the German–Jewish Experience* (Baltimore: Johns Hopkins University Press, 1990) and Michael Rothberg's recent *Multidirectional Memory: Remembering the Holocaust in the Age of Decolonization* (Stanford: Stanford University Press, 2009).

16. In a sublime essay on literary estrangement, for example, Svetlana Boym has shown how Arendt's reflections on 'distance, freedom and the banality of evil' are performed in her writing in much the same way as Victor Shklovsky's writing embodies the technique which he described. See 'Poetics and Politics of Estrangement: Victor Shklovsky and Hannah Arendt', *Poetics Today*, 26.4, Winter 2005, pp. 581–611.
17. Arendt, 'The Image of Hell', p. 200.
18. Felman, *The Juridical Unconscious*, p. 9.
19. Arendt, letter to Karl Jaspers, 2 December 1960, *Hannah Arendt, Karl Jaspers Correspondence*, p. 410.
20. Rebecca West, 'Greenhouse with Cyclamens III', in *A Train of Powder: Six Reports on the Problem of Guilt and Punishment in Our Time* (Chicago: Ivan R. Dee, 1955), p. 246.
21. Muriel Spark, *The Mandelbaum Gate* (1965; Harmondsworth: Penguin, 1967), p. 177.
22. Arendt, 'The Image of Hell', p. 200.
23. Ibid., p. 200.
24. Giorgio Agamben, *Means without End: Notes on Politics*, trans. Vincenzo Binetti and Cesare Casarino (Minneapolis: University of Minnesota Press, 2000), p. 16.
25. For recent accounts of the tensions between nationalism and cosmopolitanism in modernism and late modernism, see Jed Esty, *A Shrinking Island: Modernism and National Culture in England* (Princeton: Princeton University Press, 2004); Pericles Lewis, *Modernism, Nationalism and the Novel* (Cambridge: Cambridge University Press, 2000); and Richard Robinson, *Narratives of the European Border: A History of Nowhere* (Basingstoke: Palgrave, 2007).
26. Arendt, *The Origins of Totalitarianism* (1951; New York: Schocken, 2004), pp. 369–70. Hereafter abbreviated as *OT*.
27. See, for example, Richard Bernstein, 'Hannah Arendt on the Stateless', *Parallax*, 11.1, 2005, pp. 46–60; Wolfgang Heuer, 'Europe and its Refugees: Arendt on the Politicization of Minorities', *Social Research*, 74.4, 2007, pp. 1159–72; and Jennifer Hyndman, *Managing Displacement: Refugees and the Politics of Humanitarianism* (Minneapolis: University of Minnesota Press, 2000). For an arresting Arendtian critique of Agamben's appropriation of Arendt, see Patricia Owens, 'Reclaiming "Bare Life"?: Against Agamben on Refugees', *International Relations*, 23.4, 2009, pp. 567–82.
28. Patricia Owens connects the refugees' decision to repeat political violence on the level of body and voice to a specifically Arendtian understanding of the possibilities of politics in the era of the refugee. Owens, 'Reclaiming "Bare Life"'.
29. Joseph R. Slaughter, *Human Rights, Inc: The World Novel, Narrative Form and International Law* (New York: Fordham University Press, 2007).

30. Ravit Reichman, *The Affective Life of Law: Legal Modernism and the Literary Imagination* (Stanford: Stanford University Press, 2009), p. 11. As to Reichman's suggestion that twentieth-century law was built on a 'scaffolding of affect', I can only hear the author of *The Human Condition*, famous for its squeamishness about a promiscuously emotive social roaming roughshod over politics, mutter a firm 'I should hope not.' Reichman argues that the development of twentieth-century law was built on tort's premise of redressing injury. This is certainly an important part of the history of the rise of the trauma trial. I am less convinced, however, that this legal development was built on the sensibility of the modernist novel, or that it was central to the thought of Arendt and West.
31. Gillian Rose, 'Athens and Jerusalem: a tale of three cities', *Mourning Becomes the Law* (Cambridge: Cambridge University Press, 1996), p. 26.
32. Rose, 'Love and the State: Varnhagen, Luxemburg and Arendt', in *The Broken Middle: Out of our Ancient Society* (Oxford: Blackwell, 1992), pp. 152–238.
33. Rose, 'Athens and Jerusalem', p. 39.
34. Felman, *The Juridical Unconscious*, p. 3.
35. Mary McCarthy, 'Medina', in *The Seventeenth Degree* (London: Weidenfeld & Nicolson, 1974), p. 347.

Part I: Writing After Nuremberg

'An event that did not become an experience': Rebecca West's Nuremberg

> For the law, like art, is always vainly racing to catch up with experience.
>
> Rebecca West, *The Meaning of Treason*[1]

> How much easier would we journalists have found our task at Nuremberg if only the universe had been less fluid, if anything had been absolute, even so simple a thing as the sight we had gone to see – the end of the trial. And we saw it.
>
> Rebecca West, 'The Birch Leaves Falling' (1946)[2]

Figure 1 Rebecca West's Visitor Pass for the International Military Tribunal at Nuremberg. Reproduced by kind permission of the Special Collections, McFarlin Library, University of Tulsa.

leleine Jacob races down the corridors of the villa in the gardens
he *Schloss*, her black and white hair flying, tatty espadrilles flap-
ᶢ on the marble floor. She should not be here, this clever, haggard,
Jewish woman correspondent, any more than the other women writers
crowded into the villa's rooms. The women who once lived there, wrote
Rebecca West, also staying in the villa while she covered the Nuremberg
trial for the London *Telegraph* and the *New Yorker*, 'would have
refused to believe that these ink-stained gipsies had earned the right to
camp in their stronghold because they had been on the side of order
against disorder, stability against incoherence' ('BL' 99). The gipsies
and the Jews, the women, are running in the halls that once embodied
the most 'primitive fantasies' of the Nazi dream. The scene is typical
of West's writing about what she called in her epic, *Black Lamb, Grey
Falcon* (1941), the 'yeasty darkness' of the European death drive.[3] The
forces of order and justice are found in the disorderly and contingent;
the bad-taste historiography of European imperialism is countered by
the telling of small stories that hint towards the possibility of political
justice, of a Jewish woman, for example, running to witness the first
major war crime trial in history.

Yet the fact that West looked outside the courtroom to the dorms of
the trial's women correspondents for an image of postwar justice is not
just an example of her late modernist literary method. Her writing on
the Nuremberg trial is a record of an absence at the very centre of what
was intended to be the most emphatic dramatisation of postwar justice.
For all that today Nuremberg is evoked as the event that inaugurated
a new era of international justice, what kind of experience such a trial
could be was unclear in 1945. One of 'the greatest tributes power paid
to reason', in American Prosecutor Robert J. Jackson's famous opening
words, everyone understood that Nuremberg represented the return of
the law. More difficult to imagine was the crime on trial. It is because
of this difficulty about imagining – a sense that something was only
partly being felt – that West would later describe the trial as an aesthetic
failure. Nuremberg, she wrote, 'was an unshapely event, a defective
composition, stamping no clear image on the mind of the people it had
been designed to impress. It was one of the events which do not become
an experience.'[4] Understanding what turns a trial from a legal event
into a historical experience is a – if not the – key question for war crime
and genocide trials. To transform reason into aesthetics is to demand
not only that justice is done, but also that it is felt to be done by a community of witnesses, victims, perpetrators and bystanders. The idea that
historical justice has a particular experiential form, and that war crime
trials are a distinctive kind of legal theatre, is now a commonplace.

Today most agree that it is through hearing the testimony of victims that the need for justice is felt most keenly. The truth commission, pioneered in South Africa, in which both victim and perpetrator testimony is central, has replaced the war crime trial for countries making the transition into peace.

Nuremberg, however, took place in a time before 'the era of the witness'.[5] In fact, the trial self-consciously downplayed the role of witness testimony. Famously, Jackson insisted that mainly material evidence – documents, memos, photographs and, a first in legal history, film – should be used in the proceedings. The voices of witnesses were deemed to be too open to question; only a material archive would make the court believe the unbelievable. Pushed by Jewish organisations on the absence of Jewish voices at the trial, Jackson also confessed that he wanted to avoid turning Nuremberg into 'a vengeance trial', thus, as historian Donald Bloxham points out, playing into the stereotype of the vengeful Jew, albeit unintentionally.[6] Madeleine Jacob might have witnessed Nuremberg, but she would have discovered few like herself called upon to bear witness in the courtroom. One of the few Jewish witnesses at Nuremberg, for example, was Marie Claude Valliant-Couturier, a member of the French resistance, who gave the first testimony about the murder of Jewish children at Auschwitz. Despite its compelling nature, Valliant-Couturier's testimony was not widely reported.

Whatever its considerable claims to justice, the unintended moral scandal of the Nuremberg trial, as contemporary historians have demonstrated, was its failure to address the murder of the Jews as genocide, to the dismay, among others, of the first historian of genocide, Raphael Lemkin, who had campaigned vigorously for its inclusion in Nuremberg's mandate.[7] Instead, Nuremberg's legal originality rested with two charges unique in legal history: crimes against the peace and crimes against humanity. In the end, it was the charge of aggressive war-making, the crime against peace, which stuck in the legal judgement of the court. The Nazi genocide was taken as evidence of the very worst of inter-state aggression, but not unique of itself (famously the trial restricted itself to trying only those crimes against the Jews which were executed during the war), and only incidentally an act against any transnational or universal 'humanity'. As the French judge, Henri Donnedieu de Vabres, later put it: the 'category of crimes against humanity which had entered the Tribunal's jurisdiction through a small statutory door, evaporated in the judgment.'[8] It was as though the law had produced one of its most original and political of historical forms – the international war crime trial – in response to a crime it could not, in the end, bring itself to pass judgement on.

One reason for beginning this book with West at Nuremberg is because she allows us to catch a glimpse, as it were, of what it meant to respond to genocide in the pre-history of the era of the witness. Passionate about justice, deeply preoccupied with the fate of democratic Europe, West was both a defender and a critic of the trial. At once a coda to her history of European imperialism, *Black Lamb*, and an epigraph to her Cold War fascination with the crime of treason, West's Nuremberg writing is difficult to place. In a sense, it is as transitional as Nuremberg itself, occupying the short period between the hopes of building a better, more just world, represented by the trial, and the hardening politics of the Cold War. A second reason for beginning with West, however, rests not so much with her politics, which are always larger than life (one is never in any doubt about what West thinks is right), than with her writing. Always, in more than one sense, extravagant, West's prose has an extraordinary talent for tunnelling into the dark places of her age. In a not entirely warm review of her 1948 book, *The Meaning of Treason*, Lionel Trilling wrote of the tension between this verbose intensity, which he calls, marvellously, West's 'hectic lavishness', and her politics: 'Miss West's prose seems to unconsciously know, what Miss West's conscious mind prefers not recognize,' he remarks.[9] West herself had already described a similar textual process in *Black Lamb*: 'Art cannot talk plain sense, it must sometimes speak what sounds at first like nonsense, though it is actually supersense.'[10] An unconsciously knowing, 'supersensual' writing, I argue here, is particularly well placed to register the unconscious structures of feeling that simmered both inside and outside the courtroom in Nuremberg. It also allows us to ask a key question for this study: before the Holocaust became the crime to define crimes against humanity, before the suffering of its victims signified, what did it mean to try and experience justice? What was being 'felt' at Nuremberg if it was not the suffering of victims?

Conceived in melodrama

What is being felt here, West writes, in the first article she filed from Nuremberg for the *New Yorker*, 'Extraordinary Exile', is largely boredom: a 'citadel of boredom', in fact, is how she describes the Palace of Justice.[11] The meticulous legal conduct of the trial, the minute itemising of documents and the deliberately sober and measured speeches, as other commentators noted, may well have led to a certain dulling of proceedings for those lacking the discipline of a legal imagination. But it is not just legal boredom that West evokes in her report. Nuremberg's is a peculiarly temporal state of boredom. On the one side are the members of the tribunal, aching for the end of the trial, for the final switch to be pulled on the war machine; on the other are the defendants, committed to continuation of tedium as a means of staying alive just a little longer. It is death, then, that gives this tedium its particularly agonising shape: death sentences to be passed, the incalculable deaths read about in memos and directives, seen in photographs and in film footage of the camps, deaths future, deaths past.

But these deaths seem to have no depth. This, at least, is one way of reading West's extraordinary descriptions of the Nuremberg defendants in her first report. Far from representing an unfathomable abyss, an unknowable evil, what is so disconcerting about these new criminals is their rude obviousness. They are 'crudely', not profoundly, 'wreathed in suggestions of death'; they present, writes West, 'the blatant appearance that historical characters, particularly in distress, assume in bad paintings' ('EE' 34). If this is a new kind of evil, it is one that can be expressed only in surfaces of appearances; in the fading of colour and texture of skin, for instance, in flesh once plump now hanging loose. West was not alone in dwelling on the appearance of the perpetrators. Both Martha Gellhorn and Janet Flanner were similarly drawn to the slack jaw of the Reich's anti-Semite in Chief, Julius Streicher, for example, or Rudolph Hess's horribly knobbly, madly cropped skull in their contemporary reports.[12] This conspicuous attention to appearances reminds us that Nuremberg was not only the first international war crime trial, but the first really internationally visible – and visual – trial in history. The defendants were photographed so frequently that some took to wearing sunglasses as protection against the flashbulbs (thereby adding, albeit inadvertently, another accessory to Nazi iconography). 18,000 photographs were prepared as evidence. Images of the infamous shrunken head and tattooed skin from Buchenwald were reproduced in newspapers across the world.[13]

But West's almost obsessive attention to the surface detail of the defendants does more than simply register a mid-twentieth-century shift to a predominantly visual legal culture. These men's appearances announce what they believe, she says; and what they believe is grotesque, corrupting and yet, more chillingly, shallow. This is a depthless deathliness: an infinitely citable evil. Like the *Schloss* temporarily housing Nuremberg's correspondents, the defendants are part of a German fairy tale turned gothic melodrama. Thus the Reich's banker, Schacht, 'might be a corpse frozen with rigor mortis into an attitude which would make it difficult to fit him in his coffin', while 'neat and mousy' Baldur von Shirach, the Hitler Youth Leader, appears as 'if he were Jane Eyre' (West will compare two later Allied trials to *The Mysteries of Udolpho*) ('EE' 34) ('GC III' 239). With the 'coarse, bright skin of an actor who has used greasepaint for decades, and the preternaturally deep wrinkles of the drug addict', Hermann Goering 'adds up to something like the head of a ventriloquist's dummy' ('EE' 34). A Marseille brothel madam, a tout in a Paris café offering tickets to a Black Mass, West's Goering seems to have slithered off the pages of Djuna Barnes's late modernist classic, *Nightwood* (1936): 'even now his wide and woodenish lips sometimes smack together in smiling appetite' ('EE' 35).

Nuremberg's perpetrators are the final agents in a history that West had identified in her epilogue to *Black Lamb* as being like 'the delirium of a madman, at once meaningless and yet charged with dreadful meaning'.[14] Meaningless and yet charged with dreadful meaning is an apt way, perhaps, of describing what it might have meant to 'experience' Nuremberg in 1946. As Lawrence Douglas has argued, part of the difficulty that the trial had with dealing with evidence that lay before it, was reflected in the tendency for crimes against humanity to be described as though they were crimes of atavism; a primal savagery to be corrected by the conquering forces of law and civilisation. 'How can we explain how Germany', the French Prosecutor, Menthon, asked in his opening address, 'could have come to this astonishing return to primitive barbarism?'[15] This is West's yeasty darkness again. But the question put by Menthon, 'how can we explain how', as its repeated adverbs nervously hint, remained unanswerable within the terms of the trial. West's sense of the depthlessness behind the trial's appearances was not hers alone.

One of the more bizarre instances of visual and epistemological surface-play in the trial, for example, occurred with the screening of the film *Nazi Concentration Camps*, comprising atrocity footage from the camps shot by US Signal Corps. As the film was shown to a darkened courtroom, the prison psychologist, G. M. Gilbert, and his assistant were positioned to watch the reactions of the defendants, specifically to look at their faces – at how they appeared – as they looked at the film. The expectation was that the perpetrator-spectators might betray signs not only of guilty complicity but also, more visibly, of a shame that might reconnect them to humanity, or not, in an early example of the trial by screen evidence of atrocity which has now become standard in war crime trials. The defendants mostly comply; what is expected of them, despite (or because of) the horrors on display, is, after all, pretty normative behaviour. Some shudder, others gasp, some look away – all but Hess, who, writes Gilbert, 'glares at the screen looking like a ghoul with sunken eyes over the footlamp' (the vaudeville description could be West's), and Goering, who similarly effortlessly slips into the role of melodramatic villain: 'It was such a good afternoon,' he complains later to Gilbert. 'And then they showed that awful film, and it just spoiled everything.'[16] A chilling indifference with a malevolent hint of self-parody: small wonder Goering's comment is quoted so often in the trial literature. But if Hess's and Goering's self-performances are so apt, this is not least because the terms of the trial, in part at least, create their roles for them. If there was an 'aesthetic' at Nuremberg, it took the form of a gothic nightmare framed within the more blatant moral certainties of melodrama.

West, then, is doing more than giving the trial the colour lacking in its legal correctness. The very lavishness of her writing puts pressure on the surface of things as part of a drive to yield a meaning, a moral meaning, that otherwise seems hauntingly absent. In this, her Nuremberg reports conform to Peter Brook's influential definition of melodrama (gothic's more optimistic close cousin).[17] While both gothic and melodrama share a fascination with 'evil as a real, irreducible force', the real subject of melodrama, Brooks argues, is the collapse of the morally sacred in the modern world.[18] Its elaborate gestures, over-blown moral conflicts, preoccupation with surfaces and excessive theatricality are all there in an attempt to re-animate the moral occult: to restore ethical meaning by putting pressure on what the surfaces of things can signify. To say that aspects of the trial lent themselves to melodramatic description is not necessarily to trivialise the event; it is rather to demonstrate a moral absence. Three years later in her book on treason, West similarly argued that secularisation meant that new ways needed to be developed for thinking about the law's sacred authority:

> [P]agan and Christian alike realized that the law should be at once the rec-
> ognition of an eternal truth and the solution by a community of one of its
> temporal problems; for both conceived that the divine will was mirrored
> in nature, which man could study by the use of his reason. This is the faith
> which has kept jurisprudence an honest and potent exercise through the ages,
> though the decline in religion has made it necessary to find other and secular
> names for its aims and technique.[19]

One way of reading West's cultural modernism, with its anthropological eye for the subterranean meanings that bind peoples together (and drives them apart), is as an effort to discover and forge secular names for the divinity of the law. For West, the law is meaningful in so far as it drama-tises the desires, transgressions and taboos of a community. 'It's a queer art form this religion,' she wrote in *The Strange Necessity* (1928), 'and in its mixture of ritual and dogma and didactics as impure as opera.'[20] Without this impure opera – which is the genealogical definition of melodrama – the law would simply be a prohibition capable of exerting no more moral or imaginative force than a parking violation (West's example). Crimes have to be felt to be wrong; there has to be a symbolics of transgression and correction.

Impure operas, therefore, are what make the law meaningful. How much more excessive, we might ask, does that opera have to be when the law struggles with a crime it can barely comprehend? West possibly may be one of the first, but she will hardly be the last writer to respond to the Holocaust with the overblown gestures of melodramatic representation. Witnessing the Eichmann trial some sixteen years later, Muriel Spark too will draw on its resources (as I argue in Chapter 3). More recently, Amos Goldberg has written of the melancholic pleasure generated by the melodrama of victim testimony; the 'excess and disbelief' once associated with the perpetrators have now shifted to their victims (thus, in yet another cruel twist, making them yet again the objects not subjects of history).[21] As Goldberg cautions, although melodrama can have a radical purpose – one effect of its use by West is to demonstrate the absence of a proper sense of the law in Nuremberg – it can just as easily pull the other way into conservatism and domestication. This is precisely what West discovered at the end of the trial when Goering ceased to function as cipher for the trial's occult meanings and threatened instead to turn the entire event actually into a melodrama with his suicide on the eve of his execution. 'It was', West writes, 'disconcerting to realize that the man's world in which Nuremberg had had its being had in effect been just as crazy as it had looked' ('BL' 103).

Goering is just what he appears to be on the surface; this is the first disconcerting thing revealed about his melodramatic exit. This shallowness is very similar to the evil Hannah Arendt will discover through Eichmann's trial – an evil, as she will put it in her defence of her thesis about Eichmann's banality to Gershom Scholem, that 'possesses neither depth or any demonic dimension' and which, thereby, is particularly and uniquely insidious: 'It can overgrow and lay waste the whole world precisely because it spreads like fungus on the surface.'[22] A fierce and uncompromising irony will be Arendt's response to this shallowness, and her way of insisting upon the necessity of finding newly meaningful forms of political justice. Justice, as West was discovering, however, was the very thing Goering had very nearly succeeded in trivialising with his outrageous death. 'I felt fear,' she writes, recalling the atrocities, the photographs of corpses, the shrunken head, soap, the passivity of people in the streets, the 'visceral mournfulness' she felt over the immanent execution: fear that Goering had turned an opera into a pantomime. ' "Oh, that one!" ' she writes, anticipating the response of Nuremberg's participants to Goering's death, '"We always knew he would get the better of us yet"' ('BL' 104).

The shallowness of evil on display in the contorted gothic grotesque of its defendants threatens to creep over the entire event (like fungus). One thing that unites the writers in the first half of this book is their resistance to this kind of spread: an insistence that the attempt to find an idiom of judgement adequate to the crime should not find itself paddling in the same depthless shallows as the crime itself. The 'reason why the Nazis in Nuremberg are so smug', Arendt complained to Karl Jaspers at the time, is because they know their guilt is so inhuman it steps over 'all legal systems'. 'We are simply not equipped to deal, on a human, political level, with a guilt that is beyond crime and an innocence that is beyond goodness or virtue.'[23] That lack of equipment, perhaps, is what makes itself felt in the melodramatic frame of the trial. Neither is melodrama only about wickedness. As Goldberg reminds us, the pathos of the absolute innocence of the victims can also drift into melodrama, suggesting not so much an engagement with the reality of suffering as a lack of political and historical imagination on the part of the spectator. It was precisely because she feared such a drift towards pathos, and away from judgement, that Arendt was so critical of the use of witness testimony in Eichmann's trial (the subject of my next chapter).

Back at Nuremberg, however, before there were witnesses, before the trauma was felt as trauma, there was only one comparable moment of pathos in the trial that was widely reported, and that was during British Prosecutor, Sir Hartley Shawcross's, final summing-up. West wrote that Shawcross's speech, widely admired and much quoted, redeemed the 'staleness' of the trial by finally giving an 'imaginative realization of what some of the mass murders meant' ('BL' 44). In fact, this realisation is based on a citation from the earlier testimony of one of Himmler's *Einsatzgruppen* commanders (another ethically jarring moment produced by the decision to avoid victim testimony). The commander had described a Jewish father talking to his son in a ditch and pointing to the sky as they wait to be shot. It is an agonising moment – Gellhorn describes the scene as 'heartbreaking and appalling'.[24] Shawcross's originality, however, lies in giving the scene not only a human, but also a specifically judicial relevance. 'You will remember,' he charges the judges, 'when you come to give your decision the story, but not in vengeance – in a determination that these things shall not occur again. The father – you remember – pointed to the sky, and seemed to say something to the boy.'[25] For the first (and possibly only) time in the trial, justice is tied to an imperative to remember the experience of the victims. 'You will remember,' 'you remember.' The idea that justice should be answerable to the memory of the victims is now so commonplace that it is difficult to grasp how novel an idea this was at Nuremberg. But if West, along with others, failed to appreciate its novelty – she quotes neither Shawcross's words nor the original testimony – this was perhaps because of the stench of corruption which had spread across the entire trial made it difficult, in the end, for this moment to be anything other than a future promise of redemption. The *Einsatzgruppen* commander may have been able to recall the unbearable pathos of the moment in his testimony, may even have felt moved to testify against his former leaders, but he had still watched the father and son being shot. 'Yeasty darkness', writes West; 'fungus', Arendt replies, from across the century.

One year after the trial concluded, West wrote on the postwar rise of anti-Semitism in London's East End for the London *Evening Standard* and, at greater length, the *New Yorker*. She begins her second *New Yorker* piece with a tart defence of Dickens, a move which is, perhaps, not so surprising after the melodrama of Nuremberg. It is a conceit of the middle classes, she writes, to despise 'Dickens because, they say, his characters are overdrawn eccentrics, conceived in melodrama and executed in caricature'.[26] Dickens told the truth about the East of London, where people really are what they appear to be: all surface virtue, as in the Jewish ice-cream seller with a steady steel in her eye as she serves a group of teenage fascists; or stupid villainy, as in Pipkin (a real name), who sweats out anti-Semitic vitriol from beneath his pomaded hair. Writing about the resurgence of anti-Semitism as though it were a Dickensian melodrama was perhaps a way of attempting to check the spread of the yeasty darkness that haunted Nuremberg. It fails. Where, in her Nuremberg reports, the sense of an insidiously spreading, rootless evil pervaded, the heroes and villains of West's East End read like an appalling caricature of the catastrophic collapse of moral value theatricalised in Nuremberg. Yitzshak Laor has written that English melodrama, 'more than it extracts tears, remains silent about a greater suffering that prevails all around. It is constituted from a kind of identification that does not demand any moral action.'[27] Casting the resurgence of Fascist anti-Semitism as a Dickensian melodrama was not West's finest moment of judgement, but it does perhaps reveal a wider difficulty in the postwar period, and one that might explain why it was that Nuremberg failed to deliver the 'experience', and hence the moral action, that its legal originality promised. One of the British prosecutors at Nuremberg, Labour MP Elwyn Jones, in an article for the *Evening Standard* entitled 'Miss West – beware!', responded to what he saw as West's failure to grasp the consequences of anti-Semitism.[28] Jones had just been back to Nuremberg to witness the Americans try the

Einsatzgruppen officers themselves. This time around there had been little to obscure the specifically anti-Semitic intent of Nazi atrocity.

By tired feet

Possibly because she felt that her writing on the trial had hit a moral impasse of its own – where does one go after melodrama? – West wrote about Nuremberg not once, but three times more in the postwar period. In the trilogy, 'Greenhouse with Cyclamens I, II and III' published in her 1955 collection, *The Train of Powder: Six Reports on the Problem of Guilt and Punishment in Our Time*, West returned to Nuremberg, and to Germany, against the background of Potsdam, the Marshall Plan, the Berlin airlift and a new flood of refugees and displaced persons. The substantial differences between West's original articles and her Cyclamen essays are little discussed in commentary on her Nuremberg writing, which has tended to either damn her for failing to recognise the horrors of the Holocaust (a charge, as we have seen, that could be levelled at the entire court) or praise her for forging a poetics of memory and loss in the literariness of her prose (a trauma writing *avant la lettre*).[29] This is to miss the extent to which the meanings of Nuremberg changed, not least for West herself, within a rapidly shifting postwar geopolitical context. If Nuremberg failed in its moral purpose, in part this was because the Holocaust was not sufficiently in the European imaginary in this period. More history was to happen before the reality of the death camps could emerge into world consciousness.[30]

As West moves through postwar Germany – its geographical spaces as well as in historical time – what is registered in her writing is not the genocide of the Jews. Neither is she in mourning for the fantasy of European civilisation, nor faith, nor narrative, nor any of the other categories of thought that are often said to be lost with the recognition of the enormity of the Holocaust. Instead of mourning, what West encounters in the later 1940s, first of all, is a quietly menacing sense that something is still missing. This is the message of the increasingly malignant greenhouse with cyclamens which makes its first appearance only in the 1950s texts. (The only 'cyclamen' in West's original reports is the 'Deep Cyclamen' in a two-thirds of a page lipstick advertisement embedded in her first *New Yorker* article.) The one-legged cyclamen gardener West discovers in the *Schloss*'s greenhouse, blindly, doggedly, dynamically pursuing his trade, is chillingly indifferent to events unfolding in the trial, just as the flowers he grows have a wildly incongruous, suggestive beauty. West had already mused over the 'mystery' that led a nation of flower lovers to the camps in her original *New Yorker* pieces. (She calls it 'the German mystery'.) 'I have to remind myself', she had reported the French doctor in charge of the atrocity relics at Nuremberg as saying, that the same people who 'tortured me at Mauthausen', 'now send me in my breakfast tray strewn with pansies' ('EE' 45). In the revised essay ('Greenhouse with Cyclamens I' is a rewrite of the two *New Yorker* pieces) West now claims that part of what made Nuremberg so ill-effective as an experience was that the evil it displayed was not singular enough. The superficiality of evil she had encountered in the courtroom turned out to be as ubiquitous as the clematis that Nuremberg's gardeners trained up the walls so that it was just at eye level.

For West, the meanings of a national culture are always best revealed in the way that a people play out their deepest mythologies in the incidents of their lives as well as in their politics. And when she moves her focus away from the courtroom to events outside it in her rewrites, in a sense she is picking up the geo-poetical analysis of Europe from where she left it in *Black Lamb*, with the 'fountain of negativism . . . at the centre of Europe'.[31] Yet far from offering something different from the melodrama of the trial, this shift to the extra-legal confirms what West had first feared at the trial: that justice was confronting something impermeable, resistant. The fountain was still 'killing all living things in search of its spray'. The gross fairy-tale-turned-gothic-nightmare that had built the *Schloss* and gave Goering his wooden grimace was still running; that is the real horror of post-Nuremberg Germany. Hence the mad old crone whom she meets on a forest path and who confides, with a leery wink, that the British Judge, David Maxwell Fyfe, is in fact a Jew, but it would take a German to see it, and hopes that Sauckel hangs for the way he brought two thousand slave labourers – 'scum of the earth, Russians, Balks, Balts and Slavs' – to her village. More devastating than this caricature, but similar in intent, is the city swimmer West spies on the river bank, and whose super-thin body has been sculpted that way through exercise, not starved and overworked ('GC I' 29–30, 51–4). Even a woman, met again on a path in the woods, who bursts into tears of rage upon hearing of Streicher's death sentence, responds not with empathy for his victims, but with a memory of being forced to listen to his 'gibbering filth about the Jews' ('GC I' 55). There are more ways than one of making people disappear; the dead can be expelled from memory as well as humanity (the Jews, in the case of the worst of Nuremberg's blindness, from their own massacre).[32]

West re-writes as though she were aiming not, as with most redrafts, to give more depth to her writing, but to flesh out an absence. Like the statues in Berlin's *Tiergarten* which reproach the animate with their innocence, what is not there is made present by what remains. Germany is haunted in this writing, not by the past (which in any case is by no means past enough to be history), but by an occult sense of something amiss. 'There was a strange pattern printed on this terrain,' West writes, 'and somehow its meaning was that the people responsible for the concentration camps and the deportations and the attendant evocation of evil must be tried for their offences' ('GC I' 17). 'Somehow its meaning was . . .': what – or perhaps who – was it that was calling out for justice? And where, we might also interpret West as asking here, can that call for justice be experienced if not in the courtroom itself? On the pavement outside the Museum of Gothic Art in Nuremberg lies the huge head of a toppled Jehovah; instead, West writes, 'of scrutinizing the faces of men, He stare[s] up at the clouds, as if to ask what He himself could be about'. This, perhaps, is what the law looks like when it has yet to invent new secular names for its sacred power: a gothic melodrama played out amid the strange patterns in the ruins; a bemused God reproached by the voices of children as they swim 'in the chlorinated river that wound through the faintly stinking rubble' ('GC I' 16).

Missing persons, missing justice; it is not as though West, any more than the people she encounters, knows what it is that is absent. It is rather as though everybody is stuck at the scene of a crime that they know has been committed, yet cannot name. Neither does knowing who was responsible ease the sense that something is still missing. Visiting Hitler's bunker in Berlin, West is unnerved by a piece of Allied graffiti chalked on the walls. The British were given to drawing 'Chads' during the war: little bald-headed men, whose noses peered quizzically over walls bearing the complaint 'What no' – soap, sugar, fags – 'or whatever it was that was most drearily lacking'. On the blackened walls of Hitler's air raid shelter, one solider had 'drawn a Chad who looked over the wall and said, "What no Führer?"' The drawing, writes West, 'came out ghostly white on the black wall. It was as if one stood in a train that was quietly running into hell' ('GC I' 39). The present tense here says it all: the trains are still running. Who, however, is the 'one' who is standing on this train? If West seems to make an identification with the victims of the Holocaust it is, I believe, an entirely unconscious one – which might be its power. Art, remember West once said, cannot always talk plainly; it sometimes has to run ahead into super-sense. Read straightforwardly, the passage reads as cack-handed appropriation of the trains into hell that, yet again, boots out the victims. Or you could read it as the silent possession by the dead – whose absence I have been tracking throughout this chapter – of the unseeing living.

In another sense, of course, West's prose understood exactly what it was doing in this later writing. If the unconscious of her writing is inhabited by Nuremberg's failures, consciously West is emphatic that it is, above all, the cruel compromises of the Cold War that have diminished the trial's moral and didactic power. Since *Black Lamb*, West had been convinced that the real political threat to the world was the inward turn of European imperialism; and, like Arendt, she had no hesitation in recognising that Soviet totalitarianism and Nazi totalitarianism were part of the same historical phenomenon.[33] In retrospect, she now writes, at Nuremberg there was a 'certain irony, and certain warning' implicit in the Soviet Judge's (Iona Nikitchenko, who had presided over the worst of Stalin's show trials in the 1930s) reading 'the part of the judgment that condemned the Germans for their deportations: for taking men and women away from their homes and sending them to distant camps' ('GC I' 51). By the time she writes her second Cyclamen essay in 1949, that irony has fundamentally refigured what West describes as Nuremberg's 'pattern of guilt', as the Potsdam Conference unleashed a new wave of population transfers across Europe. The newly displaced joined the former camp inmates and slave labourers in a rapidly changing Europe; the dead and suffering, whose absence had haunted the Nuremberg trial, had new company.

In the final chapter of the first edition of *Origins of Totalitarianism*, Arendt connected 'absolute evil' with 'invention of a system in which all men are equally superfluous'. It is this, perhaps, that constitutes the crime that Nuremberg, in the end, could not try:

> to deprive men of their human condition and leave them alive, to expel the living from humanity and the dead from the memory of history seem to constitute the first crime in the long and sinful history of mankind that is a greater sin than murder itself. (*OT* 624)

Note here Arendt's correlation between expelling the dead from 'the memory of history' and the removal of the living from humanity; there is continuum, she suggests, between the crime of historical erasure and this crime against humanity. This, I think, was the unspoken correlation hidden amid the charges of atavism and barbarity in the shallow melodrama of Nuremberg; what the trial could not finally bring itself to pass judgement upon, in other words, was a crime in which the world was still horribly complicit. And this, I would also argue, is what makes itself most strongly 'felt' in the unconscious of West's prose: not the unnameable trauma of the Holocaust, but what Arendt describes as the world's 'silent conspiracy' with the 'instruments of totalitarianism' – the missing persons.

As Arendt clearly understood, and as West perhaps was at least unconsciously aware, it was this superfluity of human persons that had made the genocide of the Jewish people possible. But people did not simply disappear into 'holes of oblivion', however much the administrators of the death factories wanted it to look that way. They were put there by the inter-war emergence of another new category of persons: the stateless – those who, Arendt argued, were deprived of the right to have rights conferred by the nation state (*OT* 376).[34] The invention of the new charge of 'crimes against humanity' at Nuremberg was necessary not simply in response to unimaginable atrocity, but precisely because nation states had systematically withdrawn rights from their own people, as blithely demonstrated in the most breathtaking way by the Nuremberg 'Laws'. (Putting the law back into Nuremberg the city was one of the trial's more theatrical historical aims.) There is, as Arendt also argued, and more recently Giorgio Agamben after her, a very short path from the refugee to the death camp.[35] In this sense, the necessity for Nuremberg was also born at the failed Evian Conference of 1938 where, under Roosevelt's initiative, a last desperate bid was made to try to 'solve' Europe's refugee problem (in part created, in another grim irony, by the 1919 Minorities Treaties). One of the key players at Evian was West's close friend, the American journalist, Dorothy Thompson, with whom West was to travel across Germany in 1949. Author of the widely influential *Refugees: Anarchy or Organization?* (1938), Thompson was one of the first to insist that the 'refugee problem' was not simply one of 'international charity', but fundamentally 'a problem of international politics'.[36] Both women would have been acutely conscious of Nuremberg's inability to legislate against what was proving to be an on-going history.

As though caught within a now-you-see-it-now-you-don't historical mirage, just as crimes against humanity 'evaporated' in the final judgement of Nuremberg, even as the trial took place, the stateless of Europe rematerialised in camp after camp. While the politics of states and statelessness continued to shape the legal proceedings at Nuremberg – the British government, for example, vetoed a proposal asking Chaim Weizmann to give the court a statement about the final solution, for fear of destabilising British rule in Palestine – the Paris Peace Conference and Potsdam relentlessly created new categories of displaced person.[37] People originally imported as Nazi slave labour from the East now preferred to move into the camps recently vacated by Jews en route for Palestine than to return 'home' to Soviet occupation. While from the East itself, the German minorities were expelled 'back' across to the West. '[A]ll of them are willing to go anywhere but home,' wrote Janet Flanner in the *New Yorker*.[38] By the time West revisited Germany in

1947 there were 762 UNRRA (United Nations Relief and Rehabilitation Administration) refugee, displaced person and transit camps. (In 1945 there had been 227.)[39] When she returned again with Thompson in 1949, the Berlin airlift was firmly in place and the city was 'the largest prison ever known' ('GC II' 140).

'The Germans', West wrote in her second Cyclamens essay, 'served us by taking the way of a grave sin against the refugees' ('GC II' 135). The uneasy, to say the least, moral equivalence implied here between the deportations to the death factories (genocide) and the fate of Europe's remaining, and new, refugees might be one reason why recent criticism has tended to overlook her later writing on Nuremberg. West, however, was hardly alone in playing the postwar 'guilt game', to use Donald Bloxham's phrase. If Nuremberg failed to impress many Germans it was, indeed, because they felt their guilt was balanced by their own suffering.[40] This, in a sense, is also West's uncomfortable ideological point: if there is an unseen but none the less felt moral guilt after Nuremberg, it is, she writes, 'related to the persons present in Germany as displaced persons, expellees, and refugees' ('GC II' 126). What happens, however, against the implication of moral equivalence, if we read this instead as a kind of historiographic doubling? The missing persons, those banished from historical memory, return – not, it is true, in themselves but in a new wave of superfluous persons. Some of this new wave, writes West, arrived in a camp in Bavaria to find that the Jewish community who had occupied the camp previously had been driven to use every piece of wood available to make the packing cases that would take their meagre possessions with them to Palestine. It is hard not to hear, in this story of a new generation entering a camp stripped bare by its departing inmates, something of a quiet shift in the moral tectonic plates of recent history: as though, once more, West's writing runs ahead of its ideological moment into a time, no less of a nightmare than the one she is in, in which it is the camps, and not the people, which are a permanent feature of the world.

This, in fact, is the message that is told by the only Jewish voice we get to hear in all of West's writing about the Nuremberg trial and its aftermath. 'At last', says one of the few who have returned to Berlin, the city has learnt 'what totalitarianism is'. 'At last?' West asks sceptically (as well might we): 'They ought to have learned that long ago. There was stinking pile of evidence which should have taught the deaf and the blind' ('GC II' 154). What the stinking pile of evidence had concealed, however, was that the fact that persons could be disappeared from humanity had insinuated itself into the world. (Those left stateless in the immediate postwar period were not recognised as political refugees until

1951.)[41] Precisely what made the inclusion of 'crimes against humanity' so significant at Nuremberg (whatever the eventual fate of the charge), Arendt argued, was that it promised to address this new space of radical and absolute illegality. Crimes against humanity are not like other crimes of war, however atrocious. They are distinguished by the attack they make on the only right that transcends our rights as citizens: the right 'never to be excluded from the rights granted by his community' – an absolute 'exclusion', which differs from other forms of oppression. We lose this right, Arendt notes, not when we are put in jail, for there we are still within the law, but when we are sent to the concentration camp, where we are 'excluded from that whole sphere of legality where rights spring from the mutual guarantees which alone can insure them' (*OT* 628). Hence, for Arendt, the need to imagine a new law capable of guaranteeing this right to have rights. Without divine law to guide us, and with natural law discredited, she writes, the 'greatness of this task is crushing and without precedent' (*OT* 629).

West also sees – although 'sees' is perhaps not quite the right word for a writing that so frequently rushes ahead of itself – that it is in a repeated history of expulsion and absence that the meanings of Nuremberg might begin to be felt. Where Arendt never ceased to make demands on political and legal justice, however, West takes a different route. In a striking passage, and one that recalls the image of Madeleine Jacob running through the corridors of the former citadel of Nazi kitsch with which I began this chapter, West finally discovers the 'meaning' of Nuremberg in the tired bodies of a group of Berliner women trade unionists. Former anti-Nazis turned anti-Communists, it is the 'everyday violations' of civil rights in the East that enrage and inspire these women.

> To say in this room 'I was at the Nuremberg trial', would not have meant anything to [them] [West writes], and indeed, it would have presented them with an argument less developed than their own. There men had made a formal attack on the police state. But these women had incarnated the argument. They were discussing the matter with their bodies as well as their minds ... By tired feet and leaking shoes, and by the watering of mouths over missed meals, these women had learned with their whole being that justice gives a better climate than hate. Aching, they saw a vision of a state that should think each citizen so precious that it would give him full liberty to be himself, provided only that he did not infringe the liberties of others to be themselves; a government that would love the individual. This is the democratic faith, and it was to this they owed their allegiance. Because the learning had come to them through their whole beings, their children would grow up with it in their blood. Mother had fair hair. She cooked good liver dumplings. She was a garment worker. She kept us when we were little. She found freedom a necessity. As she got older she got slightly deaf. She died at seventy. So a tradition is established. ('GC II' 159)

There is much in this passage to like. Away from the melodrama of Nuremberg, West reanimates political justice through the suffering bodies of historical subjects; by 'tired feet and leaking shoes . . . these women had learned with their whole being that justice gives a better climate than hate'. Anticipating the turn from abstract law to lived experience in more recent feminist definitions of rights, at last the empty categories of legal thought have bodies emptied into them. Yet, precisely because West's writing here is fully conscious of its ideological biases, to my ears this powerful evocation to the lived experience of rights is compromised by its language of 'faith', 'blood' and 'tradition'. A loving nation state with an established tradition: such is the necessity West finally takes from Nuremberg – what the bodies of the women 'incarnate', and what the fair-haired mother who thinks freedom as necessary as good liver dumplings is intended to demonstrate. But what, we might ask, about the citizens of that putative state who do not grow up with its call to democracy in their blood? This question returns in the trial West reports on immediately after Nuremberg for the *New Yorker*, the lynching trial of white racist vigilantes in Greenville in 1947. One year on, in this piece West clearly struggles with the fact that the law cannot confer rights in a racist culture, however 'democratic', and however much she might want to believe that it might. 'The trial had not the pleasing pattern, the agreeable harmony and counterpoint, of good legal process, however much the judge tried to redeem it.'[42] The defendants were acquitted. Even as West rediscovers justice in the Berlin women in 1949, one can sense the dead, the half-dead, camp inmates old and future, the extra or non-citizens as they slide, once more, out of moral and political range.

In *Origins of Totalitarianism* Arendt writes of her 'ironical, bitter and belated confirmation of the famous arguments with which Edmund Burke opposed the French Revolution's Declaration of the Rights of Man'. Burke had argued that the idea of inalienable rights was a flimsy abstraction; far better, he claimed, to rely on a concept of the 'entailed inheritance' of rights which spring from 'within the nation' (*OT* 380). The camps had (almost) proved Burke grotesquely right; that dilemma – or perplexity – is the starting point for her later work on rights, justice and judgement. (The State of Israel, for Arendt, is evidence of the bitter truth that human rights can only be protected by the restoration of national rights, as we will see in the next chapter.) West reaches the same conclusion – but without the irony or bitterness. Nationalism, she had written in the epilogue to *Black Lamb*, 'is simply the determination of a people to cultivate its own soul, to follow the customs bequeathed to it by its ancestors, to develop its traditions according to its own instincts.'[43] It had been a colossal error to confuse nationalism with imperialism, she writes briskly; had the West supported the small states created after the First World War, such as Czechoslovakia and, of course, her beloved Yugoslavia, European history might, she claims, have turned out a little less yeasty.

In the end, it is this Burkean faith in the power of the nation state that underpins West's sense that Nuremberg failed to become an experience. Nuremberg was a 'defective composition' really because 'it was international, and international law . . . is a mist with the power to make solids as misty as itself' ('GC I' 49). From the start, the trial was something of an anomaly in West's trial writing corpus. By the end of 1946, she had already published four trial reports on the crime which was to obsess her well into the late twentieth century: treason. In the trials of traitors such as Norman Baillie-Stewart, John Amery and William Joyce, West discovered an idiom of judgement she thought most appropriate to the political and moral demands of a treacherous age in the Burkean traditions of national law and custom.[44] 'According to tradition and logic, the state gives protection to all men within its confines, and in return exacts their obedience to its laws; and the process is reciprocal,' she wrote in defence of the prosecution of William Joyce (Britain's 'Lord Haw Haw').[45] The drama that unfolded in a modern treason court made the laws and customs of the nation newly sacred for a secular world; that is why West liked them so much. They showed how communities resolved their 'temporal problems' while affirming the 'eternal truth' of the law because they had the authority of culture and tradition at their command. Treason trials give us back the law without melodrama.

West writing on Nuremberg, however, I have been arguing here, does not always pull in the direction of her politics. Supplementing in her prose what the trial could see but not say, West gave one of the first critiques of the extent to which Nuremberg's radical jurisprudence failed to find an imaginative form adequate for its moral ambitions; hence the melodrama of a prose that wants to insist on the possibility of a moral meaning lying latent beneath the legalism of the court. West's mode of excess, her super-sensual 'hectic lavishness', is also her mode of historical critique. Rushing ahead of the law, and frequently ahead of herself, West's writing registers the absence not just of the victims of the Holocaust, but also of a Europe that, despite its best efforts, can no longer legislate for humanity (if it ever could) against its own territorial proclivities.

I began this chapter with an image of a woman running. I want to end it with another breathless dash through history, this time through the frontiers of both writing and the nation state. 'I have run after myself like an excited *douanier* and insisted on searching myself because I have observed myself behaving in a suspicious manner,' West had written in the wonderful passage which concludes her 1928 book of criticism, *The Strange Necessity*. It is an image of modernist cosmopolitanism, but it is hard not to hear also more sinister footfalls of the psychic dislocation that was to accompany so many millions of dashes across the borders in the years to come. 'Not only am I wandering in the universe, without visible means of support, I have a sort of amnesia, I do not clearly know who I am . . . what I am . . .' But in losing herself in her writing, West also discovers something like an ethics of unconscious living. 'I know something that I have not yet told my mind, that within me I hold some assurance regarding the value of life, which makes my fate different from what it appears, not lamentable, grandiose.'[46] Something of value emerges, West is saying, when I am at my least present to myself, when I run, when I write.

Seven years later West locates a similarly forgetful type of grandiosity in what she calls 'the International Ideal'. Written in the crisis days of the mid-1930s, 'The Grandeur and Necessity of the International Ideal' is West's check on her own belief in the mystical power of the nation state. It is only when nations recognise what they are not, where they fail, she argues, that anything like the Augustinian ideal of neighbourly love can emerge.[47] For a brief moment in Nuremberg the nations forgot themselves. Had they not, West wrote, 'a gaping hole would have appeared in our moral system'; and the Nazis would have succeeded in creating a 'ruin so general that it would have consumed all courts of law' ('GC III' 245). But what West's Nuremberg prose seems to 'unconsciously know', to recall Trilling's formulation, and what her belief in the mystical powers of the nation state anxiously seeks to repress, is that if the law is to recover itself fully in a totalitarian age it must learn to listen to the footsteps of those who run still, out of historical and legal memory and into oblivion. 'From time to time,' West had reflected about the experience of writing about Europe's descent into chaos in *Black Lamb*,

> out of the text there emerged little black figures which postured on the white paper beside it, achieved a group which was magical, an incantation of death, and ran back again into the text which carried on its story of the main and legitimate historical process.[48]

The lesson she took with her from Nuremberg was that the little figures were still running.

Notes

1. Rebecca West, *The Meaning of Treason* (1941), as cited by Ravit Reichman, *The Affective Life of Law: Legal Modernism and the Literary Imagination* (Stanford: Stanford University Press, 2009), p. 103.
2. West, 'The Birch Leaves Falling', *New Yorker*, 22 October 1946, p. 99. Hereafter abbreviated as 'BL'.
3. West, *Black Lamb, Grey Falcon* (1941; Harmondsworth: Penguin, 1994), p. 1102.
4. West, 'Greenhouse with Cyclamens III', in *A Train of Powder: Six Reports on the Problem of Guilt and Punishment in Our Time* (Chicago: Ivan R. Dee, 1955), p. 246. The three 'Greenhouse with Cyclamens' essays from this collection are hereafter abbreviated as 'GC I', 'GC II' and 'GC III'.
5. Annette Wiviorka, *The Era of the Witness* (Ithaca, NY: Cornell University Press, 2006).
6. Donald Bloxham, *Genocide on Trial: War Crime Trials and the Formation of Holocaust History and Memory* (Oxford: Oxford University Press, 2001), p. 67.
7. See especially Bloxham, *Genocide on Trial* and Lawrence Douglas, *The Memory of Judgment: Making Law and History in the Trials of the Holocaust* (New Haven, CT: Yale University Press, 2001).
8. Henri Donnedieu de Vabres, 'The Nuremberg Trial and the Modern Principles of International Criminal Law', *Perspectives on the Nuremberg Trial*, ed. Guénaël Mettraux (Oxford: Oxford University Press, 2008) p. 241.
9. Lionel Trilling, 'Treason in the Modern World', *Nation*, 10 January 1948, p. 46.
10. West, *Black Lamb*, p. 1129.
11. West, 'Extraordinary Exile', *New Yorker*, 23 August 1946, p. 34. Hereafter abbreviated as 'EE'.
12. Janet Flanner, 'Letters from Nuremberg', in *Janet Flanner's World: Uncollected Writings, 1932–1975*, ed. Irving Drutman (New York: Harcourt Brace Jovanovich, 1979), pp. 98–127; Martha Gellhorn, 'The Paths of Glory' (1946), in *The Face of War* (1959; London: Granta, 1999), p. 22.
13. See Douglas, *The Memory of Judgment* for a detailed discussion of Nuremberg's use of visual material.
14. West, *Black Lamb*, p. 1114.
15. Quoted in Douglas, *The Memory of Judgment*, p. 85.
16. G. M. Gilbert, *Nuremberg Diary* (1947; New York: Da Capa, 1995), p. 45.
17. Always attuned to the task of disclosing modernity's numinous forces – the occult, the mythic, the unconscious – West was drawn to the power of the melodramatic imagination throughout her career. In novels such as *The Return of the Soldier* (1918) and *The Fountain Overflows* (1956), for example, she forged a new alliance between psychoanalysis and the melodramatic mode. Later, in novels such as *The Birds Fall Down* (1966), she would recast early twentieth-century European political history as melodramatic intrigue. In 1957 West wrote of the extreme extent to which Henry James, the subject of her first work of criticism in 1916, 'identifies

evil with vulgarity'. Something very similar could be said of her treatment of Nuremberg's Nazis back in 1946. See *The Court and the Castle: Some Treatments of a Recurrent Theme* (New Haven, CT: Yale University Press, 1957), p. 205.

18. Peter Brooks, *The Melodramatic Imagination: Balzac, Henry James, Melodrama, and the Mode of Excess* (1976; New Haven, CT: Yale University Press, 1995).

19. West, *The Meaning of Treason* (1949; London: Phoenix, 2000), p. 23.

20. West, *The Strange Necessity, Essays and Reviews* (1928; London: Virago, 1987), p. 161.

21. Amos Goldberg, 'The Victim's Voice and Melodramatic Aesthetics in History', *History and Theory*, 48, October 2009, pp. 220–37.

22. Hannah Arendt, 'Letter to Gershom Scholem', in *The Jewish Writings*, ed Jerome Kohn and Ron H. Feldman (New York: Schocken, 2007), p. 471. Ravit Reichman has also noted the correspondence between West's emphasis on the depthless nature of the defendants and Arendt's later thesis on the banality of evil. As Reichman points out, West 'actively fashions this banality itself' in her descriptions of the men in the dock (*The Affective Life of Law: Legal Modernism and the Literary Imagination* (Stanford: Stanford University Press, 2009), p. 116).

23. Arendt, letter to Karl Jaspers, 17 August 1946, 43, in *Hannah Arendt, Karl Jaspers Correspondence 1926–1969*, ed. Lotte Kohler and Hans Saner (New York: Harcourt Brace, 1992), p. 54.

24. Gellhorn, 'The Paths of Glory', p. 228.

25. Quoted in Gilbert, p. 246. Gilbert makes Shawcross's the last words of his account of the trial, letting the image resonate across the silence of the conclusion of events. Lawrence Douglas reads the speech as a crucial moment of legal defamiliarisation during which the court was finally invited 'to see the victims in a manner almost entirely overlooked by the prosecution – as a people' (*The Memory of Judgment*, p. 94).

26. Rebecca West, 'Heil Hamm! – II', *New Yorker*, 14 August 1948, p. 26.

27. Quoted in Goldberg, 'The Victim's Voice', p. 234.

28. Elwyn Jones, 'Miss West – Beware! We Cannot Stop Fascism by Stopping our Ears', *Evening Standard*, 8 October 1947, p. 6.

29. In one of the first essays on West's Nuremberg writing, Margaret Stetz discusses 'a massive omission or even evasion' of the Holocaust in her writing ('Rebecca West and the Nuremberg Trials', *Peace Review*, 13.2, 2001, pp. 223–4). More recently Ravit Reichman has argued that West's writing gives 'memory' to the experience that is elided in the courtroom. I agree with Reichman that West is attempting to supplement the trial by forging a particular kind of sensibility in her writing. I find it hard, however, to see West as constructing 'sites of memory' in this work which, as I read it, is pressed far too close to its historical moment for the Holocaust to emerge as memory – or, indeed, as an 'experience' in terms West would be able to recognise. Reichman's thesis is based on an unfortunate conflation of the early and later Nuremberg writing; the 'landscape of seepages' she describes, for example, only emerges in West's redrafting and tends not to remedy but to confirm a sense that justice is not yet able to experience the Holocaust (Reichman's chapter does not mention the original

New Yorker reports and seems to suggest, incorrectly, that the bulk of the 'Greenhouse with Cyclamens' material is derived from the *Daily Telegraph* reports) ('Committed to Memory: Rebecca West's Nuremberg', *The Affective Life of Law*, pp. 103–34). A recent exception to the conflation of West's Nuremberg writing is Debra Rae Cohen's fine reading of how the substantial revisions in the later writing are part of 'a new minatory arc' of 'interventionist witnessing' designed to foreground West's concern with the Soviet threat. See Debra Rae Cohen, 'Rebecca West's Palimpsestic Praxis: Crafting the Intermodern Voice of Witness', in *Intermodernism: Literary Culture in Mid-Twentieth Century Britain*, ed. Kirsten Bluemel (Edinburgh: Edinburgh University Press, 2009), p. 157.

30. Dan Stone, *Constructing the Holocaust: A Study in Historiography* (London: Valentine Mitchell, 2003).
31. West, *Black Lamb*, p. 1083.
32. Both Bloxham and Douglas have detailed the extent to which Jewish victims frequently dropped out of Nuremberg's legal proceedings. The commentary on the film *Nazi Concentration Camps*, as Douglas wryly observes, distinguished itself by mentioning the word 'Jew' just once (*The Memory of Judgment*, p. 57). Bloxham reports that the French prosecution's summing-up speech managed to refer to the 'seven million persons' killed at Auschwitz (*Genocide on Trial*, p. 101).
33. Arendt and West met on occasion, but did not get on. Arendt thought there was something 'profoundly hysterical about' West. It is tempting to think of West's writing on totalitarianism as a 'hysterical' version of some of Arendt's observations: not only because of its overblown claims and fears, but also because of the way it displays the symptoms of its own unease in the density of its metaphors, allusions and allegories. See Hannah Arendt, letter to Mary McCarthy, 4 April 1962, *Between Friends: The Correspondence of Hannah Arendt and Mary McCarthy 1949–1975*, ed. Carol Brightman (London: Secker & Warburg, 1995), p. 127.
34. I discuss Arendt's reading of rights in terms of statelessness in more detail in Chapter 4.
35. Arendt, 'We Refugees', *The Jew as Pariah: Jewish Identity and Politics in the Modern Age*, ed. Ron H. Feldman (1943; New York: Grove, 1978); Giorgio Agamben, 'We Refugees', trans. Michael Rocke, http://www/egs.edu/faculty/agamben-we-refugees.html, accessed 23 June 2009, published in English as 'Beyond Human Rights', *Means Without End: Notes on Politics*, trans. Vincenzo Binette and Cesare Casarino (Minneapolis: University of Minnesota Press, 2000), pp. 15–28.
36. Dorothy Thompson, *Refugees: Anarchy or Organization?* (New York: Random House, 1938), p. 10.
37. Douglas, *The Memory of Judgment*, p. 78.
38. Janet Flanner, 'Displaced Persons', in *Janet Flanner's World*, p. 150.
39. Tony Judt, *Postwar: A History of Europe Since 1945* (2005; London: Pimlico, 2007), p. 28.
40. Bloxham, 'Defeat, Due Process, and Denial: War Crimes Trials and Nationalist Revisionism in Comparative Perspective', in *Defeat and Memory: Cultural Histories of Military Defeat in the Modern Era*, ed. Jenny Macleod (Basingstoke: Palgrave, 2008), p. 120.

41. With the 1951 Geneva Convention.
42. West, 'Opera in Greenville', *The Train of Powder*, p. 93.
43. West, *Black Lamb*, p. 1101.
44. The treason reports were also all originally published in the *New Yorker*.
45. West, *The Meaning of Treason*, p. 23.
46. West, *The Strange Necessity,* p. 198.
47. West, 'The Necessity and Grandeur of the International Ideal', in *Woman as Artist and Thinker* (1935; Lincoln: iUniverse: 2006), p. 55.
48. West, *Black Lamb*, p. 1103.

Chapter 2

The Man in the Glass Booth: Hannah Arendt's Irony

I was really of the opinion that Eichmann was a buffoon. I'll tell you this: I read the transcript of his police investigation, thirty-six hundred pages, read it, and read it very carefully, and I do not know how many times I laughed – laughed out loud! People took this reaction in a bad way. I cannot do anything about that. But I know one thing. Three minutes before certain death, I probably still would laugh. And that, they say, is the tone of voice. That the tone of voice is predominantly ironic is completely true. The tone of voice in this case is really the person.

Hannah Arendt[1]

In one of the opening sequences of Rony Brauman and Eyal Sivan's film, *The Specialist* (1999), cut from original documentary footage from his 1961 trial in Jerusalem, Adolf Eichmann can be seen diligently cleaning his glasses. Finished, he brings them to his nose and then pauses; he has forgotten that he is already wearing a pair. If Eichmann cannot see out of his booth for multiple planes of glass, neither can the viewer get a clear look at him. Throughout the film, reflected back at us from the glass are the faces of the trial's audience in Jerusalem, many of them survivors, living ghosts in a glass pane. In another scene the documentary, *Nazi Concentration Camps*, first shown at Nuremberg, is played to a darkened courtroom. As Eichmann blinks into the mid-distance, looking but not seeing, the black-and-white images in the film are cast back on to the glass of his booth: a grey face among white corpses.

The Specialist is inspired by Hannah Arendt's famous account of the trial, *Eichmann in Jerusalem: A Report on the Banality of Evil*, originally published, like Rebecca West's reports on Nuremberg, in the *New Yorker* and, to great controversy, as a book in 1963. Eichmann had been deflecting the lives, sufferings and judgements of others long before he was plucked from Argentina by Israeli Special Forces and dropped into his glass box. It is in this non-reflective – in all senses – thoughtlessness that Arendt, famously, locates the banality of his evil; whence his pretentious buffoonery, and whence too the bitterly black ironic laughter that, as Arendt explains to Günter Gaus in the quotation above, defines her encounter with Eichmann. That irony is the subject of this chapter.

As Arendt saw it, the task of the trial was to find a mode of judgement that was adequate to the new kind of criminal that Eichmann represented: the fatally non-reflective administrator of genocide. Jerusalem, she thought, was entirely the right place for this endeavour, since nowhere else, not Nuremberg, nor any of the other occupied countries that had held Nazi trials after 1946, had shown willing to put the genocide of the Jewish people on trial.

> It seems to me [she wrote enthusiastically to Karl Jaspers before the trial] that we have no tools except legal ones with which we have to judge or pass sentence on something that cannot even be adequately represented within legal terms or in political terms. That is precisely what makes the process itself, namely the trial, so exciting.[2]

Back in 1946, Jaspers had cautioned Arendt about the dangers of claiming that the Nazi crimes 'explode the limits of the law'. A guilt that goes beyond criminal guilt, he warned, 'inevitably takes on a streak of "greatness" – of satanic greatness'. 'It seems to me', he writes, setting Arendt on the path which will eventually give her book on Eichmann its famous subtitle, 'that we have to see these things in their total banality, in their prosaic triviality.'[3] With the Eichmann trial, Arendt saw the opportunity for legal reason to work, not beyond, but at its limits; in recognising the genocide of the Jewish people, she hoped, the law could also begin to legislate against crimes against humanity in a meaningful way.

But if Arendt saw Jerusalem as the natural birthplace of a new, radical and ambitious form of international law, the Israeli prosecution team, led by the hugely charismatic Gideon Hausner, had different ideas about the kind of trial Eichmann should have. To start with, it was not really the case that Eichmann was on trial at all, since his guilt was obvious to everyone including Eichmann himself ('not guilty in the sense of the indictment' was his plea – the same given by the Nuremberg defendants). Instead of Eichmann's guilt, the trial put the suffering of victims at its moral, legal and imaginative centre. Testimony became the driver for justice as, for the first time in legal history, juridical process was tied to the claims of collective memory. Where Nuremberg, in Rebecca West's words, was an event that failed to become an experience, the Eichmann trial demonstrated how the experience of traumatic memory could become a legal event in its own right.

The effects on the postwar generation were profound. For Susan Sontag, the trial 'was primarily a great act of commitment through memory and the renewal of grief', clothed 'in the forms of legality and scientific neutrality'.[4] 'It was during the Eichmann trial', Geoffrey Hartman has written, 'that I first understood the power of personal witnessing.'[5] Not so, however, for Arendt, whose bleak laughter has long rung hollow in the ears of many. Arendt's ironic tone, her critics claim, is a vicious mode of defence: a cold-hearted carapace of bitter reason thrown up against the atrocious history of unbearable suffering dramatised most poignantly in the sixty-two days of harrowing witness testimony that made the Jerusalem trial unique.

Yet if Arendt's tone was wrong in *Eichmann*, this was not (or perhaps not only) because she was distancing herself from the suffering of his victims. What Arendt feared, rather, was that the sanctification of their suffering within the prosecution's case obscured the crucial judicial challenge presented by the trial.[6] When Brauman and Sivan show the outlines of the faces of survivors reflected back in the glass of Eichmann's glass box, they are repeating in visual terms the problem that the trial instead presented to Arendt: if we fail to understand Eichmann's catastrophic lack of judgement, his inability to see, his victims are condemned to remaining little more than living ghosts in the reflecting surfaces of a trauma that knows no limits. Judgement, not trauma, then, is the question that frames the Eichmann trail for Arendt.[7] To judge is also to speak, and speech, Arendt argued in *The Human Condition* (1958), is the form of political action *par excellence*.[8] With this thought in mind, it might start to matter very much how one actually speaks of someone like Eichmann. Arendt's irony, I argue in this chapter, is more than just style or symptom; it is the form that thinking has to take in the face of such thoughtlessness as a prelude to bringing Eichmann's trial back into the world of political judgement. That the tone of voice is predominantly ironic in *Eichmann in Jerusalem*, and that that irony is Arendt's 'person', turns out to be her unique response, both scandalous and ethical, to the judicial crisis she witnessed in the trial.[9]

Grey cats

One of the paradoxes of the Eichmann trial was that while nobody really doubted that the defendant was guilty (even Eichmann declared himself as 'guilty before God'), the guilt of others not in the glass box dominated discussion of it. From Eichmann's ludicrous self-aggrandising claims that his death would serve as an example to all future anti-Semites and at the same time relieve Germany's youth of its guilt complex, to Ben Gurion's 'We want the nations of the world to know [. . .] and they should be ashamed', the trial took place in a highly charged culture of grief and expiation in which Eichmann's guilt was not only a given, but even on occasion an irrelevance too.[10] Ben Gurion again: 'the fate of Eichmann, the person, has no interest for me whatsoever. What is important is the spectacle.'[11] Arendt pointedly set herself against a culture in which, as she put it, with characteristic bitter precision, 'all cats are gray and we are all equally guilty', both because she was sceptical about how the trial was being manipulated politically by the Israeli state and, more profoundly, because the collapse of judgement into an over-generalised guilt culture revealed what she described as 'a quite extraordinary confusion over elementary questions of morality' (*EJ* 297, 294). It is, then, something of another paradox that Arendt's own name should have been pulled into this culture of promiscuous culpability. Several commentators have reported instances of the para-praxis 'Hannah Eichmann' uttered in public meetings and conferences, providing an all-too-neat unconscious answer to the grotesque question posed by a headline in the *Nouvel Observateur* on the occasion of the translation of extracts from *Eichmann in Jerusalem* into French in 1966: 'Hannah Arendt: Est-Elle Nazi?'[12]

A significant part of Arendt's distrust of the culture of expiation came from her sense that a politics which could not think about culpability properly, one that could no longer judge, gravely underestimated the extent of the moral collapse that made a criminal like Eichmann possible in the first place. It was the totality of this collapse that Arendt so urgently wanted his trial to register: one so total that, as she put it, 'this new type of criminal [. . .] *hostes humani generis* [an enemy of humanity] commits crimes that make it well-nigh impossible to know or feel that he is doing wrong' (*EJ* 5). Eichmann, Arendt wrote to her husband, Heinrich Blücher, was '*nicht einmal unheimlich*' – not even uncanny.[13] The chief administrator of the Final Solution was neither satanic nor stupid; he was simply, and catastrophically, thoughtless. But in finding him banal Arendt was not, as her critics have claimed, trying to normal-ise Eichmann by depriving him of an aura of evil. Just because he was not *unheimlich* did not mean he was *heimlich*. Rather Eichmann was the platitudinous enigma through which Arendt began the work of trying to think through the question of judgement.

As the historian David Cesarani points out, where discretion might have been the better part of historical valour, and despite a historically

Figure 2 From *The Specialist* (1999), Rony Brauman and Eyal Sivan.
Reproduced by kind permission of Eyal Sivan.

untimely cold and his glass booth, this particular enemy of humanity just could not stop talking. Indeed, it was Eichmann's bad talk, his torturous mashing of dialects, his verbosity, his never-ending strings of garbled exculpation that seemed to grate most on the nerves of the court.

> I should like to tell the Accused [admonishes an exasperated Moshe Landau, the Presiding Judge, at one point] that style is a personal matter, but if we are to understand him he must use shorter sentences [. . .] It is clear to us that, in German, the predicate comes at the end of the sentence, but it takes too long to reach the predicate.[14]

For Arendt, Eichmann's verbal vacuity was related directly to the problem of judgement. His verbosity not only lacked situational judgement (the sense to know when to shut up), but its weightlessness also betrayed an absence of the ability to imagine others that is at the core of judgement itself. With a penchant for self-regarding clichés and a gift for the circumlocutory obscenity of Nazi speech, throughout his trial Eichmann performed the only version he had of himself in a darkly comic homage to linguistic idealism. 'The longer one listened,' Arendt wrote, 'the more obvious it became that his inability to speak was closely connected with an inability to *think*, namely, to think from the standpoint of somebody else' (*EJ* 49). This was speech that was drearily and obscenely context-free. 'In his mind there was no contradiction between 'I will jump into my grave laughing' appropriate for the end of the war [Eichmann's favourite catchphrase for his joy at being responsible for the death of 'five million Jews'] and 'I shall gladly hang myself in public as a warning example for all anti-Semites on this earth [his new postwar-adjusted catchphrase at the trial]' (*EJ* 53).

Accusations that, by emphasising Eichmann's ridiculousness, Arendt downplayed the significance of his crimes miss the point that, for her, his verbal thoughtlessness was no mere grating peccadillo masking the true extent of his evil, but the very direct consequence of the severance between thought, action and language which distinguishes the structure of his evil itself. When Arendt writes, famously, that Eichmann 'merely never realized what he was doing' (whence the 'banality' with which he executed his actions – not, as some have assumed Arendt to be saying, the banality of those actions themselves), she also means that he was operating in a context where language has lost its connection to thought and judgement (*EJ* 287). The 'net effect' of the 'language rules' of National Socialism, Arendt argues, 'was not to keep these people ignorant of what they were doing [the rules do not contrive to lie] but to prevent them from equating it with their old, "normal" knowledge of murder and lies [the rules contrive to disconnect language from judgement, that is, from a language that can say this is "right" or "wrong"]' (*EJ* 86). Such is Eichmann's absolute identification with this linguistic structure that, as Arendt later puts it, even when he 'knew that what he had once considered his duty was now called a crime [. . .] he accepted this new code of judgement as though it were nothing but another language rule'.[15] The Nazi marionette can dance to any tune: which is precisely what makes his banality so insidious. Later Arendt will describe this thought-defying banality as spreading like 'fungus'.[16]

However (and this is often the point at which her tone begins to get under the skin of her critics), it was not only Eichmann's appallingly guiltless verbosity that bothered Arendt; the threat of linguistic meaninglessness also haunts the pages of *Eichmann in Jerusalem*. From her concern about the quality and appropriateness of the translation of German into Hebrew on the very first page, Arendt exhibits an acerbity over linguistic matters which runs right the way through the book. This is not merely verbal fastidiousness or, as some have charged, the snobbish disdain of the Western European intellectual. Arendt is dismayed about the way that language seems to run away from historical meaning in the Eichmann trial because such linguistic sliding confirms her sense that the Holocaust has torn language away from judgement in some sort of profound and potentially irreversible way. The more the languages of the trial try to represent the trauma, for Arendt, the less it is actually able to connect with the reality (in all its at times incomprehensible complexity) of the crime of mass extermination.[17] It was this worry that was at the heart of Arendt's contentious rejection of the prosecution's presentation of the trial as an act of collective mourning.

Arendt was hardly the only commentator to criticise the verbose rhetoric of the State Prosecutor, Gideon Hausner, but she was probably his most vehement detractor.[18] 'When I stand before you here, judges of Israel, in this court, to accuse Adolf Eichmann, I do not stand alone. With me stand six million prosecutors' (*EJ* 260). From his opening statement, to his decision to rest most of the prosecution case against Eichmann on the testimony of survivors, it was Hausner who turned the trial into the consciousness-raising event it became. For many present the sheer rhetorical ambition of Hausner's opening speech, which began with the persecution of the Jews by the Pharaohs and continued to occupy a further three sessions of the court, was by turns profoundly moving and, at first, a little baffling; much of this story had been told before, after all, and not least in Israel. But as another observer at the trial, the Dutch–Jewish writer, Harry Mulisch, observed, adding anything new to the history of anti-Semitism was not Hausner's aim; it was rather 'his intention to disclose, to give the world a memory'.[19]

Arendt thought that Hausner's memory-giving was an unwelcome distraction from the question of naming Eichmann's guilt: 'It was bad history and cheap rhetoric,' she snaps in her commentary on his speech. The effect of Hausner's language, she continues, was to suggest that Eichmann 'was only an innocent executor of some mysteriously foreordained destiny' (*EJ* 20). Once more, or at least so it appeared to Arendt, an apparently weightless rhetoric, this time in the form of a history of relentless persecution and suffering, gobbled up the question of judgement, leaving language uncharged to wander through moral and historical categories at will. ' "Don't you think" ', asked Eichmann's defence lawyer, Dr Servatius (Arendt thought he was like a Georg Grosz character), a few sessions after Hausner's opening statement, ' "that irrational motives are at the basis of the fate of this people? Beyond the understanding of a human being?" '[20] (*EJ* 20). For Arendt, the banality of this kind of understanding was made possible by the extent to which the Israeli prosecution could not see what was absolutely specific about the Nazi genocide of the Jews: that it was not simply the most horrible act in an on-going history of anti-Semitism, but a new crime committed upon the body of the Jewish people, a crime against humanity.

The great virtue of the trial at Jerusalem was that it named the very thing that Nuremberg could not bring itself to judge: the genocide against the Jewish people. But, for Arendt, the prosecution at the Eichmann trial similarly risked obscuring the specific nature of the crime through its rhetorical appeal to the history of anti-Semitism. At one point, Arendt comments wryly, Eichmann's lawyer actually uses the prosecution's own logic to rehearse a theory also popular in Egypt in 1961: that Hitler was compelled to murder the Jews in order for the State of Israel to exist. It is Arendt herself, of course, who is repeating the anti-Semitic analogies here; none the less, her sense that an affectively charged history of anti-Semitism is inadequate to the task at hand cuts to the core of her unease about the trial's ability to speak to the crime being prosecuted in Jerusalem.

In this context, Arendt's repeated claims about the importance of the authority of the law itself in the trial are perhaps not surprising. 'The purpose of a trial is to render justice,' she states testily in the epilogue to *Eichmann*, 'and nothing else; even the noblest of ulterior purposes [. . .] can detract from the law's main business: to weigh the charges brought against the accused, to render judgement, and to mete out due punishment'[21] (*EJ* 253). But it was not only legal judgement that was at stake here for Arendt. The very nature of the trial called out of a new affirmation of judgement in a wider sense. 'If you say to yourself in such matters: who am I to judge?' she wrote in a set of notes she made for a discussion of *Eichmann*, '– you are already lost.'[22] Something rather complicated is going on with judgement in *Eichmann in Jerusalem*. On the one hand Arendt wants to demonstrate its absence from the languages of the trial, specifically Eichmann's and Hausner's. On the other, it seems, judgement alone is capable of standing outside of the trial's competing narratives, as if an as yet unspecified form of judgement can confer on the trial the meaning Arendt in 1961 thought was absent.

For Arendt, then, prosecution was wrong to focus on 'what the Jews had suffered, not on what Eichmann had done' because this detracted from the task of defining new terms of judgement after the Holocaust (*EJ* 6). But, as her critics have countered, it does not necessarily follow that a focus on what Eichmann had done should preclude a consideration of the suffering of his victims. While it is one thing to criticise the 'ulterior purposes' of the prosecution or the Israeli state on the grounds of an objectionable politicisation of trauma, which is also partly Arendt's point here, it is another to appear deaf to the voices of survivors who, however they are represented by the prosecution, are none the less history-tellers in their own right.

The testimonies of the prosecution witnesses at the trial, at least ninety of them survivors, many of whom had published accounts of the Holocaust, took place between 24 April and 12 June. To put this in perspective, sixty-two sessions of the Eichmann trial were given over to witness testimony, compared to the thirty-three and a half sessions in which Eichmann was on the stand (*EJ* 223). In the United States the trial was watched almost live thanks to a contract with NBC, while ABC provided a daily hour-long summary. (By contrast, few in Israel were actually able to watch the trial on TV.)[23] It was this unprecedented focus on witness testimony that made the Eichmann trial such a unique historical and legal narrative act. Whereas the Nuremberg Trial had deliberately avoided the inclusion of victim testimony on the (dodgy) grounds of unreliability and hearsay, the Eichmann trial made witnessing the central plank of the prosecution's case. The effect of those testimonies was to resonate way beyond the courtroom.

Arendt is sceptical about some (but by no means all) witness testimonies in the trial, both because she is wary of the more explicit propaganda motives in, for example, calling representatives of Aliyah Beth, an organisation which organised Jewish escape into Palestine (Arendt herself worked with Youth Aliyah in Paris in the late 1930s), and also because she thought that painting 'the general picture' through witness testimonies did everything to document the suffering of survivors but potentially nothing to establish the specificity of Eichmann's crime. This scepticism not only put her out of step with most of her peers, but also remains today as the reason why, for many, Arendt seems to have missed the point of the trial entirely. For recent theories about the politics of injury (theories that in part are derived from the trial itself), testimony is central to post-Holocaust ethics. The testimony of survivors not only is where we encounter past traumas, but also reveals the limit of what it is possible for us to understand about the injuries of others. At the same time as it has an ethical provenance, because it shuttles between the law and narrative, the act of testimony is also where history, in a culturally experienced rather than an explanatory sense, is often now taken to be. Because testimony names the previously unnameable, it also unsettles certainties about what it actually means to understand history.[24] It follows that to turn a deaf ear to the testimonies of survivors is to miss precisely what was most significant about the Eichmann trial as an entirely new kind of legal and historical event.

Such, indeed, is the criticism of Arendt that Shoshana Felman makes in her influential study of the connection between trauma and trials in the twentieth century, *The Juridical Unconscious*. Felman argues that, with the Eichmann trial, the unconscious makes its first conspicuous entry into the law, not only because of the trial's focus on survivor testimonies, but also more precisely because of the traumatic force of those testimonies. Exceeding the limits of legal conventions, procedures and narratives – hence the discomfort they produced not only within Arendt, but frequently within the courtroom itself too – the survivor-witnesses in Jerusalem gave an emphatic demonstration of how 'the unprecedented nature of the injury inflicted on victims [could not] be simply stated in a language that is already at hand,' but could be articulated only as traumatic experience.[25] When the witnesses took the stand, history was experienced as trauma within the courtroom itself.

Felman shares Arendt's sense of the inadequacy of the languages of the trial; her diagnosis of what the trial does with that failure, however, is altogether different. At the centre of Felman's criticism of Arendt is the disturbing testimony of the writer and camp survivor, Ka-Zetnik. Ka-Zetnik was the pseudonym, taken from 'KZ', the German acronym for *Konzentrationslager* (concentration camp), of the Polish-born writer, Yehiel Dinur (formerly Feiner). Little read outside of Israel, Ka-Zetnik's deeply strange sextet of memoir-novels, *Salamandra: A Chronicle of a Jewish Family in the Twentieth Century*, is partly based on his own capture, camp existence, near-death and escape. Omer Bartov has described how *Salamandra*'s 'bizarre and startling mixture of kitsch, sadism and what initially appears as outright pornography' is fused with remarkable 'insights into the reality of Auschwitz, the fantasies it both engendered and was ruled by'.[26] Ka-Zetnik's Auschwitz was not the kind of place you could describe in a court of law (was anyone's?), but was an 'other planet', out of this world, somewhere impossibly hard for the conventional codes of written language to contain. 'Reading Ka-Tzetnik', writes Bartov, 'we are in the midst of the horror; there is no control here, no embarrassment, no qualifications.'[27] Such testimony could not be further from what was required either by the court in Jerusalem or by Arendt's desire for a new language of judgement.

The different ways in which Arendt and Felman write about Ka-Zetnik's testimony, a difference of both tone and historiography, illustrate just how far Arendt's writing is from an age of testimony that the Eichmann trial itself played such a huge part in inaugurating.[28] Arendt's testy impatience with what she saw as Ka-Zetnik's distracting theatrics was shared by Moshe Landau, the Presiding Judge, who struggled to persuade Ka-Zetnik to respond to the court's questions. This is how Arendt describes the Judge's interruption of Ka-Zetnik's long and, in both her and Landau's terms, legally irrelevant testimony:

> And when he had arrived at the 'unnatural power above Nature' which had sustained him thus far, and now, for the first time, paused to catch his breath, even Mr Hausner felt that something had to be done about this 'testimony,' and very timidly, very politely, interrupted: 'Could I perhaps put a few questions to you if you will consent?' Whereupon the presiding judge saw his chance as well: 'Mr. Dinoor, *please, please,* listen to Mr Hausner and to me.'

In response, the disappointed witness, probably deeply wounded, fainted and answered no more questions. (*EJ* 244)

Arendt's deliberate bathos hits its target just before he hits the floor. (Felman writes of Arendt's 'most sarcastic', 'most funny' style, in this passage.)[29] Arendt is scathing because she sees Ka-Zetnik's collapse as symptomatic of the failure of a certain kind of witness testimony in the trial to tell the story as it should be told. Only a few in her view, such as Zindel Grynzspan, father of the assassin of Ernst vom Rath (whose death in Paris was the pretext for igniting *Kristallnacht*) and who was beaten over the Polish border in the October of 1938, had the ability to discriminate, to simplify, to tell the story with what Arendt calls 'an innocence of heart and mind that only the righteous possess' (*EJ* 229).

For Felman, Arendt's discrimination between different kinds of witness testimony amounts to a failure of reading or, to put it bluntly, a failure of empathy. 'What Arendt's irony illuminates', she argues, 'is how the law is used as a straightjacket to tame history as madness'.[30] (Note the way that irony and the law are yoked together here.) By contrast, Felman reads the incident as an example of what it means to give voice to the transmission of trauma. Here is her reading of the same scene:

> When the judge admonishes Dinoor from the authoritarian position of the bench, coercing him into a legal mode of discourse and demanding his cooperation as a witness, K-Zetnik undergoes severe traumatic shock in reexperiencing the same terror and panic that dumbfounded him each time when, as an inmate, he was suddenly confronted by the inexorable Nazi authorities of Auschwitz [. . .] The call to order by the judge urging the witness to obey – strictly to answer questions and to follow legal rules – impacts the witness *physically* as an invasive call to order by an SS officer. Once more, the imposition of a heartless and unbending rule of order violently robs him of his words, and, in reducing him to silence, once more threatens to annihilate him, to erase his essence as a *human* witness. Panicked, K-Zetnik loses consciousness.[31]

No irony here, then – which is precisely Felman's point. In the spectacle of his fainting, Ka-Zetnik slips out of the 'straightjacket of the law', and so exceeds both its terms and Arendt's irony. But what does it mean to articulate 'history as madness' in a context where, as Felman and Arendt would both agree, language is struggling to re-establish a relation with thought and judgement? Whether or not Ka-Zetnik is re-traumatised in the courtroom, this albeit different kind of unthinking from Eichmann's – the unconscious unthinking of trauma – opens up not just a 'cognitive abyss', in Felman's words, but in Arendt's terms a moral and political one too. If Moshe Landau can be an SS officer, in what sense can

Ka-Zetnik's collapse have what Felman calls 'legal meaning'? Hannah Arendt, Hannah Eichmann, Moshe Landau, Moshe Eichmann – *est-il Nazi?* Are all cats grey in the unconscious vernacular of the trauma trial?

For Arendt, the point about the trial was not just that it should objectively establish Eichmann's guilt, but also that in so doing – and this is where it failed in her eyes – it should give due measure to the absolute historical uniqueness of his acts; Eichmann had to be made accountable for a crime that had no precedent. Ka-Zetnik's collapse might well, in Felman's words, encapsulate 'the quintessence of the trial as a site of memory to the trauma of extermination', but it would not, from Arendt's perspective, help us think the crime itself.[32] While its drama has everything to do with memory and history and, importantly, with the ethics of how we encounter traumatic memory, Ka-Zetnik's literal passing out in the courtroom leaves begging the question of how the crime should be, not just experienced or memorialised, but thought about or judged, in Arendt's terms.

Commenting on the 1958 revised edition of *The Origins of Totalitarianism*, Arendt had described how she had been troubled when she was writing that book by having to practice a kind of history-writing that had, at the same time, to recall and destroy the object of study:

> I felt as though I dealt with a crystallized structure, which I had to break up into the constituent elements in order to destroy it. The image bothered me a great deal, for I thought it an impossible task to write history, not in order to save and conserve it, but on the contrary, in order to destroy. (*OT* 617)

Arendt is responding to an obligation both to remember and to judge: an obligation that also reveals a kind of necessary destruction, something akin to what Robert Cover has described as the inescapable violence of judgement.[33] It was this 'impossible' task that Arendt wanted the Eichmann trial to have its share in writing. As important as conserving the memory of the crime, for Arendt at least, the trial should also destroy the moral, political and ontological conditions that made the crime possible: hence the necessary, exhilarating vertigo, as she put it in her letter to Karl Jaspers, of judging 'without banisters'.

In her later writing, Arendt will push the activity of judging even closer to the task of history-writing. 'If judgement is our faculty for dealing with the past,' she wrote in *The Life of the Mind*, 'the historian is the inquiring mind who by relating it sits in judgement over it.'[34] Arendt is emphatically not saying that history can be the ultimate judge; for her, that conceit fell at the moment history showed that it could also transmute into the ideology of totalitarianism. Rather, judging and writing after the Holocaust call for a different kind of history-telling. Hence, perhaps, Arendt's sense in the 1960s that writing about Eichmann was itself a new form of history-writing: a writing that not only judges the crime, but which also puts the author on trial in relation to it. 'I would never be able to forgive myself', Arendt wrote to Jaspers, 'if I didn't go and look at this walking disaster face to face.'[35]

That face-to-face encounter, however, as we have seen, precluded an encounter with trauma.

> It now appeared [Arendt wrote scathingly of the culture of expiation that characterised the furore following the first publication of her writing on the trial] that the era of the Hitler regime, with its gigantic, unprecedented crimes, constituted an 'unmastered past' not only for the German people or for the Jews all over the world, but for the rest of the world, which had not forgotten this great catastrophe in the heart of Europe either, and had also been unable to come to terms with it. (*EJ* 283)

Irony again. (Justifiably Felman reads this passage as contemptuously poor psychologising.) But if Arendt was impatient with the pathos implied in the concept of traumatic history as it emerged in the courtroom in Jerusalem, it does not necessarily follow that her attachment to judgement, nor indeed her irony, is a repudiation of the extraordinary difficulty of narrating the trauma of the Holocaust. As much as for contemporary trauma theory, for Arendt too the task of thinking after Eichmann – of thinking in the wake of Eichmann's profound thought-lessness – begins with reason's ends, not with a re-assertion of its moral and legal transcendence. One reason for returning to Arendt's writing today (and why her thought is at the centre of this book) is because she offers a way to think, and hence to judge, that is bound neither to the ethical claims of the relentless demands of an impossible-to-reconcile trauma, nor to a politics premised on, but not in the end sufficiently answerable to, that suffering.

If Arendt did not understand psychoanalysis (or a psychoanalysis that she herself characterised as clumsily deterministic), what she certainly did understand was the power and complexity of political love (the *amor mundi* to which her biography owes its title) precisely as a response to a trauma which is not only criminal and historical, but which cuts to the heart of what it means to think, to be a speaking being, in a world that can no longer make judgements. This is why the lesson Arendt took from Eichmann, I suggest in the rest of this chapter, was indeed not one about the power of witness testimony, but one about the necessity of re-imagining the relations between language and thought and, in turn, between narrative and judgement.

Oratio obliqua

When Adolf Eichmann stood beneath the gallows on 31 May 1962 he did two things. First, in accordance with SS tenets, he re-affirmed that he was not a *Gottgläubiger*, and therefore did not believe in an after-life. This statement was then followed by one final elated speech act: 'After a short while, gentlemen, we shall meet again. Such is the fate of all men. Long live Germany, long live Argentina, long live Austria. I shall not forget them.' Thus immured in the treacle of his own verbiage, Eichmann finally swung. 'In the face of death,' Arendt remarks, 'he had found the cliché used in funeral oratory. Under the gallows, his memory played him the last trick; he was "elated" and forgot that this was his own funeral' (*EJ* 252). This ultimate act of 'word-and-thought'-defying banality, for Arendt, summed up the legacy of the Eichmann trial. Eichmann was not a stupid man, she later wrote, but what he had, and what made his evil possible, was 'a curious, quite authentic inability to think' ('TM' 159). Arendt is not simply saying that if Eichmann had thought carefully he would have realised that his two statements contradicted one another, any more than she had claimed that had he thought a bit harder about where he actually was in 1961 he might not have defended himself as 'the victim of a fallacy'. Thought would not have restored linguistic mastery for the simple reason that the language rules Eichmann plays under were contrived precisely to exclude the corrosive effects of reflection. Accordingly, Eichmann does not reflect upon language, but borrows it in manic acts of linguistic defence. To an extent, some day-to-day linguistic pilfering is always necessary. If we were to respond to the claim that we should think when we speak all the time, Arendt wrote in her 1971 essay, 'Thinking and Moral Considerations', 'we would soon be exhausted; the difference in Eichmann was only that he clearly knew of no such claim at all' ('TM' 161).

The question that concerned Arendt in the years following the Eichmann trial was as follows: if evil is not radical, as she had earlier claimed in *Origins of Totalitarianism*, but unthinking or thoughtless, is it not possible that the activity of thinking could act as a prophylactic against the catastrophic collapse of conscience? 'Is our ability to judge', Arendt wrote in 'Thinking and Moral Considerations', 'to tell right from wrong, beautiful from ugly, dependent upon our faculty of thought?' ('TM' 160). What is so arresting about Arendt's answers to this question in this essay is her insistence that the kind of thinking she has in mind absolutely does not belong to rational mastery – judgement is not simply an assertion of reason, it is rather reflective and imaginative.[36]

Following Kant's distinction between reason and the urge to think 'beyond knowledge', Arendt aligns thinking not with faith, which is where Kant puts those questions that cannot be known by reason alone, but with what she calls, after Heidegger, 'the destruction of all possible foundations of metaphysical systems'[37] ('TM' 164). Hence, thinking is reason's other scene. Thinking is not mastery, but perplexity; it is not instrumental, but happily provisional (what I think today will be undone tomorrow). When I think, I shed my identity: '*Tantôt je suis,*' Arendt quotes Valéry, '*tantôt je pense.*' Sometimes I am, sometimes I think ('TM' 165). Thinking removes the self from the world of appearances and casts it into one of disappearances and representations. 'An object of thought', Arendt writes, 'is always a re-presentation, that is, something or somebody that is actually absent and present only to the mind which, by virtue of imagination, can make it present only in the form of an image' ('TM' 165). Thinking, then, is akin to fantasy and imagination. To think is also to desire, which is why, Arendt also says, thinking is a profound kind of love: 'Love by desiring what is not there establishes a relation with it' ('TM' 179). Thinking, then, although Arendt does not quite put it like this in her essay, is a form of affectivity that brings our relationship with objects and concepts 'out into the open'.

This is something quite different from the legal positivism and anachronistic faith in universal reason that some of her detractors have been quick to read in Arendt's attachment to judgement in the Eichmann trial. Here the limits of reason are not so much challenged by the 'cognitive abyss' (to repeat Felman's words) of traumatic testimony, as deconstructed by a 'noncognitive, nonspecialized sense' (Arendt's) of thinking ('TM' 187). Such thinking neither makes sense of Eichmann's crimes, nor delivers justice to his victims; it grounds nothing and is incapable of founding moral concepts. But the wind of thought (Arendt borrows the image from Socrates) brings with it a warm moral and political breeze. Thinking (Arendt uses this verb at least three times in her essay) 'defrosts' language out of its petrified state, not so much so that it can directly recover the capacity to judge, but so that we can attend to its otherness as a prelude to some kind of judgement.

Arendt's precedent here is the aporetic Socratic dialogue in which words rediscover their meanings not because Socrates knows the meaning of, for example, the word 'house', but because what the dialogues teach us is that once you stop to think about the word 'house', once you repeat it, things, as Arendt puts it, begin to 'get slippery', 'nothing stays put anymore, everything begins to move.' So it is we discover that the word 'house' is not merely the place which is always and forever hopelessly untidy, but also (and again after Heidegger) houses thoughts about dwelling: 'it is a word that could not exist unless one presupposes thinking about being housed, dwelling, having a home' ('TM' 172). This sort of non-cognitive thinking reveals what words surrender when they are spoken too soon (the wild existential ambition of 'I want a new house,' the darker politics of the 'problem of social housing', for instance). Indeed, another way of describing what Arendt is trying to get at here, although she would have disliked the implications, would be to say that thinking reveals the existence of something like a linguistic unconscious.

To think is therefore also to be temporarily released from the shell of social, political or, indeed, legal identity. I talk to myself; 'I am', Arendt writes, 'inevitably *two-in-one* – which incidentally', she adds, 'is the reason why the fashionable search for identity is futile and our modern identity crisis could be resolved only by losing consciousness' ('TM' 184). But while thinking causes the social and political subject to fade, it is also because thinking compels one to listen to one's inner voice that thinking reminds us that we are persons with a conscience. Thinking, therefore, is also a path back to judgment and, hence, politics. 'I am a villain. Yet I lie, I am not. / Fool, of thyself speak well. Fool, do not flatter,' soliloquises Richard III, another clowning war criminal, who none the less differs from Eichmann because Richard's inner dialogues reveal him to be a truly wicked villain since he acts in spite of himself ('TM' 185). Eichmann, by contrast, is neither properly wicked nor irredeemably stupid; rather, and far more troublingly, he is capable of infinite evil because when he speaks there is, quite literally, no one else home. To this extent, Eichmann is pure social and linguistic identity. (Indeed, by Arendt's reading, it should be he and not Ka-Zetnik who loses consciousness in the courtroom in Jerusalem.)

Eichmann's trial had made the activity of thinking, and its absence, newly and politically conspicuous. Thinking about thinking, in this context, is both Arendt's retroactive response to the trial and, like thought itself, an act of destructive political love. 'This destruction', Arendt concludes her essay, 'has a liberating effect on another human faculty, the faculty of judgement, which one may call, with some justification, the most political of man's abilities' ('TM' 188). Judgement returns in Arendt's thought here not as the imposition of legal reason, but as the offshoot of the very activity repressed by the language rules of National Socialism: thinking. Arendt, then, rediscovers judgement not, as her critics sometimes suppose, in the universalist language of the law or within the transcendence of reason, but in something more like reason's dream world, in the reflective imaginative activity of judging particulars.

> If thinking, in the two-in-one of the soundless dialogue, actualizes the difference within our identity as given in consciousness and thereby results in conscience as its by-product [Arendt writes], then judging, the by-product of the liberating effect of thinking, realizes thinking, makes it manifest in the world of appearances where I am never alone and always much too busy to be able to think. The manifestation of the wind of thought is not knowledge; it is the ability to tell right from wrong, beautiful from ugly. And this indeed may prevent catastrophes, at least for myself, in the rare moments when the chips are down. ('TM' 189)

If here, as elsewhere, Arendt defends what could be described as the otherworldliness of thought, as Julia Kristeva has put it, it is 'not so it can disappear in an unnameable, affected, and even potentially tyrannical solipsism', but rather 'to infuse the dialogue of thinking into the very political space in which thinking is used as a means of distinguishing good and evil'.[38] 'When the chips are down', we must hedge our bets not on what is incomprehensible to reason, but on understanding how the intricate ways in which we differ from ourselves as thinking and speaking subjects can revive the political through the exercise of judgement.[39]

As Arendt would go on to argue in her lectures on Kant, while one might think alone, when we judge we do so as a member of the community. It is the figure of the 'judging spectator' who turns a historical event into a political one.[40] It was, of course, as a judging spectator that Arendt had written *Eichmann in Jerusalem*. In another essay, directly provoked by the controversies following the book's publication, 'Truth and Politics' (1967), Arendt addressed the question left implicit in *Eichmann* and raised again in 'Thinking and Moral Considerations': what narrative mode is most suited to the perplexities of judgement? Responding to a political culture that rewrites history by trading in open lies, such as, she writes with a clear aim at her critics, 'the case of rewriting contemporary history under the eyes of those who witnessed it' (note the way Arendt emphatically re-instates herself as an historical witness or judging spectator here), in this essay Arendt evokes the figure of the 'truth-teller'.[41] With its conspicuous echoes of Walter Benjamin's storyteller (Arendt was to publish her introduction to the Schocken Books' collection of Benjamin's essays, *Illuminations*, barely one year later), Arendt's truth-teller, like her dead friend's narrator, gives form to contingency. 'Who says what is', Arendt writes, 'always tells a story, and in this story the particular facts lose their contingency and acquire some humanly comprehensible meaning' ('TP' 545). While the truth-teller remains aloof from politics, by giving narrative to truth she also brings historical judgement back into the political:

The political function of the storyteller – historian or novelist – is to teach acceptance of things as they are. Out of this acceptance, which can also be called truthfulness, arises the faculty of judgement – that . . . in Isak Dinesen's words, 'at the end we shall be privileged to view, and review, it' – and that is what is named the day of judgement. ('TP' 572–3)

As several commentators have noticed, this passage is resonant with Arendt's earlier praise for the matchless simplicity of Zindel Grynzspan's witness testimony in *Eichmann*. 'This story', Arendt had written about Grynzspan's simple and almost unbearably moving witness account, 'took no more than perhaps ten minutes to tell, and when it was over – the senseless, needless destruction of twenty-seven years in less than twenty-four hours – one thought foolishly: Everyone, everyone should have his day in court' (*EJ* 229).

It hardly needs to be said that this is an altogether different tonal response from Arendt's scathing account of Ka-Zetnik's testimony.[42] In her reading of this passage, Felman detects here both Arendt's grief for her own history of brutal exile, and also haunting whispers of the dead Benjamin; 'remarkably and deeply moved', Felman interprets, Arendt 'steps out of her boundaries and (for a moment) pleads against her own puristic, legalistic emphasis on strict legal relevance'.[43] But if it is true that Grynzspan reveals the power of traumatic testimony to Arendt, it is not quite clear how we are meant to hear that 'foolishly' ('one thought foolishly: Everyone, everyone should have his day in court').

Arendt clearly does not think the testimony of the righteous is somehow foolish. But neither is this 'foolishly' simply a self-distancing adverbial garb with which Arendt seeks to protect herself from the traumatising effect of Grynzspan's words. On one level, Arendt thinks her thought foolish because, just as Benjamin's storyteller is a vanishing voice in a world of over-information, Grynzspan's testimony illuminates the extent to which, to let Benjamin's famous words from 'The Story Teller' chase Arendt's, 'the epic side of truth, wisdom' has died in direct proportion to the devaluation of experience that he thought characterised modernity, and that Arendt found in the ruin of categories of thought and judgement revealed by totalitarianism.[44] So while a storyteller such as Grynzspan is a clearly a figure of redemption, what Arendt discovers 'in the endless sessions that followed' his testimony, what makes her first thought 'foolish', was actually, as she puts it, 'how difficult it was to tell the story – at least outside the transforming realm of poetry' (*EJ* 229). It is not so much the case that Arendt thought all the other witnesses were somehow irrelevantly inelegant compared to Grynzspan, then, but that the force of his story rested precisely in its ability to throw the difficulty of testifying into such sharp relief. In other words, Grynzspan's testimony demonstrates not the fact that, if everyone had their day in court, then somehow a new type of justice would be done, but the opposite: how achingly fragile truth-telling, in this sense, actually is.

In another and indeed related sense, when Arendt thinks 'foolishly', she is also, in some senses 'speaking the fool'. To ascribe foolishness to one's thoughts is a rhetorical act of self-doubt. When I describe myself as 'foolish', I am also scrutinising myself; as in the 'two-in-one' of thinking, I am voicing my own duplicity. The natural idiom for this kind of doublespeak is irony – the very mode of address that many of Arendt's readers have found so intensely inappropriate about *Eichmann in Jerusalem*. 'It is that heartless, frequently almost sneering and malicious tone with which these matters, touching the very quick of our life, are treated in your book to which I take exception,' wrote Gershom Scholem to Arendt in a heated exchange following the publication of the book.[45] Arendt replies, specifically to the charge that she had described Eichmann as a 'convert to Zionism': 'I never made Eichmann out to be a "Zionist." If you missed the irony of the sentence – which was plainly in *oratio obliqua*, reporting Eichmann's own words – I really can't help it.'[46] Many, with Scholem, have read in Arendt's irony a self-distancing disdain for the representation of the suffering of survivors. But I want to conclude by suggesting instead that Arendt's irony is at the heart of her response to the trial; and that, indeed, for those who lack the eloquent simplicity of the truth-teller, when the chips are down irony might well be the narrative mode most appropriate for the writer who wants not only to encounter the past, but to judge it.

Arendt is hardly unconscious of her own stylistic prejudices and knows that she has an important precedent in the much-chequered history of ironic thought. In her 'Thinking and Moral Considerations' essay she cites Socrates' exemplary ironic demonstration of how he teaches his students to think: 'It isn't that, knowing the answers myself I perplex other people,' Socrates states marvellously; 'the truth is rather that I infect them also with the perplexity I feel myself' ('TM' 173). Denise Riley begins her defence of the politics of irony with the same quotation, noting that although Socratic irony is often reviled for its haughty philosophical superiority, where the speaker simulates ignorance in order to reveal what they already know, the truth is that irony is as frequently 'self-disparaging'. Socrates, writes Riley, 'enacts the clinical irony which clarifies a true perplexity.'[47] Far from 'straightjacketing' madness in the name of the law, then, it is perhaps more helpful to think of irony as reason's psychoanalyst; and hence as a possibly more benign presence in the business of legislating for historical injury.

To speak in *oratio obliqua*, in indirect speech, is to speak double; it is an act of repetition which extricates the statement from its context, allowing it, as in Arendt's account of thinking, to get slippery, to slide out of its unthinking habitat, and to become something else on the lips of its imitator. So when Adolf Eichmann declares to the court (in Jerusalem) that he is a reader and admirer of Herzl's *Der Judenstaat*, Arendt parrots back: 'Theodor Herzl's *Der Judenstaat*, which converted Eichmann promptly and forever to Zionism' (*EJ* 40). Arendt not only reminds us of Eichmann's situational irony (needlessly, perhaps, given the context), but through her own verbal irony ('promptly and forever') deflates Eichmann's injurious pomposity and sends this utterly thoughtless Nazi utterance back to its source. But what she thus echoes back (and what Scholem could not hear) is now stripped of its original context. It is no longer Eichmann's statement; in Arendt's words it has become something else, something critical, something scornful – something, Arendt might have said, positively and politically judgemental.

Judging Eichmann in an ironic manner is not that controversial; nor is it, given his skills at self-parody, particularly difficult. Arendt was hardly the only commentator to think he was a buffoon. What is difficult about *Eichmann in Jerusalem* is that Arendt tends to write the majority of her reports on what was said at the trial in *oratio obliqua*. 'To the matter of which you speak', writes Scholem, 'it is unimaginably inappropriate [. . .] I detect, often enough, in place of balanced judgement, a kind of demagogic will-to-overstatement.'[48] But what would a writing appropriate to a 'balanced judgement' be in this context? Idith Zertal has argued that what Scholem was responding to in Arendt's language was also her 'contempt for the sublimity, the numinous sanctity of the Holocaust' which was such a crucial part of the national politics of the trial.[49] This is clearly why Arendt would also choose, for example, to report the State Prosecutor, Gideon Hausner's, words using indirect speech, precisely to create ironic distance from what she saw as bad politics. But Arendt was also aware, I think, of how swiftly an ethics of story-telling, an ethics which today is frequently placed at the centre of the encounter with trauma, can be made available to a politics of redemption which might not, in the end, serve the cause of the suffering it evokes.

Irony, as W. G. Sebald once noted, 'operates on the borders of what language can convey'.[50] Sebald was writing with reference to Jean Améry, a survivor-writer also known for his acerbity and rejection of pathos. Arendt too thinks and judges on that border. Read this way, her irony is not so much a refusal of suffering as the opposite: a register of the seriousness of an engaging with hurt. Describing irony's close relation to injury, Riley quotes the following piquant exchange from Schlegel's novel, *Lucinde*:

> *Julius:* I understand it. I even believe it. A joke can make a joke about every-thing; a joke is free and universal. But I'm against it. There are places in my being, the deepest ones in fact, where for that reason an ordinary hurt is unimaginable. And in those places a joke is intolerable to me.
>
> *Lorenzo:* So the seriousness of these places is probably not completely perfect yet. Otherwise there would be irony there by now. But for that very reason irony exists. You'll only have to wait awhile.[51]

Riley glosses the passage: 'Lorenzo is implying that irony will arise spon-taneously within that injury which has been compelled into an intensity of self-contemplation.' Thinking is the name Arendt gave to a similarly intense self-contemplation: a thinking that refuses the incomprehensibil-ity of trauma in the name of political judgement. It is in this sense too perhaps that irony is Arendt's testimony to the Holocaust: the way she finally manages to look at it, 'face-to-face'. 'That the tone of voice is predominantly ironic is completely true,' remember Arendt later admit-ted of the writing in *Eichmann in Jerusalem* in her interview with Gaus. 'The tone of voice in this case is really the person.'

It is telling, finally, that when Arendt presents her own judgement against Eichmann in her book (an act, according her critics, of extraor-dinary arrogance) she does so by putting quotation marks around her own words. Arendt had wanted Eichmann to be tried specifically for crimes against humanity (the crime that slipped to the margins of Nuremberg's final judgement). 'The question is', Arendt had written to Jaspers, 'would things be different if we had a law against *hostes humani generis* [enemies of humanity] and not only against murderers and similar criminals?'[52] The danger inherent in Hausner's approach was that, in seeing in Eichmann's crimes yet another, albeit the most cata-strophic, atrocity in the history of anti-Semitism, the prosecution elided the unprecedented nature of a crime which directly attacked 'human diversity as such'. For Arendt, Eichmann foremost was guilty of 'a crime against humanity, perpetrated upon the body of the Jewish people', and it is in these terms that she ventriloquises her own judgement. First, she rejects Eichmann's defence that he was at best an incidental villain whose only crime was to follow orders. (It was not Arendt who claimed Eichmann was innocent because he was banal, as some of her critics have wrongly charged, but Eichmann himself.) ' "What you meant to say was that where all, or almost all, are guilty, nobody is," ' Arendt responds. Even if eighty million Germans had planned and executed the killings with such meticulous care, she adds, ' "this would not have been an excuse for you," ' echoing, quite precisely, the judgement actually arrived at in Jerusalem in June 1961. She then adds her own:

> 'And just as you supported and carried out a policy of not wanting to share the earth with the Jewish people and the people of a number of other nations – as though you and your superiors had any right to determine who should and should not inhabit the world – we find that no one, that is, no member of the human race, can be expected to share the earth with you. This is the reason, and only reason, you must hang.' (*EJ* 270)

The language here is universal – 'we find that no one, that is, no member of the human race, can be expected to share the earth with you.' It is difficult to see how it could be otherwise since (as Ben Gurion knew as well as Kant) it is not possible to make judgements outside of some kind of communal consensus. Or as Arendt put it herself in her lectures on Kant: 'When one judges, one judges as a member of community.'[53]

But Arendt is very far from asserting the domination of universal judgement over the particularity of historical injury here. Her peroration is also an act of self-citation which is not, as most legal judgements by definition have to be, illocutionary. Arendt's judgement makes nothing happen. It is quite literally suspended between those quotation marks which punctuate the distance between the historical crime and what Arendt saw as the distracting politics of the trial. The marks neither outpace the irony of the rest of the book with a plea to a voice of integrity, nor are they fully ironic. If Arendt judges for all in her final testimony to the Eichmann trial, it is not because she fears madness or the incomprehensibility of trauma and wants to escape back into the law, but because she thinks the crime itself *is* an attack on all. But the quotation marks also suspend the time of this judgement, as if to say, as Lorenzo does to Julius in *Lucinde*, that the seriousness that belongs to the crime of the Holocaust is not yet perfect, as if in the end Arendt herself, like the court in Jerusalem, is still waiting for the day of judgement.

Notes

1. Hannah Arendt, ' "What Remains? The Language Remains": A Conversation with Günter Gaus', in *The Portable Hannah Arendt*, ed. Peter Baehr (Harmondsworth: Penguin, 2000), pp. 15–16.
2. Arendt, letter to Karl Jaspers, 2 December 1960, *Hannah Arendt, Karl Jaspers Correspondence 1926–1969*, ed. Lotte Kohler and Hans Saner (New York: Harcourt Brace, 1992), p. 410.

3. Jaspers to Arendt, 19 October 1946, p. 62.

4. Susan Sontag, 'Reflections on *The Deputy*', in *The Storm Over The Deputy*, ed. Eric Bentley (New York: Grove, 1964), p. 119.

5. Geoffrey Hartman, *The Longest Shadow: In the Aftermath of the Holocaust* (Basingstoke: Palgrave, 2002), p. 22.

6. As Idith Zertal has argued in her provocative recent study of the troubling relations between trauma, grief, collective memory and national politics in Israel, Arendt's irreverence was not towards the victims, but towards the sanctification of their suffering within the emerging politics of Israeli nationhood. Idith Zertal, *Israel's Holocaust and the Politics of Nationhood* (Cambridge: Cambridge University Press, 2005).

7. Arendt's focus on the problem of judgement in the wake of Eichmann is well documented in contemporary political theory. For an excellent exegesis and interpretation of the development of judgement in Arendt's thought, see Ronald Beiner's 'Interpretative Essay' in his edition of Arendt's *Lectures on Kant's Political Philosophy* (Chicago: University of Chicago Press, 1992), pp. 89–156. See also Seyla Benhabib, 'Judgement and the Moral Foundations of Politics in Hannah Arendt's Thought', *Political Theory*, 16.1, 1988, pp. 29–51 and her *The Reluctant Modernism of Hannah Arendt* (2000; Lanham: Rowman & Littlefield, 2003), pp. 172–92. I am indebted too to Elisabeth Young-Bruehl's narrative of the changing role of judgement in Arendt's life in *Hannah Arendt: For Love of the World* (New Haven, CT: Yale University Press, 1982).

8. Arendt, *The Human Condition* (1958; Chicago: Chicago University Press, 1998), pp. 178–81.

9. In an attentive reading of the 'scandal' of Arendt's tone, Deborah Nelson has read Arendt's repudiation of suffering in *Eichmann* across to her later critique of suffering in *On Revolution*. Suffering, for Arendt, threatens to flood the thought necessary to counter the profound thoughtlessness of totalitarianism as she describes it in *Origins*. But in an arresting twist, Nelson also links Arendt's ironic repudiation of suffering to the inability to think the Holocaust. See Deborah Nelson, 'Suffering and Thinking: The Scandal of Tone in *Eichmann in Jerusalem*', in *Compassion: The Culture and Politics of an Emotion*, ed. Lauren Berlant (London: Routledge, 2004), pp. 219–44.

10. Arendt, *Eichmann in Jerusalem: A Report on the Banality of Evil* (1963; Harmondsworth: Penguin, 1994), p. 10. Hereafter cited as *EJ*.

11. Quoted in Zertal, *Israel's Holocaust*, p. 107.

12. As reported to Arendt in a letter by her friend, Mary McCarthy, 21 November 1966, *Between Friends: The Correspondence of Hannah Arendt and Mary McCarthy 1949–1975*, ed. Carol Brightman (London: Secker & Warburg, 1995), p. 198. Brightman reports the literary historian Alan Wald inadvertently slipping up and referring to 'Hannah Eichmann' in a conference on Mary McCarthy at Bard College in 1993 ('Introduction: An Epistolary Romance', p. xxvii). For accounts of responses to *Eichmann in Jerusalem*, see Richard I. Cohen, 'A Generation's Response to *Eichmann in Jerusalem*', in *Hannah Arendt in Jerusalem*, ed Steven E. Ascheim, (Berkeley: University of California Press, 2001), pp. 253–80, and Elizabeth Young-Bruehl, 'Cura Posterior: *Eichmann in Jerusalem*', in *Hannah Arendt*, pp. 328–58.

13. Cited in Elisabeth Young-Bruehl, *Hannah Arendt*, p. 329.

14. Cited in David Cesarani, *Eichmann: His Life and Crimes* (London: Heinemann, 2004), p. 273.

15. Arendt, 'Thinking and Moral Considerations', in *Responsibility and Judgment*, ed Jerome Kohn (1971; New York: Schocken, 2003), p. 159. Hereafter cited as 'TM'.

16. Arendt, 'Letter to Gershom Scholem', in *The Jewish Writings*, ed Jerome Kohn and Ron H. Feldman (New York: Schocken, 2007), p. 471.

17. Noting that Arendt was witness to the worst atrocities of the twentieth century, Patricia Owens reveals how the complexity of reality in Arendt's writing opens up a kind of ethics that demands a constant scrutiny about the limits of the comprehensible ('The Ethic of Reality in Hannah Arendt', in *Political Thought and International Relations: Variations on a Realist Theme*, ed Duncan Bell (Oxford: Oxford University Press, 2008), pp. 105–21). For a brilliant account of how Eichmann's unthinking provides a counter and mirror to Arendt's own complicated understanding of reality, see Rei Terada, 'Thinking for Oneself: Realism and Defiance in Arendt', *ELH*, 71.4, Winter 2004, pp. 839–66.

18. Cesarani writes of 'Arendt's irrational zeal in finding fault' in everything Hausner said, although Cesarani himself concedes that the 'thoroughness' of Hausner's opening address cleared the court of journalists after several days (*Eichmann: His Life and Crimes*, p. 47).

19. Harry Mulisch, *Criminal Case 40.61, The Trial of Adolf Eichmann*, trans. Robert Naborn (1961; Philadelphia: University of Philadelphia Press, 2005), p. 47.

20. Young-Bruehl, *Love of the World*, p. 332.

21. Arendt's apparent adherence to the transcendent authority of the law has attracted criticism from legal scholars. In a compelling essay on the competing narratives of history and justice in the Eichmann trial, Leora Bilsky argues that Arendt failed to appreciate how Hausner's tactics also constituted an unprecedented challenge to conventional jurisprudence by insisting not only on the story but on the importance of who tells it. With her conventional prejudice for visual documented evidence, Arendt is deaf to this new kind of justice which, Bilsky argues, works through 'a double gesture of imputing responsibility to the perpetrator by responding to the words of the victims'. Arendt, in other words, wanted to use the law to contain the incomprehensible (Leora Bilsky, 'Between Justice and Politics: The Competition of Storytellers in the Eichmann Trial', in *Hannah Arendt in Jerusalem*, pp. 232–52).

22. Cited in Young-Bruehl, *Love of the World*, p. 339.

23. Cesarani, *Eichmann: His Life and Crimes*, p. 254.

24. I am drawing here from Dori Laub's classic essay, 'An Event Without a Witness', in Shoshana Felman and Dori Laub, *Testimony: Crises of Witnessing in Literature, Psychoanalysis, and History* (New York: Routledge, 1992), and from Cathy Caruth's *Unclaimed Experience: Trauma, Narrative and History* (Baltimore: Johns Hopkins University Press, 1996), and her essay, 'Parting Words: Trauma, Silence and Survival', in *Between the Psyche and the Polis: Refiguring History in Literature and Theory*, ed Michael Rossington and Anne Whitehead (Aldershot: Ashgate, 2000).

25. Shoshana Felman, *The Juridical Unconscious: Trials and Traumas in the Twentieth Century* (Cambridge, MA: Harvard University Press, 2002), p. 124.

26. Omer Bartov, *Mirrors of Destruction: War, Genocide, and Modern Identity* (Oxford: Oxford University Press, 2000), pp. 188–9.

27. Ibid., p. 195.

28. For a legal history of the significance of testimony in the trial, see Douglas, *The Memory of Judgment: Making Law and History in the Trials of the Holocaust* (New Haven, CT: Yale University Press, 2001), pp. 95–182.

29. Felman, *The Juridical Unconscious*, p. 142.

30. Ibid., p. 145.

31. Ibid., p. 146.

32. Ibid., p. 9.

33. Robert M. Cover, 'Violence and the Word', in *On Violence*, ed Bruce B. Lawrence and Aisha Karim (Durham, NC: Duke University Press, 2007), pp. 292–313.

34. Arendt, *The Life of the Mind* (1971; New York: Harcourt Brace Jovanovich, 1978), p. 216.

35. Arendt, letter to Karl Jaspers, 2 December 1960, pp. 409–10.

36. Arendt addressed these questions in greater detail in her final book, *The Life of the Mind*, following the lectures she gave on late Kant at the University of Chicago just after the publication of *Eichmann*, the New School in 1970, and the Clifford lectures in Aberdeen in 1973. The New School lectures are now published in Arendt, *Lectures on Kant's Political Philosophy*.

37. In much of this Arendt is following Heidegger's emphasis on the non-instrumental nature of thought. But smuggled into this writing is a critique of what she saw as her former teacher and lover's historically ill-judged (to put it mildly) reification of thinking at the expense of action, particularly political action. Arendt herself, by contrast, pointedly retrieves thinking for politics by aligning it with judgement. The relation between Heidegger and Arendt is a constant current pulling under her experience of the Eichmann trial and her later work on thinking and judgement, but is beyond the scope of the present study. For contrasting accounts of the relation between Heidegger and Arendt's writings, see Benhabib, *The Reluctant Modernism of Hannah Arendt*, and Dana Villa's *Arendt and Heidegger: The Fate of the Political* (Princeton: Princeton University Press, 1996).

38. Julia Kristeva, *Hannah Arendt*, trans. Ross Buberman (New York: Columbia University Press, 2001), pp. 153–4.

39. Mary McCarthy, Arendt's friend and the final editor of *The Life of the Mind* after her death, edited Arendt's repetition of 'when the chips are down' out of the version of 'Thinking and Moral Considerations' that made it into that book.

> 'When the chips are down': I cannot say why the phrase grates on me and particularly coming from her, who, I doubt, ever handled a poker chip. But I can see her (cigarette perched in holder) contemplating the roulette table or *chemin de fer*, so it is now 'when the stakes are on the table'

– more fitting, more in character. (Mary McCarthy, 'Editor's Postface', *The Life of the Mind*, p. 248)

By contrast, I prefer the thought of Arendt describing herself as a poker player, caught in the agony of indecision, finding a way to make the judgement that comes from somewhere at the back of the mind yet will determine everything that follows. It is not the gambler, but the player forced to act who Arendt is identifying with here.

40. Arendt, *Lectures on Kant's Political Philosophy*, pp. 65–72.
41. Arendt, 'Truth and Politics' (1967), in *The Portable Hannah Arendt*, p. 564. Hereafter cited as 'TP'.
42. See Nelson for a close reading of how Arendt both conveys and cancels her emotion towards Grynzspan's testimony in this uncharacteristic passage ('Suffering and Thinking', p. 227).
43. Felman, *The Judicial Imagination*, p. 238.
44. Walter Benjamin, 'The Storyteller', in *Illuminations*, ed. Harry Zohn (New York: Schocken, 1970), p. 87; Hannah Arendt, 'Understanding and Politics', *Partisan Review*, 20, 1953, p. 388.
45. ' "Eichmann in Jerusalem": Exchange of Letters Between Gershom Scholem and Hannah Arendt' (January 1964), in *The Jew as Pariah*, ed. Ron H. Feldman (New York: Grove, 1978), p. 241.
46. Arendt, 'Letter to Gershom Scholem', in *The Jewish Writings*, p. 468.
47. Denise Riley, *The Words of Selves: Identification, Solidarity, Irony* (Stanford: Stanford University Press, 2000), p. 147.
48. Scholem, *Jew as Pariah*, p. 142.
49. Zertal, *Israel's Holocaust*, p. 153.
50. W. G. Sebald, 'Against the Irreversible: On Jean Améry', in *On the Natural History of Destruction*, trans. Anthea Bell (London: Hamish Hamilton, 2003), p. 156.
51. Riley, *Words of Selves*, pp. 161–2.
52. Arendt, letter to Jaspers, 23 December 1960, *Hannah Arendt, Karl Jaspers Correspondence*, p. 417. Eichmann was tried under Israel's Nazis and Nazi Collaborators (Punishment) Law, 1950, designed originally to try Jewish collaborators who had come to Israel (none were convicted).
53. Arendt, *Lectures on Kant's Political Philosophy*, p. 75.

Chapter 3

Fiction in Jerusalem: Muriel Spark's Idiom of Judgement

> It was a highly religious trial.
>
> Muriel Spark, *The Mandelbaum Gate*[1]

> When it comes to moving from one side of Jerusalem, which is Jordan, to the other side, which is Israel, the world of dream sets in.
>
> Martha Gellhorn, 'The Arabs of Palestine'[2]

Hannah Arendt and Muriel Spark missed each other by just one day in Jerusalem in the June of 1961. Spark attended the Eichmann trial between 26 and 28 June for the *Observer* newspaper. No reports for the paper seem to have appeared. Instead, Spark was to place the trial at the 'desperate heart' of her most historically ambitious and aesthetically awkward novel, *The Mandelbaum Gate* (1965). The first four chapters of the novel were published in instalments in the *New Yorker* in 1965. Codas to Arendt's reports on the trial published in the magazine four years earlier, like *Eichmann in Jerusalem*, Spark's fictions of Jerusalem run an uncomfortable line between the act of witnessing Eichmann's trial and the question of what the trial said – or demanded – about being a Jew, or in Catholic convert Spark's case, a half-Jew, in relation to modern Israel in the early 1960s.

Both writers produce dissident answers to this question. Where Arendt responded to what she saw as the sanctification of the suffering of survivors in the prosecution's case with a critically judging irony, Spark interrogates the power of fiction itself to make meaning out of what she calls the 'bottomless pit' revealed by Eichmann's trial (*MG* 283). Where Arendt's acerbic style was taken as indifference to the suffering relived at the trial, a carapace of bitter reason that also questioned her Jewishness (Gershom Scholem accused her of lacking *Ahabath Israel* or a 'love of the Jewish people'), Spark's decision to use Jerusalem in

1961 as the setting for a recasting of the pilgrimage genre as an exuberant thriller-cum-farce similarly missed the historical point for some of her critics.[3] In terms that echo criticisms of Arendt's cold cleverness, Alfred Kazin, for instance, described Spark's pilgrimage as 'dispassionate'. Subsuming what he referred to as 'the unnaturalness of the situation' in Israel–Palestine to the theoretical obsessions of a theologically driven plot, *The Mandelbaum Gate*, he wrote, was frothily ill-suited to the seriousness of the times at hand.[4]

Spark's biographer, Martin Stannard, reports speculation that the hostile reception of *The Mandelbaum Gate* by American Jewish intellectuals may have influenced Spark's decision to leave New York, where she had been working under the auspices of the *New Yorker* since her return from Israel in 1961.[5] In an odd echo of the way Spark's religion became entangled with questions of her race, bizarre rumours about Arendt's apparent 'conversion' to Catholicism also circulated around New York at the same time. The melodramatic quality of such 'canards', as Arendt described the story of her alleged conversion, is pretty characteristic of the deeply felt and occasionally histrionic intensity of the debates and arguments, political and religious – and frequently political as religious – generated by Eichmann's trial.[6] The trial was always going to be more than a legal theatre, and was always going to demand answers that exceeded its secular jurisdiction. And while the trial itself was not opera, the debates, myths and narratives that developed in its wake frequently restaged its moral and historical dramas with an operatic intensity. The ways in which that intensity is dramatised in Spark's novel is the subject of this chapter.

Unlike many who were drawn to Eichmann's trial as an arena for the secular staging of justice, Spark went to Jerusalem with questions of religious and racial identity uppermost in her mind. Whereas Arendt was caught out by the extent to which her reading of the trial became the occasion for interrogating her identity as a Jew, Spark had the question of identity firmly in front of her even before she stepped on the plane. In 1963, the same time that *Eichmann in Jerusalem* was published in book form, the *New Yorker* published Spark's autobiographical short story, 'The Gentile Jewess', the title under which Spark also wrote much of *The Mandelbaum Gate*. 'There were so many half-Jews that I knew and I thought this is a whole way of looking at life, a whole consideration worth writing about,' Spark stated in a late interview with Martin McQuillan. 'That's what I wrote about, and I went to the Eichmann trial for the *Observer*.'[7] To the half-Jew, or to the Jew perhaps, as Arendt was to put it, while having no strong connections to the community, 'for whom, however, the fact of their Jewishness is not a matter of indifference', there was indeed a way of looking at life, and of looking at the Eichmann trial, that was well worth writing about.[8] The difficulty Spark had in writing her novel, however (unusually, it took her over two years), the peculiar form it eventually took (Spark later repudiated the novel on the grounds of its shapelessness), testify to just how problematic this perspective was in pre-1967 Israel.[9]

A great part of that difficulty rested (and rests) with the 'unnaturalness of the situation', as Kazin put it, of post-Mandate, post-1948, post-Nakba and post-Holocaust Israel. It was the specifically genocidal nature of the Nazi crime, the crime against the Jewish people as Jewish people, which the Eichmann trial revealed to the world. But few in Jerusalem in 1961 could have failed to note how the politics of race, religion and identity pervaded not only the trial, but also the entire region. As Eichmann in his glass box feebly affected to turn his murderous anti-Semitism into a sympathetic, if unfortunately perverted, Zionism, elsewhere the categories of race, creed and nationality were caught up in newly intense dramas. Jerusalem in 1961 was no place for what Spark describes as the 'non-conforming alliance' of race and creed possible in Britain (*MG* 29). Jerusalem, rather, was a place of dangerous absolutes. This is how Saul Ephraim puts it to Spark's heroine, Barbara Vaughan, in the novel:

> 'You're British. Well that's alright, more or less. You're a Catholic convert – OK. But you're a half-Jew as well. The three together are a lot.'
> 'I should have thought being a half-Jew would be held in mitigation for the rest.'
> 'You ought to know better.'
>
> (*MG* 31)

Frequently viewed to one side of the febrile politics of race, religion and identity that surrounded the Eichmann trial, much criticism (particularly British) has cast *The Mandelbaum Gate* as a novel that affirms the freedom of the self from categories of religion and race. Whether couched in terms of postmodern liberation or within more modest claims about the independence of the individual conscience, this affirmation of freedom is assumed to be Spark's response to the moral abyss opened up in the Eichmann trial. In this chapter I suggest that this is too easy a response to the questions generated by the trial and, in turn, by the book itself. For Spark there is no escape from the intensities of race and religion. Part theological, part secular melodrama, Spark's idiom of judgement rests instead with the extravagant powers of fiction. Such an idiom demands that we read Spark not as somehow apart from the operatic fictions generated by Jerusalem in 1961, but as a responding to them directly and deeply. The droll eccentricity that infuriated some of her critics (no American would have written a novel like this, Kazin comments; such wry detachment only comes from an old literary culture), but has given succour to others who think such detachment points to the survival of the liberal (read 'English') novel, turns out to be something of a lure. Neither beside the historical point nor loftily rising above it, Spark's apparently dispassionate humour is the measure of the real seriousness of what she discovered in Jerusalem in 1961.

At the Eichmann trial

Freddy, a British diplomat, crosses from Jordan into Israel via the Mandelbaum Gate. With a bumbling insouciance familiar in late colonial Oxbridge males, he notes in passing the political intensity at the Gate, wishes the Israelis and Arabs could be more moderate, and turns to the real task at hand, determining whether a bread-and-butter thank-you poem should be a rondeau or a triolet. But within weeks Freddy will taste the delights of immoderation. Crossing back through the Gate, he enters a fugue state, sleeps with Suzi, the androgynous blue-eyed Arab free spirit, cracks a Pro-Arab anti-Semitic British spy ring, and is fortuitously freed from the tyranny of his 'Ma' when she is knifed to death by her long-suffering servant. Meanwhile, Barbara Vaughan, the Gentile–Jewess and Catholic convert, in love with an archaeologist divorcee, sits atop of Mount Tabor, the alleged site of Christ's transfiguration, pondering her identity. 'I go on, she thought, with questions and answers in the old Hebraic mode, chanting away to myself' (*MG* 50). Barbara too slips through the Gate to complete her pilgrimage disguised as an Arab woman servant. A bout of scarlet fever and a cathartic beating of a British anti-Semitic spy in a Jordanian brothel later, Barbara returns to Israel, having decided to marry her divorcee in defiance of her Church. A fortunate decision, it turns out, for by a fateful birth-certificate plot-twist, it happens that, as Harry was really Catholic all along, his first marriage is void. Meanwhile, Barbara's schoolmistress colleague, the existentially minded Ricky, finds love and Islam in the copious arms of the travel-insurance-spy agent Joe Ramdez, whose son, Abdul, runs illegal sandals and pilgrims across Potter's Field with his friend Mendel Ephraim, with whom he eventually opens a café in Tangier.

It is not difficult to see why some readers should have thought the extravagant plotting of *The Mandelbaum Gate* made distastefully light of the situation in Jerusalem in 1961. 'It is the story of an escapade', wrote Sybille Bedford, somewhat breathlessly, in an enthusiastic contemporary review, 'and the theme, essentially, is libera-tion. Liberation and identity. Liberation from *an* identity.'[10] If liberation from identity was the main driving force behind the novel, then the absurdity of its espionage/pilgrimage plotting, the guises and double guises, masquerades and veils would be all part of its generic piece. The Cold War spy-thriller genre had long used the lying intrigue of other nations as a clammy background for the adventures of the freely deter-mining Western liberal. With the disastrous Lavon affair (a botched Israeli counter-terrorism plot that targeted British and US interests in Egypt) rebubbling in the early 1960s, pipelines being laid under the Negev Desert (another 'plot' to drain water away from Arab lands), the ascent of Nasser and Arab nationalism, and deals with the French over Algeria, it could be said that Spark had captured the fevered intensity of pre-1967 Israel rather well.

The Eichmann trial, however, and its role in the novel, makes such a reading difficult, or, at the very least, qualifies its emancipatory claims. However light Spark's tendency to farce seems to make of Israel, just as attending the trial was to throw her into a personal crisis, the plots in which her characters find themselves are contrived in direct response to the trial. 'Something', writes her biographer 'seems to have happened to her in Israel, something abstractly investigated in *The Mandelbaum Gate.*' Sleepless and tearful upon her return, at the time Spark was unable to discover why she felt so wretched. Only later did she link her depression to the experience of attending the trial.[11] Throughout her immaculately maintained archive, there is a sense that something is missing, something that cannot quite be told, about Spark's passage through Jerusalem. I won't tell you now about the trial, she writes to her agent, John Smith, from her hotel room in Tel Aviv, or about my car crash with an insufferable guide who insisted on showing me the cement factories of the new Israeli state and not the Holy sites I had come to see.[12] She does not, it seems, really tell anybody very much about her journey to Jerusalem.

However, there is much in the novel that is directly autobiographical. 'I am really interested essentially in the Holy Land,' Barbara says to her similarly insufferable Israeli guide. 'This is the Holy Land,' he replies (*MG* 24). When he then asks Barbara why she has chosen to become a Catholic and turn her back on her people, Barbara feels 'her personal identity to escape like smoke from her bones' (*MG* 27). History, and in particular the trial, mix this metaphor into a deathly dark twist: if the guide's interrogation of Barbara's *Ahabath Israel* questions her iden-tity as a Catholic convert, just down the road in Jerusalem the smoke from the death camps was being recalled by a generation for whom the questioning of one's racial identity was not an option. As the guide makes clear to Barbara (as one suspects his real-life model did to Spark too), it was not just Eichmann who was on trial in Jerusalem, nor an indifferent world, but the post-Holocaust generation of Israeli-Jews, Diaspora-Jews, half-Jews, convert-Jews … anyone for whom their Jewishness was not a matter of indifference.

Attending the trial for the *Observer* was part of a wider project, both to prepare for Spark's next novel, 'The Gentile-Jewess', and, as a fairly recent Catholic convert, to visit the Holy Land. Unlike other writers and reporters, then, Spark went to the trial with mystery in mind. The surprise, perhaps, and possibly the source of her deep unease in Israel, was to discover one of the most profound mysteries, not so much in its religious sites, but unravelling itself in the secular halls of the People's House of Justice. As the Chief Prosecutor, Gideon Hausner, clearly understood and intended, the Eichmann trial was to be an event of Biblical proportions. Recall his moving and powerful opening statement: 'When I stand before you here, judges of Israel, in this court, to accuse Adolf Eichmann, I do not stand alone. With me stand six million prosecutors' (*EJ* 260). For the prosecution, the trial had not only a historical, but also a Messianic purpose: to tell the history of the persecution of the Jewish people; to transform the Holocaust from an unnameable festering trauma in the history of Israel, into a collective myth of suffering and redemption. 'For a stage of the pilgrimage you might go to the Eichmann trial,' suggests Barbara's cousin, the international lawyer, Michael Aaronson.

> 'I haven't been', she said.
> 'I know. That's what I'm saying.'
>
> (*MG* 175)

'This trial is part of the history of the Jews,' adds Saul Ephraim (*MG* 175). In a mirror image of the ways in which the Holocaust was lifted into narratives of suffering and redemption within the trial itself, then, in Spark's novel too, brute history is encountered through the sense-conferring powers of fiction and memory-making.

Spark attended the part of the trial in which Eichmann was being cross-examined, thus missing what Saul Ephraim in the novel describes as 'the impassioned evidence from the survivors of the death-camps' witnessed by Arendt (*MG* 177). Eichmann's own testimony was the trial's 'boring phase'; few could tolerate the grinding mendacity of his defence and many journalists had left. But if missing the dramatic testimony of the survivors put Spark at a distance from the affective drama at the centre of the trial, she was no less convinced that its real horror rested with the suffering of listening by earphones to translations of Eichmann's convoluted arguments. I want first to turn to this scene in the novel, not least because it is here, in the courtroom, that most readers locate the prompt for Barbara's journey through the Mandelbaum Gate, and hence the moral direction of meaning in the novel as a whole:

Eichmann was being examined day by day by his own counsel, in a long-drawn routine, document by patient document. Many journalists had gone home. Barbara was not prepared to be taken in by the certainty, immediately irresistible, that this dull phase was in reality the desperate heart of the trial. Minute by minute throughout the hours the prisoner discoursed on the massacre without mentioning the word, covering all aspects of every question addressed to him with the meticulous undiscriminating reflex of a computing machine. Barbara turned the switch on her earphones to other simultaneous translations – French, Italian, then back to English. What was he talking about? The effect was the same in any language, and the terrible paradox remained, and the actual discourse was a dead mechanical tick, while its subject, the massacre, was living. She thought, it all feels like a familiar dream, and presently located the sensation as one that the anti-novelists induce. Or it is like, she thought, one of the new irrational films which people can't understand the point of, but continue to see; one can neither cope with them nor leave them alone. At school she usually took the novels and plays of the new French writers with the sixth form. She thought, repetition, boredom, despair, going nowhere for nothing, all of which conditions are enclosed in a tight, unbreakable statement of the times at hand. She had changed her mind, without awareness at the moment, of any disruption in the logic of personal decision, but merely allowing herself to recognize, in passing, that she would inevitably complete her pilgrimage to the Holy Land. This mental fact was the only one that seemed able to throw light on the ritualistic lines which the man in the glass box was repeating or to give meaning to her mesmerized presence on the scene.
  Bureau IV-B-4. Four-B-four
  I was not in charge of the operation itself, only with transportation. . . .
  Muller needed Himmler's consent.
  I was not in a position to make any suggestion only to obey orders.
  And technical transport problems.
  Strictly with timetables and technical transport problems.
  I was concerned strictly with timetables and technical transport problems.
  Bureau IV-B-4. Four-B-Four-IV-B-4
  [. . .]
  Presently, a slight hesitation occurred in the court proceedings, a pause. The counsel for defence looked courteously towards the tribunal, as if waiting for one of the judges to say something, while they, in turn, were under the impression that he was about to speak. The presiding judge then leaned forward and accompanied a sign for the lawyer to proceed with a brief remark in German. 'What are we waiting for?' duly said the English translator's voice in the earphones.
  – What are we waiting for?

– We're waiting for Godot.
The lawyer proceeded: 'I come now to the matter of the Jewess Cozzi –'
It was a highly religious trial. (*MG* 177–80)

As anyone who has read even just a few pages of the transcripts of the Eichmann trial will appreciate, particularly those reporting his cross-examination, Spark gets unnervingly close here to reproducing the benumbing sense of tired nausea that accompanies the effort of trying to listen in one's head to what is being said (and it is always an effort).[13] The dead mechanical tick of language that drains history of life: Hannah Arendt was not alone in thinking Eichmann's a murderous discourse, all the more fatal for its banality. 'Whose words killed men because those men were words', runs a line from Michael Hamburger's poem about Eichmann.[14] A good part of this passage is reproduced verbatim from Eichmann's actual testimony and lifted directly from Spark's copies of the trial's translated transcripts (given to all attending journalists daily). As well as being at its dramatic centre, therefore, the trial scene as a piece of living history sticks out in the novel; or rather the novel has stuck this piece of history on to its fiction. Always a magpie, Spark frequently grafts the events of her day into her writing; one of the pleasures of reading the press cuttings in her *Mandelbaum* archive is tracking the absurd-sounding story to the really absurd incident in the novel.[15] Rarely, however, does Spark cite from her sources so directly and immediately. This is not a fictionalisation of history so much as a place where history, for a moment at least, refuses to be incorporated into fiction. As Bryan Cheyette has put it, by reproducing the transcripts verbatim, it as if Spark is saying that 'nothing can be added to the historical record.'[16]

Something else does, however, have to be added to the fictional record in order for this incursion of a hard little chunk of the indigestible real into the novel to be made meaningful in a way that Eichmann's words fail to mean. The question posed by this passage, in other words, echoes the question posed by the trial itself: what kind of narrative can we create in response to Eichmann? If Eichmann's language is murderous to its core, what kind of writing can make the massacre live? Although Spark's laconic homage to the *nouveau roman*, *The Driver's Seat* (1970), is only a few years away, something about her response to the trial meant that *Mandelbaum* was not permitted to slip off the historical or moral hook by wrapping up the absurdist agony of the times in a tight, unbreakable statement. The response to Eichmann's bad theology is not (not in Jerusalem in 1961, at any rate) the negative theology of the *nouveau roman*. Or at least not quite. Spark was not left waiting for Godot at the trial of Adolf Eichmann. She was waiting on God.

The evidence in this part of the trial was brought forward by Eichmann's defence lawyer, Dr Servatius, in an ill-fated effort to demonstrate Eichmann's administrative insignificance. The atrocities Spark heard about in the courtroom between 26 and 28 June were mainly committed against children: the Lidice children, for example, out of whom only three were considered fit for 're-Germanisation'. Eichmann had nothing to do, apparently, with the fate of the remaining ninety-one. The children from Düsseldorf: did Eichmann order that they should wear the yellow star? He was not authorised to do so. Of the five thousand children sent from Hungary, only forty-three made it to Palestine; did Eichmann know the fate of the remaining? They were sent to 'a different destination'. No doubt Servatius had chosen cases concerning children in order to highlight some imaginary tenderness on Eichmann's part. More often than not, evidence of Eichmann's alleged mercy backfired; boasting about the fact that he had kept children with their families by raising the age a boy could be turned in a slave labourer from ten to fourteen, for example, Eichmann conveniently forgets that those children who got to stay with their mothers invariably also got to die with them rather sooner than their fourteenth birthday.[17]

None of this is written into the novel. Spark does not do pathos, not even at the major trial of the Holocaust (especially not, for reasons which will become clear, at the major trial of the Holocaust). But if the children remain outside of Spark's narrative, her repetition of the circumlocutory obscenity of Eichmann's speech carries their living massacre like an invisible scar, and the catastrophic disjuncture between form and content, the vehicle of Eichmann's deathly speech and its terrible tenor, remains. One possible reason why Spark could not turn this novel into a tight unbreakable statement of the absurdity of the trial was because something in Israel prevented her from closing that gap with language, as if the sense of the massacre, and the demands it makes on those now witnessing it, had to be kept alive. It is because she wants to find a way of keeping the wound between speech and atrocity open, that Spark, like Arendt, is so focused on Eichmann's speech. On the copies of the trial transcripts in her archive, she has diligently marked every instance of Eichmann's evasive loquacity: 'The idea was that these mandatory language formulations were for the use in the files themselves,' Eichmann at one point attempts to explain the intricacies of Nazi speech to Judge Halevi. 'They were applicable for the outside. When one had to discuss these things . . . Then these mandatory formulations automatically entered the files.' 'When registering the deportation of the Jews, one must not mention the final destination, but also say emigrated,' he adds, helpfully.[18] There are pages of this, each particularly obscene convolution carefully marked by Spark's pen. In her letter to John Smith from Tel Aviv, Spark apologises for the length of one of her sentences; she's caught the habit from Eichmann and his lawyer, she says.[19] As with Arendt's fastidious focus on the linguistic infelicities of the trial, for Spark too it is as if a deathly meaninglessness threatens to overwhelm any sense that can be made of the event. Among the source material for *The Mandelbaum Gate* in Spark's archive are well-thumbed pages of Arendt's five reports for the *New Yorker*.

As for many of those who witnessed the trial, Spark, then, came away charged – and the sense of a forceful moral injunction here is perhaps not to be underestimated – with the task of finding a form of meaning, and a form of writing, adequate to its 'desperate heart'. The trial scene, in this respect, is not just one step on Barbara's pilgrimage, a bit of local colour in an early 1960s theological romp, but the transfiguring historical event that defines the form that the rest of the novel will take: the exuberant passage not only of the novel's two main characters, but of the text itself through the Mandelbaum Gate into the feverish dream world of Eastern Jerusalem. As Frank Kermode astutely pointed out in his review of the novel, if the drainage of meaning in the Eichmann trial is at the novel's desperate heart, Spark's most immediate response is a redemptive celebration of the power of fiction to transfigure historical reality: a power that also belongs, and of course by no means coincidentally, to Jerusalem itself, site of Christ's transfiguration into myth and original place of the pilgrimage genre in Western literature.[20]

As Maurice Halbwachs argued in his classic study of the narrative origins of collective memory-making, with the emergence of the Christian pilgrimage narrative, the absolute judgements dramatised in the Old Testament give way to the storytelling 'on a human level' of the New. Judging became telling, obedience to the law a narrative adventure of faith and spirit.[21] For a Jew turned Catholic convert writing under the shadow of the Holocaust, it is not difficult to see why a fictional pilgrimage might be an especially tempting genre with which to attempt to redeem the catastrophe that has decimated one's race with the narrative power of one's faith; 'the scriptures were especially important to the half-Jew turned Catholic. The Old Testament and the New, [Barbara] said, were to her as near as she could apply to her own experience the phrase of Dante's vision – "bound by love into one volume"' (*MG* 26).

The bonds of love, however, are frequently bloody. The Christianising of Jewish sacred sites that accompanied the development of the pilgrimage, as Spark well knew, was also a way of narrativising acts of historical violence. From the Crusades on, pilgrimage literature is characterised by a passionate intensity that carries with it the violent history of its origins, albeit recouched in the passion of faith. *The Mandelbaum Gate* is no exception here; the novel does not so much come up with the idea of pilgrimage as a solution to the historical catastrophe of the Holocaust ('I feel a terrible need to do something positive . . .,' Barbara says after her visit to the trial) as find itself swept along, in a fast-moving bloody narrative which pays scant attention to the intentions and deliberations of its pilgrims ('and if I'm going on a pilgrimage, I'm going on a pilgrimage, that's all' (*MG* 182)). There is 'something mechanical about the force that retains people around a sacred place,' writes Halbwachs, of the force that propels pilgrims.[22] Similarly, Spark's characters do not so much experience their journey as hallucinate it in states of fevered disjunction: 'there will be bloodshed,' intones Freddy repeatedly, and there is.

Despite her author's evident fascination with the violent otherworldly force of her pilgrimage across Jerusalem, many readers have been curiously keen to see Barbara's journey in terms of rather reasonable forms of religious compromise. D. J. Enright, for example, in a sympathetic contemporary review, reads the novel in terms of a 'chastened Christianity'. 'Hope' after Eichmann, he concludes, 'lies with those who, though committed to their faith, preserve their own "private judging" individualities, and are able to respect other individuals who are otherwise committed.'[23] Pleas for religious tolerance frequently imply that there is something to be 'tolerated' about the other's faith (hence their back-handedness). By contrast, being a Jew for Barbara is 'inherent', 'in the blood', just as her faith is a 'dangerous gift'; these are not things to be 'tolerated', they just absolutely are. Yet even Spark's most avowedly Catholic critic reads the moral of the story in the exercise of Barbara's individual conscience; her decision to marry Harry, hence, makes her a disobedient believer (in contrast to Eichmann's fatally blind obedience), who keeps her faith alive, if not dangerously so, in the hope that God 'will ratify her own decision' later.[24] Hedging one's moral and theological bets on a conveniently agreeable God seems a pretty tepid response to the call to judgement, whether it be God's himself ('I know of thy doings, and find thee neither cold nor hot,' thunder the lines from *Apocalypse* across the novel (*MG*, 21, 44, 50)) or the more secular forms of judgement so clearly demanded by Eichmann's trial. And it is clearly no answer to the Lidice children.

If readers have been quick to find forms of compromise in a novel which is so unashamedly uncompromising, this is a reflection not just of the prevailing liberalism of mid-century literary criticism, but also of the way similarly reasoned affirmations of the importance of individual judgement over the tyranny of thoughtless obedience characterised many secular responses to the Eichmann trial itself. Martha Gellhorn, for instance, in a piece on the trial written for the *Atlantic*, writes of Eichmann as a 'warning that the private conscience is the last and only protection of the civilized world'.[25] Gellhorn's framing of the trial as the occasion for a re-engagement with Enlightenment values is fairly typical of moral reactions to the trial. 'The private conscience is not only the last protection of the civilized world,' she concludes her piece, '[i]t is the one guarantee of the dignity of man. And if we have failed to learn this, even now, Eichmann is before us, a fact and a symbol, to teach the lesson.'[26]

Spark, too, was well aware of the didactic importance of the trial in secular terms. In her writing notebook to the second part of the novel, the part she found so difficult to complete, she has copied the following famous passage from Kant's essay, 'Perpetual Peace: A Philosophical Sketch': 'Every man is to be respected as an absolute end in himself; and it is a crime against the dignity that belongs to him to use him as a mere means to some external purpose.'[27] Kant's parsing of moral reason was at the heart of the endeavour to legislate for crimes against humanity in the postwar period, from Nuremberg to the drafting of the Declaration of Human Rights in 1948, to the Eichmann trial and beyond. What Spark does with this passage in her novel, however, is far more ambitious than a simple endorsement of a free-thinking liberal conscience (which, in any case, by the middle of the twentieth century had proved itself a pretty poor defender of the dignity of man).

If Kant is in her notebooks, rather, it is because Spark needs to understand what respecting a man as an absolute end in himself can mean in a world where absolute ends can emerge with such uncompromising violence. This violence in the novel is both political and temporal, and a-temporal and theological. The 'and' here is important; *Mandelbaum*'s exuberant form, its intense and frequently ludic plotting and fevered sense of moral purpose, are derived precisely from the effort to marry the otherworldly and the worldly. The point at which they meet is also the novel's point of least resistance: the moment at which the characters and the plot itself threaten to topple into a kind of delirium produced from the sheer effort of being in Jerusalem in 1961.

When, in the second part of the novel, Barbara finally feels all 'of a piece, a gentile Jewess, a private-judging Catholic, a shy adventuress', this is not, as is often assumed, because she is exercising her private conscience over either the historical allegiances of her race or the dogma of her faith, and thus proving herself through her pilgrimage to be unlike Eichmann (a surprisingly common contrast noted by critics – did anybody seriously worry that they were like Adolf Eichmann in 1961?).

Rather it is because 'she had caught some of Freddy's madness . . . flowering in the full irrational norm of the stock she also derived from' (*MG* 164). Freddy's is the madness of late English colonialism, 'coast memory', the cold-historical sweat of diligent administrators in hot places; but the 'currents of horror, unidentifiable, unknown to experience' that charge through his body in Jerusalem also gesture both to the darkness at the heart of the trial itself, and to a feverish occult menace that pervades the text (*MG* 124). English colonialism, the legacy of the Mandate, the Holocaust, the Eichmann trial, the unnatural intensity of present-day Israel–Jordan, all are linked indissolubly in Spark's novel, albeit obscurely. As I argue in the rest of this chapter, it is this same obscurity, the sense in which the occult presses itself against the novel's historical framework, which constitutes the boldness of Spark's idiom of judgement.

The suffering of Job

'[A]ll your suffering and inconvenience of scarlet fever is God's blame.'

(*MG* 214)

I asked Alfred Kazin one day if he thought the death of six million Jews could have any meaning; and he replied that he hoped not.

Elie Wiesel, 'Eichmann's Victims and the
Unheard Testimony'[28]

One, possibly paradoxical, reason for paying serious attention to the unnerving intensity of Spark's theological ambitions in *Mandelbaum* is because of their politics. While the unnaturalness of the situation in Israel in 1961 was, as it is today, caused by human history, the meanings ascribed to those catastrophes are frequently described, understood and experienced in theological and religious terms. In this respect, Spark might be credited as being one of the first writers who fully grasped how a sense of the occult, of a meaning beyond human history and temporality, not only clouded political debate in Israel, but frequently defined it. For many, the Eichmann trial was the event that transformed the Holocaust from a historical event into a metaphysical narrative. Eichmann's was precisely a 'highly religious trial', in this respect, not only because its apparent evacuation of meaning left the court waiting for Godot, but also because new and powerful narratives about the meaning of human suffering flooded into that God-shaped hole. Spark, as I have been arguing here, understood all this keenly.

Despite the fact that the novel seems so awkwardly at odds with developing genres of Holocaust writing, then, Spark's sense of the occult meanings of the trial puts her much closer to contemporary Jewish writing than her dissident half-Jewish convert status might lead one at first to assume.[29] Survivor and writer Elie Wiesel, for example, another writer-witness at the trial, wrote in similar terms to Spark on how the 'absurdity' of Eichmann's acts 'transcended his person and placed him outside of temporal justice'.[30] The trial failed, in Wiesel's eyes, as had so many discussions of guilt and justice in the wake of the Holocaust, because it was incapable of registering the extreme extent to which it 'splashed its guilt' over everyone. The trial normalised the catastrophically abnormal; 'the earth had trembled and men had stayed the same.'[31] For Wiesel, the particularly bitter irony left in the trial's small wakes was that only people prepared to discuss this a-temporal, extra-juridical guilt in terms appropriate to its magnitude were, in fact, the least guilty and the most suffering: the survivors whose tragedy, writes Wiesel, 'is the tragedy of Job before his submission: they believe themselves guilty, although they are not'.[32] 'Pray for those who suffer justly,' Spark writes in one of her *Mandelbaum* writing notebooks. 'Those who suffer unjustly have their reward.'[33]

As Esther Benbassa has argued in her study of the role of suffering in constructions of Jewish identity post Eichmann, the narrative of Job's suffering discovered new life both in avowedly theological interpretations of the Holocaust, which attempted to give religious meaning to the guiltless suffering of its innocent victims, and in more secular mythologisations of that suffering itself – a suffering without redemption, as Benbassa puts it, which seems to have neither a heavenly nor an earthly term. This, in a sense, is what Wiesel was already saying when he drew on the analogy of Job in his reading of the trial; because no trial, and thus no historical or political process, ever will be adequate to this suffering, there can be no earthly form of judgement made in its wake. Suffering, here at least, becomes a sacred limit which blocks historical or political redemption. Yet, as Benbassa argues, the real significance of Job's plight within Judaism lies not just with the horror of his guiltless suffering and the obscenity of a world in which God can let a man suffer for no other reason than a cheap bet with Satan, but also with Job's 'inability to grasp the meaning of it'.[34] Or, as Muriel Spark was to put it, frequently and throughout her long career, Job 'not only argues the problem of suffering, he suffers the problem of argument'.[35]

'Yet man is born unto trouble, as the sparks fly upward.'[36] It is not the representation of suffering itself which is the issue for Spark (for her, as for other religious believers, there will always be suffering) but the particular ways in which such suffering incites us to question our world. From her first novel, *The Comforters* (1956), which shares with *Mandelbaum* an uncomfortable hallucinatory allure, to the late formalism of *The Only Problem* (1984), the questions posed by Job's suffering are never far from Spark's concerns. Given that, as she wrote in a 1955 review of Jung's reading of Job, the book also marks a 'critical stage in the development of Israel', it is perhaps also not surprising that Job's suffering of the problem of argument followed Spark, so to speak, back to Jerusalem in 1961.[37] Job for Spark is as central to the history of Jerusalem as any modern-day pilgrimage; indeed, any pilgrimage made in 'the year of Eichmann', as the novel repeatedly historicises itself, is also going to have to reckon with the problem of arguing Job's suffering.

It is from the starting point of Job's arguments too that the occult in Spark's fiction, for all its cheek and love of mischief, partly derives its theological seriousness. For Spark, the Book of Job is decisive in post-exilic history because, at 'the point at which human reason cannot reconcile the fact of evil with the goodness of God, an anthropomorphic conception of God breaks down'.[38] This is the moment when mystery emerges properly into the Hebraic world. It is this mystery that Spark affirms again and again throughout her novels: in fictions which neither reconcile us to human suffering nor demonstrate the goodness of God, but consistently mark a limit point for human reason. For Spark, Job is a magnificent dramatic poem: fictional not historical, and its point, just as so often the point of fiction itself is for her, is to affirm an occult sense of mystery in the sublunary. While such occult plotting characterised Spark's writing from its beginnings, and whilst the evident pleasure she takes in such mischief increases in the later work, it is in *Mandelbaum* that Spark's fictional theory runs closest to its theological and historical sources. Kermode first observed Spark's tendency to put her characters in plots which were 'absurd like God's' in his review of the novel.[39] Where recent criticism has tended to stress the extent to which Spark thus foregrounds the caprices of fiction-making (many of her obituaries in 2006 focused on her prescient postmodernism), in this context and, perhaps, especially in the context of Israel in 1961, it seems just as important to affirm the absolute faith in mystery that lies behind that fiction-making. 'I don't claim that my novels are truth – I claim that they are fiction, out of which a kind of truth emerges,' Spark said in a much-quoted interview with Kermode in 1963, the same year she troubled over *Mandelbaum*. This is not, it seems to me, the difficult part of Spark's theory of fiction. Far odder, and quite deliberately so, is the way she next moves to underwrite the existence of absolute truth through the writing of fiction itself. She continues:

> There is metaphorical truth and moral truth, and what they call anagogical, you know, the different sorts of truth; and there is absolute truth, in which I believe things which are difficult to believe, but I believe them because they are absolute. All this is one aspect of truth, perhaps. But if we are going to live in the world as reasonable beings, we must call it lies.[40]

In a sense we could say that to read a Spark novel is to endure the suffering of argument. At some level it means accepting that there is a limit to human reason, that the arguments her fiction deals with are not going to be resolved by comparisons with human behaviour. And if Job's suffering is the paradigm for Spark's distinctive fictional theology, Jerusalem in 1961, I would hazard, is its historical source.

It is because arguing the problem of suffering takes us to the limit of human reason that Spark, unusually among post-Holocaust renderings of Job, to put it mildly, finds the book so funny. In her review of Jung's *Job* Spark attacks the way in which critics have tended to focus on the dramatic dialogues between Job and his (so-called) comforters, and Job and God in the middle section of the book, at the expense of the more traditional Hebraic prose judgements of the Prologue and Epilogue. While focusing on the dialogues between Job and God, as most Christian critics tend to, emphasises the human drama of the fiction (hence heralding the passage of Job into literature), for Spark the Epilogue is crucial both because it is the only place where God says anything really intelligible to Job (that is, to pray for those comforters who had tried to persuade Job that his suffering was due to a guilt that he just had not thought hard enough about), and because the Epilogue also contains the book's scandalously hilarious ending: God's reward to Job for his suffering by bestowing upon him large amounts of livestock, plus 'seven sons, unnamed; three daughters respectively and frivolously entitled by names which, translated, are "Turtle Dove", "Cassia" (a perfume) and "Box of Eye-paint" '.[41]

I want to draw a line from this early reading of Job to Spark's Blashfield Foundation address in 1971, 'The Desegregation of Art'. Many commentators have read her defence of satire and humour in that lecture as a post-novel defence of the brilliant deathly cold humour of *The Driver's Seat* of the year before. But the subject of the lecture, the cultish representation of suffering in contemporary culture, speaks far more directly back to Jerusalem in 1961. The vicarious identification with suffering in depictions of what in the lecture she calls (coyly) the 'gross racial injustices of our world' is in reality a block to real understanding, Spark argues. The salt tears that bowl down our cheeks blind us to the real human causes behind such suffering. And as our tears fall, the 'culture of the oppressor–victim complex' blindly perpetuates itself: 'there is always, too, the man who finds the heroic role of the victim so appealing that he'll never depart from it.' The only other lesson the victim can take from this complex, is to resolve not to be a victim: 'I suggest that wherever there is a cult of the victim, such being human nature, there will be an obliging cult of twenty equivalent victimizers.'[42] Anyone who has tracked recent debates about the depiction of suffering in post-Holocaust writing and historiography will recognise how early, and how accurately, Spark was prepared to challenge what at this point were only developing sensibilities post Eichmann.[43] If the lecture, at least in part, is a response to her own novel, far from being blind to these sensibilities, *Mandelbaum* re-emerges as a crucial part of Spark's developing critique of the cult of suffering that arose mid-century.

If the suffering of the Lidice children did not appear directly in Spark's rendering of the trial in the novel, we might now add that this perhaps was because Spark was also refusing, not the meaning of their suffering, but its depiction within a sensibility so focused on that suffering that it fails to honour its seriousness. Refusing the cult of suffering sensibility, thus, is another way of keeping the wound between form and historical content uncomfortably open – of keeping the massacre alive. Whence also, however, and even more discomfiting perhaps, Spark's humour. Unlike the anagogical humour she admires in the writing of *Job*, the humour Spark advocates in her Blashfield lecture is entirely earthly and political. Ridicule, for Spark, is a direct and exuberantly bad-tempered protest against the way false sanctifications of suffering separate us 'from the actions of our life'.[44] This is not some well-manicured lofty indictment of the absurdity of her times (a common characterisation of Spark), but a thoroughly moral defence of the seriousness of humour as a proper response to suffering. If the Eichmann trial, for Spark as for many, recast the Book of Job for a post-Holocaust world, the lesson she took away from Jerusalem was not about a suffering without term, but about the problem of finding a fictional form capacious enough for that suffering. Part of the answer to that problem (the only problem, Spark would say) resides like Job, with understanding that the plots one finds oneself mark the limits of human reason. The other, paradoxically, means resisting making such a limit falsely sacred by embracing the ridiculousness of this occult meaning of one's life. It is within that sense of the ridiculous that Spark's final answer to Eichmann is revealed.

A world of dream

> She had changed her mind, without awareness at the moment,
> of any disruption in the logic of personal decision, but merely
> allowing herself to recognize, in passing, that she would
> inevitably complete her pilgrimage to the Holy Land.
>
> (*MG* 177)

Whereas in Christian mythology Jesus takes on Job's suffering for the sake of mankind, in *Mandelbaum* the torments of the novel's pilgrims are pretty remorseless, even by Old Testament standards. The Biblical Ruth offsets suffering such as Job's with her selfless kindness and bountiful generosity; in Judaism the Book of Ruth is read on *Shavuot*, the harvest feast that celebrates the gift of the Torah. Here she appears in the perverted form of Ruth Gardnor, another of Barbara's comforters who nurses her on her sickbed, and who, despite her name, cultivates nothing but a spiteful anti-Semitism. One of the attractive things about the moral philosophy of Christianity might well be, as Barbara suggests, the way it harmonises human action despite the obscurity of motive and intention, but the characters in the second half of *Mandelbaum* have good cause to argue that its plots strain to harmonise the obscurity of actions, that they do not so much execute as find themselves in (*MG* 161).

It is the upstart young priest at the altar of the Church of the Holy Sepulchre who reminds his pilgrims of the 'supernatural process going on under the surface and within the substance of all things' (*MG* 199) in the novel. But the supernatural or occult, for Spark, is not simply otherworldly; 'I treat the supernatural', she said in a 2004 interview, 'as if it were part of natural history.'[45] While Spark launches her characters into their ludic suffering with a feverishness that matches their own, this is also a way of making history happen, or perhaps happen again, not just as farce but as ethically redemptive.[46] And for Spark the only way to make justice happen, in a novel at least, is through the occult force of fiction itself. The genre most suited to articulating the moral occult, as Peter Brooks demonstrated in his classic study, is melodrama (as we also saw in Rebecca West's melodramatic representation of Nuremberg).[47] For Brooks the melodramatic excess of the late nineteenth century signalled a kind of moral deficit. In *Mandelbaum* the inability of the Eichmann trial to make sense is finally substituted by the frenzied fiction-making of a hilariously fevered plot, driven by pseudo-causalities that make a kind of moral sense unavailable to the court in Jerusalem. But whereas in secular melodrama the occult is there to remind us what is lacking in the world, in Spark the occult returns with a fully Biblical force. In the end, there is nothing tepid, and nothing boring and repetitious, about the drama of judgement in *Mandelbaum*.

In one of the novel's final scenes, a fevered Barbara attacks the anti-Semitic British spy, Ruth Gardner, with a pair of headphones:

> Barbara threw these objects at Ruth, then in a frenzy leapt upon the woman and battered her head with the disconnected earphones of the wireless. Ruth kept saying, 'My God, please, Barbara, quiet! Quiet, Barbara, please – quiet!' Barbara scratched. Every obscene word that she had ever heard and (what was so strange) never had heard, Barbara pelted forth at Ruth Gardner. (*MG* 270)

Icons of the desire to translate justice for a new world, the defendants at Nuremberg had once worn their headphones as though they were a new form of defensive armour. In the Eichmann trial, Phillips, the makers of the headphones used, insisted that their logo be removed for fear of upsetting the neighbouring Arab market. In Spark's melodrama, the headphones seem to have lost the power to translate international history into law and have instead become weapons of attack. Or, we could say, Spark has transfigured these icons of postwar secular justice into swords of a melodramatically uncompromising intervention into the post-Holocaust history of anti-Semitism.

'I know of thy doings, and find thee neither cold nor hot; cold or hot,' chant the lines from *Apocalypse*, the most uncompromising and surreal book of the New Testament, across the novel. 'Being what thou art, luke warm, neither cold nor hot, thou wilt make me vomit thee out of my mouth' (*MG* 21). In the end, Barbara spews Ruth out: or at least spews out a judgement against her in words she 'never had heard'. There is nothing tepid, or chaste, finally, about this scene whose hysterical theatricality, at the same time, enacts Kant's moral determinism in the intensity of its violence. Instead it is as if Spark runs the trial through an occult scene of judgement precisely so as to re-invest Kant's moral judgement with a newly historical sense of purpose, as the judicial is re-imagined as a form of absolute judgement. Far from being frothily irrelevant, turning legal history into farce turns out to be a way of redeeming its sublunary deficiencies.

It is in this scene too that I think Spark gives her final answer to the Israeli guide who accuses her of repudiating her Jewishness through her conversion. Although the scene makes both moral and generic (moral as generic) sense in that it restages secular judgement in the absolute terms of melodrama, Barbara's attack on Ruth is not an act of moral agency. Nor has it anything remotely to do with the beliefs of a privately judging Catholic. Barbara amazes herself by her actions, even as she has rehearsed them in her mind. She is driven to act, just as Benny is driven to kill the tyrannical Ma, in an addition to the plot that verges on being meaningless unless we think of it perhaps as more melodramatic excess: an accretion to the moral drama that stretches the surface realities of the novel almost to breaking point. The last part of the novel is stuffed with such pseudo-causalities. (Spark apparently wrote the final stretch of the novel over a full fifty-six hours, and then collapsed.)[48] To give one particularly laden chain of associations: with a gormless nonchalance characteristic of middle England, Freddy's soon-to-be dead 'Ma' casually confuses Eichmann with a German musician she knew before the war, as if the first major war crime trial since Nuremberg were simply an occasion for the renewal of social networking. With music in the narrative air, Barbara then recalls that she last played the cello at a dinner party in the war at which she first met the Gardners and at which, she only remembers in Jordan, unusually for wartime Britain, no one was wearing a uniform. The only Jew (or half-Jew) at a soirée of anti-Semites, at the party Barbara decides, of course without then knowing why, that she will give up music. None of these associations makes any precise sense. They are not meant to. Chronology, for Spark, is never causality; the reason why one acts in the way one does can come later, or it can come without you knowing at all.[49] But Spark knows that it is out of such associations that fictions are made and that, correspondingly, it is out of such fictions that histories are fatefully, and often violently, determined.

This sense of being part of a history, Jewish history, which is lived unconsciously, was at the heart of the short story that, in a sense, first took Spark to Jerusalem, 'The Gentile-Jewess'. The memories of childhood days spent with the Jewish side of her family are also recalled in *Mandelbaum*. In the novel, however, the sepia tones of pre-war Passovers stay pretty much within the conventions of family reminiscence. 'She ees a bit of milk and meat in the same dish,' parodies Michael in a parody well aware of the codes for depicting 'Jewishness' in the twentieth-century British novel (*MG* 36). Something much stranger, however, is at work in Spark's short story. 'The scene is as clear as a memory to me,' Spark begins, suggesting not clarity, but a shifting play of the presence and absence of the past for the remembering self.[50] This sense of distance and overwhelming proximity characterises not only the narrator's memories, but also the memories that belong to her Jewish grandmother's life to which the narrator, on the one hand, is so drawn that she cannot believe she was not there: by her grandmother's side, for example, in the van that drove with the Suffragettes up Watford High Street.

On the other hand, in a characteristically Proustian gesture, it is precisely the narrator's absence from the past that attracts her to it. 'Was I present at the Red Sea Crossing? No, it had happened before I was born.'[51] The question of how one relates to a history at which one was not present, but yet which seems so overwhelmingly there in one's mind, was exactly the dilemma that the Eichmann trial raised for many Jews, and half-Jews, converts and atheists, within both Israel and the Diaspora. For Spark the trial was not, as it was for others, an occasion to renew her Jewish identity through an identification with the suffering of Eichmann's victims. As I have been suggesting here, however, it did not follow that Spark repudiated that suffering; what she grappled with in Jerusalem, rather, was the task of finding an idiom of judgement adequate to it. If the effort nearly drove her mad, as Spark herself would have been the first to recognise, this was not least because one's debts to the world frequently come not from one's identity, but from the occult side of one's head, from a place where what is least manageable about one's place in history has its own sense. And if that means that the suffering in Jerusalem in 1961 finally gets its reward in Spark's novel with an Arab called Abdul Ramdez and a Jew called Mendel Ephraim opening up a café in Tangiers together, then so be it.

Israel goes to the Vatican

For many today such an ending remains about as appropriate as God rewarding Job for all his suffering by restocking his herd and with a daughter called 'Box of Eye-paint'. Yet while the bizarrely funny endings given to us by fiction and, in Spark's case, by God, may be otherworldly, they are by no means beyond history or politics for being so. If what haunts Jerusalem in 1961 appears to come from the limit points of human reason, it is from that very same point too, Spark suggests, that a politically lived form of redemption might emerge. Jerusalem in the novel is not the only site to generate occult meanings. The seaside hippy town of Acre in the novel (and in Israel in the 1960s) draws a somewhat different kind of pilgrim:

These were lapsed Jews, lapsed Arabs, lapsed citizens, runaway Englishmen, dancing prostitutes, international messes, failed painters, intellectuals, homosexuals. Some were silent, some voluble. Some were mentally ill, or would become so.
  But others were not. Others were not, and never would become so; and would have been the flower pride of the Middle East, given the sun and air of the mind not yet to be available. (*MG* 101)

If in the year of *Mandelbaum*'s publication, 1965, the jarring double-stress on a future 'not yet to be available' suggested not a free passage, but a difficult stumbling towards such a time when the air of mind might allow the dissident to flower, then how much more so does it now.

If Spark qualifies her redemptive vision with hesitant grammar, this is because she also knows that it is from the same limit point of human reason that a more absolutist and uncompromising kind of politics can emerge. In 1973 something of the intensity of her experience in Jerusalem followed her to Rome, where she settled after leaving New York, (quite literally) in the form of then Israeli Prime Minister, Golda Meir's, visit to the Pope. The Vatican's handling of the visit was, even by the Holy See's abysmal public relations record, morally and politically botched. Having sanctioned Meir's visit diplomatically, the Vatican first put out a press statement to the effect that the meeting went well and had focused on ways of finding a peaceful solution to the 'Holy Land's' problems. Later, however, another Vatican representative told the press that the Pope had allowed the visit only so that he could lobby for the plight of the Palestinian refugees, and that in any case, the whole meeting had been entirely at the Israeli's pushy instigation. Worse still, back in Israel Meir revealed in a newspaper interview with *Maariv* that the Pope had used the occasion to lecture her on how the Jewish people, of all people, 'should conduct themselves mercifully'. Spark was incensed by the Vatican's double-dealing and barely disguised anti-Semitism. In a piece originally intended for the *New Yorker* she wrote:

> the idea that a modern Pope could be so far out of touch with reality as to start weighing in to a modern Prime Minister (the first woman head of government to be received in the Vatican) on the level of the old-time Renaissance moral admonishment of the Jews, rather gave the outsider to blink.[52]

But Spark, of course, was hardly an outsider. If the Eichmann trial had put her relation to her race on trial, when Israel came to the Vatican it was the historical institution of Catholicism itself that was called into judgement.

If Meir's visit recalled something of the intensities of Spark's 1961 visit this was not least because the melodrama that was being staged in Rome (Spark describes it as 'a Verdi opera') too had as its starting point something of the absolute occult authority that Job finally submits to God.

> The confrontation at the Vatican [Spark writes, eventually not in the *New Yorker* but in the British Catholic paper, *The Tablet*] was between two tenacious characters, each thoroughly formed by a long lifetime's dedication to

causes and cultures vastly different and yet somehow akin: basically, both the Vatican State and the State of Israel owe their conception and territorial existence to the doctrine that God says so. It is always an unarguable claim: you have to take it or leave it.[53]

I have been suggesting in this chapter that Spark's originality and political prescience in *The Mandelbaum Gate* rests with her recognition of how the business of worldly justice is both buttressed and compromised by the presence of the occult. If in the end, however, Spark retreated from the expansive and febrile melodrama of her Jerusalem novel into novels that, at least in appearance, more assuredly wrapped up their subject matter into tight unbreakable statements, this was because, perhaps, the doctrine of 'God says so' was finally easier to sustain in fiction than in lived history. By contrast, the unarguable claims of modern-day Israel/Palestine have proved themselves capable of being neither taken nor left. And Acre's dancing dissidents still wait for occult demands of absolute justice to be translated into a form of politically and historically meaningful redemption.

Notes

1. Muriel Spark, *The Mandelbaum Gate* (1965; Harmondsworth: Penguin, 1967), p. 180. Hereafter cited as '*MG*'.
2. Martha Gellhorn, 'The Arabs of Palestine', *Atlantic Monthly*, October 1961, p. 56.
3. ' "Eichmann in Jerusalem": Exchange of Letters Between Gershom Scholem and Hannah Arendt' (January 1964), in *The Jew as Pariah*, ed. Ron H. Feldman (New York: Grove, 1978), p. 241.
4. Alfred Kazin, 'Dispassionate Pilgrimage', *Book Week*, 17 October 1965, p. 2. Spark's novel was reviewed next to Jerzy Kosiniki's classic and controversial autobiographical account of the anti-Semitic violence in wartime Poland, *The Painted Bird*: an implicit comparison perhaps bound to make *Mandelbaum* appear light-weight.
5. Martin Stannard, *Muriel Spark: The Biography* (London: Weidenfeld & Nicholson, 2009), p. 319.
6. Arendt, 'Answers to Questions Submitted by Samuel Grafton' (one of Grafton's questions was about Arendt's 'conversion'), in *The Jewish Writings*, ed. Jerome Kohn and Ron H. Feldman (New York: Schocken, 2007), p. 478.
7. ' "The Same Informed Air": An Interview with Muriel Spark', in *Theorizing Muriel Spark: Gender, Race, Deconstruction*, ed. Martin McQuillan (Basingstoke: Palgrave, 2002), p. 215.
8. Arendt, 'Answers to Questions Submitted by Samuel Grafton', p. 483.
9. In a later interview Spark said of *Mandelbaum*: 'I don't like that book awfully much ... it's out of proportion. In the beginning it's slow, and in

the end it's very rapid, it races' (cited in Ruth Whittaker, *The Faith and Fiction of Muriel Spark* (Basingstoke: Macmillan, 1982), p. 79.

10. Sybille Bedford, 'Frontier Regions', *Spectator*, 29 October 1965.
11. Stannard, *Muriel Spark*, p. 245.
12. Letter from Muriel Spark to John Smith, 3 July 1961, pp. 1–3, Box Folder 1/10, Washington University in St Louis Library.
13. See www.nizkor.org/hweb/people/e/eichmann-adolf/transcripts.
14. Michael Hamburger, 'In a Cold Season', in *Ownerless Earth: New Selected Poems* (New York: Dutton, 1973).
15. In the press cuttings in Spark's archive in the McFarlin Library, for example, we find the story of Brother Daniel, a Jewish convert to Christianity, who had discovered that his Right of Return had been blocked. Brother Daniel wanted to be recognised by Israel as both a Jew and as a Catholic; his case was heard by Moshe Landau, who had also been the Presiding Judge at the Eichmann trial. There is also the case of Miss Sheila Smith, who had been captured when her boat on the Dead Sea got too close to the Jordanian shoreline. Her companion, Menahim Ophir, managed to swim back to Jerusalem.
16. Bryan Cheyette, 'Writing against Conversion: Muriel Spark and the Gentile Jewess', in *Theorising Muriel Spark: Gender, Deconstruction, and Psychoanalysis*, ed. Martin McQuillan (Basingstoke: Palgrave, 2002), p. 109. Spark was not the only writer to incorporate the trial transcripts directly in her writing. Charles Reznikoff, for example, in his long poem, *Holocaust*, pasted his work with words from many of the most disturbing witness testimonies from the trial (New York: Black Sparrow, 2007).
17. Taken from the Transcripts of the Trial of Adolf Eichmann, Sessions 79, 80, 81, Muriel Spark Archive, McFarlin Library, Special Collections, University of Tulsa.
18. Session 79, 26 June 1961, T1.
19. Letter from Muriel Spark to John Smith, 3 July 1961, p. 3.
20. Frank Kermode, 'The Novel as Jerusalem', *Atlantic Monthly*, 216, October 1965, pp. 92–8.
21. Maurice Halbwachs, *On Collective Memory*, ed. and trans. Lewis A. Coser (Chicago: University of Chicago Press, 1992), p. 210.
22. Ibid., p. 201.
23. D. J. Enright, 'Public Doctrine and Private Judging', *New Statesman*, 15 October 1965, p. 563.
24. Ruth Whittaker, *The Faith and Fiction of Muriel Spark*, p. 73.
25. Gellhorn, 'Eichmann and the Private Conscience', *Atlantic Monthly*, February 1962, p. 2.
26. Ibid., p. 17.
27. Notebook 39.5, Muriel Spark Archive, McFarlin Library, Special Collections, University of Tulsa.
28. Elie Wiesel, 'Eichmann's Victims and the Unheard Testimony', *Commentary*, 32.6, December 1961, p. 510.
29. The most immediate effect of the Eichmann trial was to give new force and legitimacy to the Holocaust testimonial genre itself. In fiction, Spark's sense that to witness the trial was to be pulled into its moral and psychic drama was shared by other Jewish writers. See, for example, Norma Rosen's

extraordinary *Touching Evil* (New York: Harcourt Brace, 1969), in which the trial's presence on American TV prompts Rosen's semi-autobiographical heroine into an intense and fevered reconsideration of her identity. Perhaps closer to Spark in terms of its sense of the mystery of the absurd, Saul Bellow's *Mr Sammler's Planet* (London: Weidenfeld & Nicolson, 1969) also takes the trial (and the 1967 war) as a point of tension and identification for Bellow's existentially aimless Mr Sammler.

30. Wiesel, 'Eichmann's Victims', p. 510.
31. Ibid., p. 514.
32. Ibid., p. 516.
33. Spark, Notebook 39.6. The same notebook contains a reprise of Spark's favourite formula for her reading of Job: 'afflicted argued the problem of suffering also suffered the problem of argument because it was beyond reason'.
34. Esther Benbassa, *Suffering as Identity: The Jewish Paradigm,* trans. G. M. Goshgarian (2007; London: Verso, 2010), p. 7.
35. Spark, 'The Mystery of Job's Suffering: Jung's New Interpretation Examined', *Church of England Newspaper*, 15 April 1955, p. 7.
36. Job 5:7.
37. Spark, 'The Mystery of Job's Suffering', p. 7.
38. Ibid., p. 7.
39. Kermode, 'The Novel as Jerusalem', p. 93.
40. 'Muriel Spark's House of Fiction', interview with Frank Kermode, reprinted in *Critical Essays on Muriel Spark*, ed. Joseph Hynes (New York: G. K. Hall, 1992), p. 30.
41. 'If we read only the prologue and the dialogue,' Spark comments, 'the effect is extremely ironical; add the epilogue and we are given that type of anagogical humour which transcends irony, and which is infinitely mysterious' ('The Mystery of Job's Suffering', p. 7).
42. Muriel Spark, 'The Desegregation of Art' (1971), reprinted in Hynes (ed.), *Critical Essays on Muriel Spark*, p. 35.
43. See in particular Esther Benbassa, 'Suffering without Hope', in *Suffering as Identity* and Carolyn J. Dean, *The Fragility of Empathy after the Holocaust* (Ithaca, NY: Cornell University Press, 2004).
44. Spark, 'The Desegregation of Art', p. 36.
45. James Brooker and Margarita Estévez Saá, 'Interview with Dame Muriel Spark', *Women's Studies*, 33.8, December 2004, p. 1036.
46. My thanks to Adam Piette for pointing out to me how Spark's commitment to the supernatural is at the same time a commitment to making history happen.
47. Brooks, *The Melodramatic Imagination: Balzac, Henry James, Melodrama, and the Mode of Excess* (1976; New Haven, CT: Yale University Press, 1995).
48. Stannard, *Muriel Spark*, p. 165.
49. In an interview with Sara Frankel, Spark says: 'What interests me about time is that I don't think chronology is causality: I don't think that the cause of things necessarily comes hours, moments, years *before* the event; it could come after, without the person knowing' (*Partisan Review*, 54, Summer 1987, p. 451).

50. Spark, 'The Gentile Jewess', *The Complete Short Stories* (Harmondsworth: Penguin, 2001), p. 347.
51. Ibid., p. 351.
52. Spark, 'The Elder Statesmen', letter from Rome, unpublished draft, Muriel Spark Archive, Box 31, MacFarlin Library, pp. 9–10.
53. Muriel Spark, 'When Israel Went to the Vatican', *The Tablet*, 24 March 1973, p. 272.

Part II: Territorial Rights

The unmentionable secret disclosed by the existence of the refugee was that the legal apparatus of the state had been superseded by the brute politics of nationalism. The refugee, Arendt goes on to note, is a curse on the fantasy of the nation state as the guarantor of equality before the law. Wishing the refugee either back to his country or incorporated into the immigrant population of your own, in this context, is indeed the grimmest of situational ironies, if by 'situation' we mean countries that play fast and loose with the law. 'Right', Hitler was to pronounce infamously, 'is what is good for the German people.'

In *Origins of Totalitarianism* Arendt developed one of the most subtle and complex critiques of how the twentieth-century's stateless ruptured historical fantasies about the inalienable sanctity of rights to emerge out of the war.[6] But Arendt also writes as the category of person she at the same time historicises. Like Koestler in his widely read memoir, or psychoanalyst Bruno Bettelheim who was to publish one of the first accounts of the psychological effects of the camps within only months of his own release from Buchenwald, for Arendt thinking and writing as a refugee was in itself a poignantly historical form of intellectual and, she might say, political action. Eighteen months after her arrival in New York, Arendt published a short essay entitled 'We Refugees'. Written just as the full horror of the Final Solution was becoming clear, and first published in the *Menorah Journal*, 'We Refugees' is one of a sequence of pieces that Arendt wrote on Jewish international politics in the crisis days of the early 1940s.[7] The essay is immediately notable for the way in which Arendt begins to outline of the critique of rights that she was to develop in *Origins*. But at least as striking is the essay's bitter-tight, unrelenting, ironic tone. In this chapter, I want to ask what it meant to write 'as' a refugee in the 1940s.

It is a question that cuts to the heart of the central theme of this book. If, as I argued in the first chapter, the Nuremberg trial failed to forge an idiom of judgement adequate to the genocide of the Jewish people, this in part was because it could not legislate against the statelessness that made it possible. The Eichmann trial responded to Nuremberg's failure to do justice to the victims of the genocide with a powerful moral theatre of remembrance. What remained wanting, however, as Arendt argued at the time, was the sense of a law capable of legislating against crimes against humanity from beyond the (frequently capricious) protection of the nation state. Against this background, to write 'as' a refugee is to do more than to testify to the suffering of statelessness. It is also to write from within the lacuna left by the law's inability to imagine a legal cosmopolitanism capable of protecting all of humanity in the postwar era.

Pointedly eschewing the pathos of exile in the doubling and distancing of its voice, Arendt's 'We Refugees' is more than a fierce protest against the condition of statelessness. It is in this early essay that we also see the development of the distinctively ironic voice that was to define Arendt's writing on Eichmann (discussed in Chapter 2), suggesting that if, indeed, judgement is a matter of style for Arendt, the origins of her particular aesthetic are to be found in the experience of radical right-lessness ('once they had been deprived of their human rights they were rightless, the scum of the earth'). While to talk of a refugee style, in this context, might be to risk sounding as historically gauche as effecting cosmopolitan statelessness in 1938 (or as apparently being emotionally detached from the testimonies at Eichmann's trial), here again the force of Arendt's political theory can be felt in her language, as her analysis of a new category of political and juridical human being – the refugee – emerges from within the complexities of her ironically charged lyricism. To be beyond the law, Arendt will later write in *Origins*, is to be cast into the 'dark background of difference' beyond the periphery of political and historical life. I read Arendt as asking what kind of imagination, and what kind of writing, can capture the perplexities of this radically new kind of human condition. In 1943, her answer to this question begins with what will become a characteristic act of linguistic disavowal.

We refugees

'In the first place,' the first line of Arendt's essay runs, 'we don't like to be called "refugees"'.[8] In the first place, then, Arendt immediately refuses the assignation that is declared in the title of her essay, 'We Refugees'. No sooner than a collective identity is claimed ('we refugees'), it is disavowed. Something of the immense distance between Virginia Woolf's cosmopolitan confidence ('as a woman I have no country') and Arendt, the refugee who will not recognise herself as such, is exposed in this quietly stated discomfort. Declaring cosmopolitan ambitions is clearly not the same thing as finding yourself in a declarative sentence. What the two writers share, however, is a pointed refusal of political and legal appellation. Just as Woolf's essay has been noted for 'cosmopolitan style' in its repeated wry questioning of the assumption that she should defend a liberal democracy against Fascism (when, as far as she and many others are concerned, that democracy is infected with its fair share of institutional and legalised barbarism), Arendt too writes 'as' a refugee, or as a refugee demonstrating why she does not like to be called a refugee, in her favoured verbal idiom, indirect speech, or *oratio obliqua*.[9]

Ever since the eighteenth century, there has been an allegiance between the subtle suppleness of textual artifice and ironic distancing, and cosmopolitan sympathies. The irony that indirect speech makes possible might be said to define the detachment available to the 'critical cosmopolitan', to borrow a phrase from Rebecca Walkowitz's study of cosmopolitan style.[10] Both the ironist and the cosmopolitan, of course, are also open to the charge of elitism, of rising above intended meaning as they rise above the parochialism of the nation state. But, as much as irony can signal lofty detachment, its semantic and vocal equivocations also render it highly suitable for voicing the experience of enforced un-attachment. 'Lying in a simple inflection of the voice', Denise Riley has written in her defence of the politics of irony, 'or of the voice slipped onto the page, [irony] generates puzzles of recognition and knowingness.'[11]

Irony produces puzzles, or perplexities, because it un-houses the voice; with irony we think we recognise what is being said, but we do not quite, because it is being said somehow differently. To speak ironically is also to indicate that one is not at home, either with the world or with oneself. It is to recite, repeat, echo, in Riley's account, those words in which the 'I' so often uncomfortably finds itself . . . as a refugee, as a woman. Whence irony's capacity to cause social trouble. Like being singled out by the newspapers for not knowing how to shop for bread and milk without being conspicuously pushy – Arendt's example in her essay of the person more accustomed to the ration queue or bread line trying to shop in New York in 1943 – the habits of irony mark the speaker out as not quite comfortable in their host nation, culture or language.

Arendt's irony in 'We Refugees' both gives vent to the rage of a 'we' torn brutally from its language, occupation and memory and, through a subtle ventriloquism, protests against attempts to normalise the position of the refugee. 'We were told to forget; and we forgot quicker than anybody ever could imagine,' she writes. Listen to the tone of the voice that slides on to the page here:

In order to forget more efficiently we rather avoid any allusion to concentration or internment camps we experienced in nearly all European countries – it might be interpreted as pessimism or lack of confidence in the new homeland. Besides, how often have we been told that nobody likes to listen to all that; hell is no longer a religious belief or a fantasy, but something as real as houses and stones and trees. Apparently nobody wants to know that contemporary history has created a new kind of human beings – the kind that are put in concentration camps by their foes and in internment camps by their friends. ('WR' 56)

,oting the interdictions (the refugee as forgetting conveniently) ,ced on events even before, so to speak, they had had a chance to ,come history and memory, Arendt's 'we' linguistically enacts its own ,.istorical un-homing.[12] This voice does not so much allow the real hidden history of the radically stateless to speak, as dramatise the fact that there is *no* position, at least no stable pronoun, to speak from. 'Apparently nobody wants to know that contemporary history has created a new kind of human beings – the kind that are put in concentration camps by their foes and in internment camps by their friends.' It is self-evident, 'apparently', that the refugee is an unwelcome new paradigm of historical consciousness, and yet this truth is also only apparent, an appearance. The disavowals are as dizzying as the protest against normalisation is sharp, as Arendt's 'new kind of human beings' speak from within the echo chamber of historical denial.

Neither is assimilation into another category, becoming another 'we', an option. In passages that make this essay, even by the standards of the early 1940s, one of the most bitterly despairing of her writings, Arendt is ruthless in her critique of the desperate non-identity politics of the figure she calls (after Bernard Lazare) the parvenu. 'We are fascinated by every new nationality in the same way as a woman of tidy size is delighted with every new dress which promises to give her the desired waistline,' she writes, as if enforced immigration were akin to a trip to Macey's (there is a conspicuous amount of shopping in Arendt's essay) ('WR' 64–5). And if the dress will not fit, if its cut turns out to be deceiving, there is always suicide. 'We are the first non-religious Jews to be persecuted,' Arendt notes, pitilessly, 'and we are the first ones who, not only *in extremis*, answer with suicide' ('WR' 59). Negative liberty, we might say, as the last refuge for the refugee.[13] Death by one's own hand, or madness: 'Whatever we do, whatever we pretend to be, we reveal nothing but our insane desire to be changed, not to be Jews' ('WR' 63). And indeed it is, in part at least, because of the 'insane' drive not to be Jewish, that the refugees of Arendt's title do not like to be called refugees: 'we don't call ourselves stateless, since the majority of stateless people in the world are Jews' ('WR' 63).

Arendt's targeting of the parvenu, a critique she had begun in her first book on Rahel Varnhagen, is entirely and boldly political.[14] None the less, her tone must have sounded harsh, not least to some of her refugee contemporaries. This aggressive bitterness is not simply the exasperation of the historian of European Jewish culture in the face of its extinction. It is also existential and linguistic. Twenty years later Arendt will describe a similar tone as, in her words, 'her person'. In her 1964 interview with Günter Gaus after the publication of *Eichmann in Jerusalem* (1963), when asked about the acerbic and, for many, offensive voice in that book, Arendt replied: 'That the tone of voice is predominantly ironic is completely true. The tone of voice in this case is really the person.'[15] Irony is no mere adornment to righteous political and historical anger, but also, as Arendt went on to argue in the wake of the Eichmann trial and, in particular, of Eichmann's banal thoughtlessness (as we saw in Chapter 2), a matter of thinking and judging in the world. To speak double, to parrot oneself ironically, is to generate the kind of perplexity necessary to thought. It is to speak as a refugee, certainly, but to the extent that one speaks 'as' one who knows what it is to be echoed in a category not of one's making.

It is also, Arendt might have said, a quiet way of insisting on the right not to be deprived of rights. For to double-voice the speech of the refugee, as Arendt does in her essay, is also to put a diacritical marker on her political and historical assignation. The stateless person, by definition, has been deprived of those rights accorded only to the legal citizens of nation states; to speak from inside that category – univocally as a refugee – would be to concede that fate existentially and linguistically, as well as politically. Arendt's double-voicedness refuses that path in 'her person'. It is this, as well as her radically extra-legal status, that makes the refugee a 'new kind of human being'.

The effect of this voice that echoes in and out of the category it so uneasily inhabits, is not just to critique the law, specifically international rights law (such as it existed in the early 1940s), but to foreground the extent to which matters of legal protection, of rights, are not only, as Arendt herself will insist, the very stuff of political life, but as such also matters of subjectivity and speech. Much like the more famous *Eichmann in Jerusalem*, with which it shares a sense of brute historical immediacy, 'We Refugees' reads as a kind fictive theatre of the law, a staging of its impasses within a drama of language. Drama, note, and not monologue; if the refugee, in Agamben's provocative formulation, has become the 'limit concept' of our time, in Arendt's essay, that limit is also experienced dialogically, between the stateless and the state-protected, between the refugee and the national or naturalised.[16] As compromised as the collective 'we' Arendt uses throughout the essay is the 'you' of her implied addressee: the non-refugee.

The immediate context for that 'you' is the readers of the *Menorah Journal* in which Arendt's essay was first published: intellectual and free-thinking Jews, whose sense of the possibilities of an American Hebraism within a 'Hellenism of nations' had established the journal in 1915, and was now being buffeted against waves that bore with them a very different experience of immigration.[17] The 'we' who are refugees, the title of her essay suggests, are not the same as the 'you' who are settled immigrants within a nation state. But in the same way as the new figure of the refugee refuses any easy assimilation into national categories, the possibility of any kind of existentially meaningful national or legal identity (national, immigrant, refugee, Jew) also begins to recede in the semantic shifting of Arendt's pronouns. By the end of the essay it becomes clear that, far from berating the 'we refugees' for their foolish, gauche, self-deceiving optimism (a reading that would be grist to the mill for the Arendt as a self-hating Jew argument that loomed so large after her reports on the Eichmann trial), Arendt's irony is also intended to indict a 'you' who is balefully blind to the historical and legal apparatus that pins the 'new kind of human being' into a language she can utter, but not own.

'But before you cast the first stone at us', Arendt writes, giving a New Testament lesson to others who would despair at the timidity of the poor parvenu, 'remember that being a Jew does not give you any legal status in this world' ('WR' 65). 'If we should start telling the truth that we are nothing but Jews', she continues, and note the far from comfortable shift from 'you' to 'we', if perhaps, we might rephrase this, we should learn to speak non-ironically, or even learn to speak 'as refugees',

> it would mean that we expose ourselves to the fate of human beings who, unprotected by any specific law or political convention, are nothing but human beings. I can hardly imagine an attitude more dangerous, since we actually live in a world in which human beings as such have ceased to exist for quite a while; since society has discovered discrimination as the great social weapon by which one may kill men without any bloodshed; since passports or birth certificates, and sometimes even income tax receipts, are no longer formal papers but matters of social distinction. ('WR' 65)

To speak 'as a Jew', to speak somewhere outside of irony and outside of the law, is a kind of linguistic and historical suicide. There is nothing, and this is where Arendt's powerful critique of rights really begins, about being merely human, about simply existing, as a Jew or as a refugee, that guarantees one any rights. On the contrary, as Marx argued, the only 'universal' rights are those accorded by the state and incidentally, therefore, are not public rights, but private entitlements to property and a freedom defined only in relation to our antagonism with others, rather than universal companionship.[18] Following Marx, Arendt twists this critique one stage further: to be stateless is to be absolutely and radically rightless. Concurrently, in a linguistic echo of this profoundly extra-juridical status, in Arendt's essay the conflation between speaking and being is pulled apart. To speak *as* a Jew in this context is not so much to *be* a Jew, to inhabit a linguistic designation as one's own, as to expose the historical paradox at the heart of the idea of human rights itself.

As she will later go on to argue in *The Origins of Totalitarianism*, in a section first published as an essay in 1949 under the title ' "The Rights of Man": What are They?', the 'calamity of the stateless' is that without political and national rights they are reduced to the 'abstract nakedness of being human' (*OT* 380).[19] Natural or self-evident rights are no protection for this 'new kind of human being'. 'If a human being loses his political status,' Arendt writes, 'he should, according to the implications of the inborn and inalienable rights of man, come under the situation for which the declarations of such rights provided.' But what the refugees of the 1940s and beyond reveal is precisely the opposite. Now it seems 'that a man who is nothing but a man has lost the very qualities which make it possible for other people to treat him as a fellow-man' (*OT* 381). With the refugee, the fallacy that rights ever existed outside of history and politics withers on 'the barbed-wire labyrinth', in Arendt's evocative phrase, into which the stateless had been drawn (*OT* 371).

Arendt, as we have seen, was already teasing out and reciting the perplexities at the heart of the concept of universal rights in her 1943 essay: foregrounding the paradoxes that come with the effort of trying to inhabit the category of human rights, politically, historically and existentially, through the very medium seen as central to democratic notions of rights, through her voice. In 'We Refugees' this voice is doubled not only against itself, but also against the conditions of its own disentitlement. As a refugee, as in fact a Jew in 1943, I have no country and as such, as rights are not natural but positive, national and political, I have nowhere from which to exist in civil, political, cultural and, we might add, linguistic terms. Except, of course, it is precisely as a writer, as a stateless intellectual claiming the right to thought, that Arendt brings her own condition into political and worldly view.

'The dark background of difference'

To suggest that the tonal estrangement of her writing enacts the critique of the law that she is also making, then, is not merely to praise Arendt's considerable rhetorical slickness (in what, after all, was her third language). It is also to understand how the refugee is not just, to recall Agamben's words, a 'new paradigm of human consciousness', not just, that is, a paradigm of what it means to be deprived of rights, politics and culture, but a person who enacts that deprivation in her speaking being. In her famous discussion of the private and public realms in *The Human Condition* (1958), Arendt reminds us that the realm of the private derives from the condition of deprivation. For the Greeks to be private, to be of the home, the *oikia*, was to be deprived of the freedoms that come from belonging to the political world.[20] Before it became a right to be protected from the political, privacy was a way of distinguishing political rights themselves – the rights due only to those in the *polis*. This intimacy between the private and the public realms (although both in Arendt's account of the decline of the public sphere have been squeezed of significance by the ubiquitous growth of the social), Arendt argues, is still manifested in the way that modern intimacy is illuminated against the background of the public realm. 'Each time we talk about things that can be experienced only in privacy or intimacy', she writes, 'we bring them into a sphere where they will assume a kind of reality which, their intensity notwithstanding, they could not have had before' (*HC* 50).

But what happens to the speaker when she speaks into a public realm where she is deprived of recognition? What happens when one writes an essay like 'We Refugees' in 1943? 'There seems to be no bridge', Arendt notes in *The Human Condition*, 'from the most radical subjectivity, in which I am no longer "recognizable" to the outer world life' (*HC* 51). She is writing about the experience of pain (love too, in a different way, Arendt says, is extinguished by publicity) but that 'most radical subjectivity' surely also recalls something of the plight of the refugee? Like the suffering or loving body, the body of the refugee is not recognised by the outer world. To speak from within the subjectivity of the refugee, then, is to bring the concealed into public light, which might be why Arendt chooses to describe such a telling as 'indecent'.

> Those few refugees who insist on telling the truth [Arendt concludes 'We Refugees'], even to the point of 'indecency', get in exchange for their unpopularity one priceless advantage: history is no longer a closed book to them and politics is no longer the privilege of the Gentiles. ('WR' 66)

The indecency of refugee style, we might say, is the writing of the vanguard, a writing back into the public and political realms from the position of the stateless.

Arendt, as should be clear by now, claims that indecent truth-telling for herself in her refugee essay. But, as much as Arendt's voice is a form of political critique, hers is not the sort of irony that allows one to rise out of the dilemmas one is revealing – which is also perhaps what makes it an example of refugee and not cosmopolitan style. Rather, Arendt's voice remains tightly enmeshed in what is also part of her historical project in the essay: to make the 'intimate life' of the refugee recognisable. In what looks, at least at first, as if it might be the first non-ironic passage of the essay we find the following evocation of the private life of the refugee:

> I don't know which memories and which thoughts nightly dwell in our dreams. But sometimes I imagine that at least nightly we think of our dead or we remember the poems we once loved. I could even understand how our friends of the West coast [of the US], during the curfew, should have had such curious notions as to believe that we are not only 'prospective citizens' but present 'enemy aliens'. ('WR' 57)[21]

These are what Arendt calls 'dark speculations': the thoughts and memories that come at one in the night. But, while the passage begins by evoking the dreams and memories of the refugee (the unconscious as speaking to me of my lost identity), it ends, again, in *oratio obliqua* ('such curious notions as to believe'), with the grimly pernicious associations that give grotesque body to the 'matters of social distinction' that, earlier in the essay, Arendt had analysed as casting the refugee into the realm of 'nothing but human'. The unconscious, by the end of the passage, is somewhere where I become 'the enemy alien' the laws of my host nation require me to be. And even though by daylight, Arendt adds, all refugees know they are only 'technically' enemy aliens and are really prospective citizens, it is precisely because these instrumental laws stop you leaving your home 'during the dark hours' that their appellation has such devastating force.

This is not just a lyrical address on behalf of the dispossessed, or a claim to privacy in a world in which to have no home, as Arendt will later put it, is to be no longer human (*HC* 59). As they shift between different levels of enunciation, between the 'I don't know' and 'I imagine' of the first sentence, to the 'curious notions' of the second, Arendt's dark speculations are illuminated by their articulation in what is actually a radically indifferent public realm. The nightmares of the refugee are not only private, they also cast light into the darkness into which, Arendt will go on to argue, modern political thought casts the stateless.

The problem of the refugee for political life, Arendt later argued in *Origins,* is that her very non-political existence illuminates 'the dark background of mere givenness': that is, a life before rights, a non-political existence – the 'background formed by our unchangeable and unique nature' which is governed not by law, but by difference (*OT* 382). This non-political condition is a reminder of how fragile the work of giving politics meaning – or turning a group of different people into a nation state of equal rights holders – actually is: which is why it can re-appear as a threat. The 'dark background of mere givenness', Arendt writes, 'breaks into the political scene as the alien which in its all too obvious difference reminds us of the limitations of human activity – which are identical with the limitations of human equality' (*OT* 382). It is this kind of pathology that accounts for the tendency for city and nation states to prefer ethnic homogeneity as a way of shoring up the political against the 'dark background of difference' (*OT* 383), the twilight realm of the non-citizen, the potential refugee. (A psychoanalyst might describe the perception of active return by a category that has in fact been cast out violently – 'breaks in' as an 'alien' – as a form of projection.) In this realm, as in the camps and in the refugee community, existence is dependent not on the law, but on the luck of friendship and the grace of love. Here, it is the simple Augustinian injunction, 'I want you to be,' Arendt says, not the political entitlement to rights, which grounds existence. To ground a politics solely on rights is to forget this merely human interchange. Whence for Arendt the paradox of the crisis of modern human rights: 'the loss of human rights is that such loss coincides with the instant when a person becomes a human being in general' and thus 'loses all significance' (*OT* 383).

But once revealed as the limit concept of rights, it is as if Arendt cannot find a language to describe this merely existing person, this refugee, which does not repeat the very rhetoric of the savage, the enemy alien, the other which, as she herself demonstrates, has been the invariable companion of the discourse of the rights of man ever since their declaration. In the very last paragraph of the 'Perplexities' section of *Origins*, Arendt writes of the danger of the ever-increasing numbers of refugees to political life as being akin, and 'perhaps even more terrifying', 'as the wild elements of nature once threatened the existence of man-made cities and countrysides'. The danger of the new One World, Arendt concludes, is 'that a global, universally interrelated civilization may produce barbarians from its own midst by forcing millions of people into conditions which, despite all appearances, are the conditions of savages' (*OT* 384).[22]

This is the cosmopolitan dream turned absolute nightmare. Between the abstract nakedness of being human and so-called human rights, between inside the polity of the nation state and outside in the refugee camp, Arendt's prose struggles to give a linguistic place to the merely human. And it is not immediately clear whether that difficulty belongs to the political world she is describing or to Arendt herself: as the force of the logic of separation and division that drives the politics of rights begins to eclipse the image of the merely existing life, the life of the refugee, which Arendt had been struggling to illuminate since 1943. This struggle – conceptual, historical and linguistic – echoes the tight knot of the historical, political and ethical entanglements that are Arendt's concern. If the refugee is consigned to a place outside of politics and law, if to be human is to be without human rights, how can she speak of her enforced non-political life without shoring up the very terms that place her there? In 'We Refugees' the nightmares of the refugee reveal a place where I can become an enemy alien to myself. In *Origins*, we could say, that syntax is repeated in the very structure of the political itself.

'Remnants of certain other peoples'

'The problem of style', Arendt wrote in defence of her method of writing *Origins of Totalitarianism*, 'is a problem of adequacy and of response.' Style thus is inextricable from understanding and judgement.[23] In the end, Arendt's critique of the rights of man produces perplexities that even her irony finds difficulty in containing. Or perhaps it is more accurate to say, perplexities that her irony generates, and possibly quite deliberately so. These puzzles of recognition no more belong simply to political philosophy than they do to biography. As Arendt's writing demonstrates, they are the perplexities that belong to those kinds of borders in the first place. How is the refugee to imagine herself if she has no political recognition? What is the style that corresponds to the 'new type of human beings' that emerged out the disaster of mid-century Europe?

I want to end this chapter by coming at this question from a different direction and returning to a figure Arendt thought had been abandoned by the refugee: Freud. Psychoanalysis, Arendt had suggested in 'We Refugees', was now out of fashion with refugees, many of whom were, of course, its first patients. People do not need ghost stories any more, Arendt notes in one of her characteristically blithe dismissals of psychoanalysis; 'it is real experiences that make their flesh creep' ('WR' 57). She might have been surprised, then, to discover that her ironic indictment of the failure of European cosmopolitanism had a precedent in Freud's writing some thirty years before. Written during the First World War, the 'explosion', as Arendt was to describe it, that tore apart 'the European comity of nations beyond repair' (*OT* 341), Freud's essay, 'Thoughts for the Times on War and Death' (1915), is both a lament for that comity and a taking apart of the narrative fantasy that once sustained it. We had expected, Freud writes (and watch that 'we' because it will turn out to be as darkly fugitive as Arendt's later use of pronouns), 'the great, world-dominating peoples of the white race upon whom the leadership of the human species has fallen, who were known to have world-wide interests as their concern', to have succeeded in finding better ways than war and barbarism to settle their differences.[24]

The racism of Freud's disappointment at the failure of the imperialist project to deliver the cosmopolitan goods turns out to be as fraught and doubled as Arendt's positioning of the refugee in her later essay; this is not to exonerate it, but to raise again a question about the linguistic provenance of cosmopolitan style, this time from that seemingly most private, most rightless, of places – the unconscious.

Where Arendt later locates in that catastrophe the failure of rights law to protect the stateless, Freud predicts the same failure in the inability of political reason to transcend violent desire. The comity of European nations, he writes, fell to pieces at the moment when the state rationalised barbarism, monopolising unconscious hostility to its own ends, and turning the figure of the foreigner, the outsider, whose visiting rights are so central to the cosmopolitan ideal, once more into the feared stranger, the enemy alien ('TT' 63). The consequences of this for the 'foreigner' were to become abundantly clear in the postwar period, when the new order produced by the peace treaties meant that 'many European states began to pass laws allowing the denaturalization and denationalization of their own citizens.'[25] Very quickly, the foreigner was to become the refugee, the enemy alien the camp inmate.

Just as with Arendt's refugee, so too in Freud's writing it is as if the 'foreigner' tracks his own imprisonment within the category of 'enemy alien' at the level of the sentence. In a striking passage which seems to speak directly to Arendt thirty years later, Freud claims that, even before the war, the fragile illusion of civilised coexistence had been under strain, by virtue of its barely constrained anti-Semitism:

> Observation showed, to be sure, that [even before the war] embedded in these civilized states there were remnants of certain other peoples, who were universally unpopular and had therefore been only reluctantly, and even so not fully, admitted to participation in the common work of civilization, for which they had shown themselves suitable enough. ('TT' 63)

For which they had shown themselves suitable enough. *Für die sie als genug geeignet erwiesen hatten.* Freud's quiet irony here is unmistakable. And it does very much the same kind of work as Arendt's. The circumlocution, 'remnants of certain other peoples', *'gewisse eingesprengte Voelkerreste'*, puts an unmistakable strain on the coherence of the 'we' of the essay.[26] What Freud's irony tells us is that the 'we' who are surprised and disappointed at the decline of the cosmopolitan ideal is not exactly identical with the implied subject of the sentence, the one to whom observation has already revealed the stain of anti-Semitism on this ideal, the subject who might even belong to the same group that goes under the name of the 'remnants of certain other peoples'.

As in his own theory of the psyche, there is a splitting in Freud's writing, as if there can be no 'we' in this sorry historical and political collectivity, any more than there can be an 'I' uninterrupted by desire in psychoanalytic speech. Yet it is not desire that is doing the interrupting here, but a type of speech that sits on the border of history and politics: the remnants of other peoples sprinkled here and there within European culture – *eingesprengte* – are also embedded within the voice of the analyst-historian, illuminated pieces of quartz in a dark crystal.[27] Just as Arendt's refugee will later find herself inside a politics that at the same time casts her across its borders, Freud's irony too puts him both inside and outside his own theory.

Dreaming of oneself as an enemy alien or as a remnant: this is the psychopathology of the crisis of international human rights which was inaugurated in the early part of the twentieth century. It is a political and historical pathology that pushes itself into language. Those who find themselves cast, without rights, into 'the dark background of mere givenness', may have only the grace of one another as their comfort, but in the bitter stresses of their speech they also dramatise how they came to be there. As I have been suggesting, these stresses are the affective and biographical markers not merely of dismal times, but of a kind of politics of language. If appeals to a universal humanity are no longer any guarantee of rights (or, in Freud's terms, if the fantasy that they ever could be is no longer workable), what Arendt will later articulate as the 'right to have rights' can perhaps be heard, at the very least as a demand, from within the strains of that speech (*OT* 376). What is voiced in both Arendt and Freud's style is not just, thus, as befits their reputations, the wry detachment of the disappointed Jewish European cosmopolitan, but something more difficult than this. Theirs, I would hazard, is a language of cosmopolitanism that works, for very necessary political and historical reasons, against itself.

Notes

1. Virginia Woolf, *Three Guineas*, in *A Room of One's Own and Three Guineas* (1938; London: Vintage, 2001), p. 206.
2. Arthur Koestler, *The Scum of the Earth* (New York: Macmillan, 1941), p. 275.
3. The best account of Arendt's time as a stateless person is Elisabeth Young-Bruehl's *Hannah Arendt: For Love of the World* (New Haven, CT: Yale University Press, 1982); see Chapter 4, 'Stateless Persons', pp. 115–63.
4. Giorgio Agamben, 'We Refugees', trans. Michael Rocke, http://www/egs.edu/faculty/agamben-we-refugees.html, accessed 23 June 2009; 'Beyond Human Rights', *Means Without End: Notes on Politics*, trans. Vincenzo

Binette and Cesare Casarino (Minneapolis: University of Minnesota Press, 2000), p. 15.

5. Cited by Arendt, *OT*, p. 358.

6. Today Arendt's critique of rights has discovered a second life in political and critical theory. The most influential of these is Giorgio Agamben's *Homo Sacer: Sovereign Power and Bare Life*, trans. Daniel Heller-Roazen (1995; Stanford: Stanford University Press, 1998), in which Agamben appropriates Arendt for his account of biopolitics. Important here also are Jacques Rancière's 'Who Is the Subject of the Rights of Man?' and Werner Hamacher's 'The Right to Have Rights (Four-and-a-Half-Remarks)', both in *South Atlantic Quarterly*, 103, 2.3, 2004, pp. 297–310 and pp. 343–56; and Paul Ricœur's 'Who is the Subject of Rights?' and 'Aesthetic Judgement and Political Judgement According to Hannah Arendt', in *The Just*, trans. David Pellauer (Chicago: Chicago University Press, 2000), pp. 1–10, pp. 94–108.

7. These writings have now been collected in full in *The Jewish Writings*, ed. Jerome Kohn and Ron H. Feldman (New York: Schocken, 2007).

8. Arendt, 'We Refugees' (1943), in *The Jew as Pariah: Jewish Identity and Politics in the Modern Age*, ed. Ron H. Feldman (1943; New York: Grove, 1978), p. 55, hereafter abbreviated as 'WR'.

9. Even Woolf's claim to 'have' no country 'as a' woman is suspended in reported speech, assigned to nameless 'outsider', not quite identical to the voice that hesitates to stake her claim to any category.

10. Rebecca L. Walkowitz, 'Critical Cosmopolitanism and Modernist Narrative', in *Cosmopolitan Style: Modernism Beyond the Nation* (New York: Columbia University Press, 2006), pp. 1–32.

11. Denise Riley, 'Echo, Irony and the Political', in *The Words of Selves: Identification, Solidarity, Irony* (Stanford: Stanford University Press, 2000), pp. 142–3.

12. The traces of Heidegger's account of *Dasein*'s radical unhomeliness too can be registered in this passage. Three years after 'We Refugees' Arendt marked her return to philosophy with an essay in which she focuses on the emphasis on homelessness in existentialism ('What is Existential Philosophy?', in *Essays in Understanding, 1930–1954: Formation, Exile, and Totalitarianism*, ed. Jerome Kohn (New York: Schocken, 1994), pp. 163–87). Seyla Benhabib has made a persuasive case for Arendt transplanting Heideggerian phenomenology into her account of the homeless conditions of totalitarianism, *The Reluctant Modernism of Hannah Arendt* (2000; Lanham: Rowman & Littlefield, 2003), pp. 35–61.

13. Arendt is far from being glib here. Young-Bruehl suggests that she contemplated taking her own life in the dark days of her time in the camp at Gurs. Young-Bruehl cites a letter Arendt wrote to Kurt Blumenfeld in 1952: 'In general, things go well; if only world history were not so awful, it would be a joy to live. But, then, that is the case anyway. At least, that was my opinion in Gurs, where I posed the question to myself in earnest and answered myself somewhat jokingly' (*For Love of the World*, p. 154).

14. Arendt, *Rahel Varnhagen: Life of a Jewess*, trans. Richard and Clara Winston (1957; Baltimore: Johns Hopkins University Press, 1997).

15. Arendt, ' "What Remains? The Language Remains": A Conversation

with Günter Gaus', in *The Portable Hannah Arendt*, ed. Peter Baehr (Harmondsworth: Penguin, 2000), p. 16.

16. Agamben, 'Beyond Human Rights', p. 23.
17. Lewis Fried, 'Creating Hebraism, Confronting Hellenism: The *Menorah Journal* and its Struggle for the Jewish Imagination', *American Jewish Archives Journal*, LIII, 1–2, 2000, pp. 147–74.
18. Karl Marx, 'On the Jewish Question', *Early Texts*, ed. D. McLellan (Oxford: Blackwell, 1971), pp. 115–29.
19. Arendt, '"The Rights of Man": What are They?', *Modern Review*, 3.1, Summer 1949, pp. 467–83.
20. Arendt, 'The Public and the Private Realm', in *The Human Condition* (Chicago: University of Chicago Press, 1998), p. 24. Hereafter abbreviated as *HC*.
21. There is an echo of this passage in a poem Arendt wrote in her native German later in 1943:

> They have risen from the standing pool of the past –
> these many memories
> Misty figures drew the longing circles of my enchainment
> around, alluring to their goal.
> Dead ones, what do you want? Have you no home or hearth in Orcus?

The poem is reproduced in Young-Bruehl, *Hannah Arendt: For Love of the World*, pp. 485–6; translation, p. 185. On the West coast refugees were also subject to the 'enemy alien' laws that put Japanese Americans in internment camps.

22. For a compelling reading of how Arendt's language here takes her thinking to the limits of Eurocentrism, see Michael Rothberg, 'At the Limits of Eurocentrism: Hannah Arendt's *The Origins of Totalitarianism*', in *Multidirectional Memory: Remembering the Holocaust in the Age of Decolonization* (Stanford: Stanford University Press, 2009). Rothberg tracks the emergence of a 'boomerang effect' between colonialism and Nazi genocide in mid-century political, philosophical and literary writing. Arendt (like Agamben after her) makes the link between the 'abstract nakedness of being human' in the camps and the bare humanity of Africa that shocked the colonial imagination, but cannot develop it into a forceful critique.
23. Arendt, 'A Reply to Eric Voeglin', in *The Portable Hannah Arendt*, pp. 159–60.
24. Sigmund Freud, 'Thoughts for the Times on War and Death', *The Pelican Freud Library*, vol. 12 (1915; Harmondsworth: Penguin, 1985), p. 62. Henceforth abbreviated as 'TT'.
25. Agamben, 'Beyond Human Rights', p. 16.
26. Freud, 'Zeitgasses über Krieg und Tod', *Gesammelte Werke 1913–1917* (1915; Frankfurt: Fischer, 1967), p. 326.
27. My thanks to Jean Boase-Beier for alerting me to this rendering of *eingesprengte*.

Chapter 5

'Creatures of an Impossible Time': Late Modernism, Human Rights and Elizabeth Bowen

> What caused the girl to express herself like a displaced person? The explanation – that from infancy onward Eva had had as attendants displaced persons, those at a price being the most obtainable, to whose society she'd be largely consigned – for some reason never appeared: too simple perhaps?
>
> Elizabeth Bowen, *Eva Trout or Changing Scenes*[1]

At almost the exact same time as Rebecca West attended the Nuremberg trial, Elizabeth Bowen travelled from Ireland to France to report on the Paris Peace Conference for the *Cork Examiner*. The conference took place amid the tired splendour of the Luxembourg Palace between 29 July and 15 October 1946, and like Nuremberg, was intended to restore some kind of lawfulness to postwar Europe. Borders between Italy, Yugoslavia, Hungary, Romania, the Soviet Union, Bulgaria and France were redefined; Italy, Romania, Bulgaria and Finland resumed sovereign state status; reparations were agreed and, after a late amendment, the signatories of the five treaties committed themselves to the 'enjoyment of human rights and the fundamental freedoms' for all people under their jurisdiction.[2] The conference, however, lacked the historical and moral intensity of Nuremberg, and was a tense, weary event. Any sense that the world's diplomats were coming together to script the final chapter of an atrocious history was quickly tempered by the realisation that they were, in fact, in an early episode in the Cold War. Even as the delegates declared fundamental freedoms for all, Europe was in the grip of a mass population transfer. The war might have been over, but the columns of people on its roads, the transit camps, the pursuit of legal identities in hastily hand-ruled ledger books kept on coming. It was in this period, historian Tony Judt reminds us, that the distinction between 'displaced persons (assumed to have somewhere, a home, to go to) and refugees (who were classified as homeless)' was introduced.[3]

There is little of this calamitous history immediately apparent in Bowen's three reports on the conference. 'I am here as a free-lance, an onlooker, granted the *entrée* to the Luxembourg by the goodwill of those who hold that novelists should be let picture history, in actual making, though they may not record it,' Bowen writes in an early draft of her reports, included alongside her three published articles by Allan Hepburn in his recent edition of her previously uncollected writings.[4] An observer, a roving eye: as the over-strained passivity of 'let picture history' suggests, Bowen is a witness who indeed does not so much record the event, let alone its political failures, as yield to its impressions.

Unlike West or Arendt, Bowen was not a political journalist; nor did she ever aspire to be (it was the 'photography of the situation' that she was interested in, she later said).[5] Neither did she have an obvious personal investment in the proceedings, as Spark clearly did at the Eichmann trial. None the less, at first glance, her attention to atmosphere, impressions and feelings jars with the conference's politics. Compare, for example, Martha Gellhorn's furious dismay at its total inability to connect with the suffering of the human beings in whose name 'justice' was being claimed.[6] Bluntly put, the kind of literary imagination in which Bowen is absorbed, the 'poetic truth' she describes as being central to the novel form, seems to be at odds with the imaginative reconstruction work with concepts of justice and human dignity the world saw itself as doing in 1946.[7] Like so many of the characters in her postwar fiction, she seems to be peculiarly out of time.

But if the ethereal qualities of her prose seem to distance her from the human tragedies being played out at the conference, and across the world, in another sense Bowen's acute sense of displacement makes her later writing very much of its time. Bowen's is not the displacement of the modernist exile; she once described the taking up of the position of the 'psychologically displaced person' of the inter-war generation as 'cerebrally brilliant but skin deep'.[8] To talk of an acute sense of displacement in her fiction is to register instead its visceral, deep and often painfully unnerving qualities. Bowen's writing enacts the homelessness it so often describes. But while her famously dislocating sentences frequently seem to be on the verge of losing their objects, something of the sense of the world is always pulled back from oblivion by the exquisite sensuality of her prose. Arendt once wrote that Husserl's phenomenology was as an attempt to 'evoke magically a home again out of the world which has become alien'.[9] The same, I think, could be said of Bowen's writing.

As we saw in the last chapter, Arendt took her reading of existential homelessness into her account of twentieth-century politics: hence the refugee who articulates her abandonment by the law and politics in the strains of her speech. In a parallel movement, Bowen takes the displaced person into the novel form, the genre through which, traditionally, Europe has imagined and legitimised its concepts of personhood. To claim that displaced persons are significant in postwar literature, as I do in the final two chapters of this book, is not simply to remark that they become conspicuous, like cappuccino machines and teenagers. It is to suggest that Arendt's 'new kind of human beings' also raise important questions about the social and political province of humanity that it had long been literature's, and in particular the novel's, business to address. If the novel was the form that once came to house the subject of rights, what (if any) kind of home could it provide for the newly stateless of the world?

Finally, in 1959, selling the home in County Cork she had always had to go to, constitutionally Anglo-Irish and yet easily peripatetic, Bowen, who once claimed that her writing was a 'substitute for something I have been born without – a so-called normal relation to society', was perhaps always well placed to unsettle assumptions about what a normal relation to home, or the nation state, might be.[10] The so-called 'normalisation' of the troublesome individual's relation to society, often assumed to be a mark of the novel form's latent conservatism, is always a hazy unfinished affair in her fiction (although neither is it entirely absent).

Until recently much criticism tended to suggest that the displaced children and gooseberry grown-ups who so gently haunt her early work lose something in their retelling in her later writing, as if it is Bowen herself and not the novel form that has run out of steam; however, in this chapter I argue that it is in her postwar writing, particularly in her final novel, *Eva Trout, or Changing Scenes* (1968), that Bowen offers her most provocative – and most affecting – image of the kind of moral and imaginative work the European novel can still do at mid-century.[11] At the beginning of what has been described as a new era of human rights, far from breezily stepping over the casualties of events such as the Peace Conference, Bowen asks us to imagine how it is possible to make the displaced person seem 'real' in the first place. In this she makes a crucial link between the postwar politics of the novel, particularly in relation to the politics of rights, and the ethics of literature.

1948: Human rights, human feelings and the mid-century novel

I want to start, however, not with displaced persons *per se*, but with the literary provenance of the rights that were intended to give a refuge to the world's homeless in the mid-1940s. In his recent book on the connection between the development of postwar human rights and the rise of the postcolonial novel, Joseph Slaughter tells the compelling story of the 'two Watts'.[12] The first Watt is Ian Watt, who in 1948 was revising his dissertation into what would become *The Rise of the Novel* (1957), the hugely influential account of how the modern capitalist individualist, with his creative and destructive capacity for self-determination, his ability to experience moral sentiments and his brutal indifference to the lives of others, was made real in the eighteenth-century English novel. Also in 1948, a second Watt, Alan Watt, an Australian diplomat, was attending the Third Social and Humanitarian Committee of the United Nations (UN) at the *Palais de Chaillot* in Paris, another Second Empire *huis clos*, where the final draft of the Universal Declaration of Human Rights (UDHR) was being revised. It was this Watt who provoked a tardy consideration of the boundaries of individualism among the Declaration's drafters when he tabled an amendment replacing the idea that 'free and full development of the personality' at the heart of the Declaration was 'enabled' by one's community, with the more determinist idea that such persons owed their free development to that community alone. The consequence was an enthusiastic debate centring on Daniel Defoe's *Robinson Crusoe* – the first Watt's paradigmatic novel of individualist absolutism.

Predictably, the delegates differed on the extent to which Crusoe's triumphant self-sufficiency depended on his society or on his own creative will. The result was a compromise that concealed a paradox: 'Everyone has duties to the community in which alone the free and full development of his personality is possible,' Article 29 finally read.[13] Everyone is free, potentially at least, but only to the extent that that freedom is made possible by their community. Slaughter's point is that *Crusoe* provided the Third Committee with an 'enabling fiction' that allowed them to formulate this paradoxical freedom as a right. Just as Defoe's novel blends self-determining individualism with a model of the new moral subject, so too does Article 29 manage to harmonise the tension between rights and obligations, self-determination and subjection. So it was, Slaughter argues, that the 'grammar' of the European *Bildungsroman* found its way into the UDHR.

As the delegates' enthusiastic seizing upon *Crusoe* might suggest, this literary-historical backward look belied a more anxious, and therefore subdued, set of questions about the type of person the war-shocked, multi-national, highly politicised UN could actually legislate for in 1948. Enlightenment consensus seemed out of the question; what emerged instead was a somewhat abashed restatement of some of its themes. Natural law, for so long the philosophical cornerstone of concepts of rights (rights are given by nature), was resuscitated for the new world order with a more mobile, and politically malleable, emphasis on personhood – hence the 'the free and full development of personality' in Article 29.[14] 'In each of us there dwells a mystery and that mystery is the human personality,' wrote the French Catholic philosopher, Jacques Maritain, a consultant on the drafting of the UDHR and a leading advocate of 'personalism'.[15] In his independent declaration of *The Rights of Man* (1940), H. G. Wells similarly offered a timely mid-century definition of rights when he stressed the necessity to protect 'that free play of the individual mind which is preservative of human efficiency and happiness' against 'uncontrolled absolutisms'.[16] Turning this mysteriously freely playing personality into positive law, and making this idea of personhood seem real enough to pass as a universal: such was the creative work demanded of the drafters of the UDHR. Small wonder, perhaps, that it was the quietly stated universalism of the more modest novel, rather than the grand foundational claims of Western philosophy, that came to stand in for some of the new judicial humanism's more precarious assumptions.

Neither, perhaps, is it a coincidence that some of the most influential accounts of the novel form emerged in this period. Georg Lukács's seminal definition of the *Bildungsroman*, *Goethe und Sein*, was first published in 1947. (Lukács had opened his earlier *Theory of the Novel* (1920) by saying that he was provoked into writing by the outbreak of the First World War, so there is a pre-history for postwar re-appraisals of the novel here too.) F. R. Leavis's *The Great Tradition* appeared in 1948, neatly balanced by the publication of Marxist Arnold Kettle's *An Introduction to the English Novel* in 1951. A. D. McKillop's *The Early Masters of English Fiction* was published in 1956, followed by Northrop Frye's *Anatomy of Criticism* and Watt's *Rise of the Novel* in 1957. In 1953, Erich Auerbach's giant, *Mimesis*, written while in exile in Turkey, was first published. Auerbach's thesis that the novel was distinguished by its embedding of persons in thick social contexts famously also bears the biographical and historical traces of the displaced persons for whose rights the UDHR was attempting to legislate.

In their very different ways, all these classics take the individual and his or her relation to society as a starting point. All also assume that the novel's originality as a literary form rests with its capacity to make that relation feel real: 'the novel's realism does not reside in the kind of life it presents,' wrote Watt memorably, 'but in the way it presents it.'[17] The same might be said for the model of personality enshrined by the UDHR. But while this literary-critical consensus both mirrors and anchors the 'textuality' of human rights, there is something conspicuously anachronistic about the way this war-shattered (literally in many cases) generation of critics and diplomats bends back to the eighteenth- and nineteenth-century novel in order to rediscover a model of the human person for the postwar and post-Holocaust period.[18] Just as there was a tendency at Nuremberg to normalise the Holocaust in order to recommit the law to the progress of human civilisation, so too for literary criticism of the novel, it was as though more recent chapters of extremist modernity were to be quickly passed over if the genre was to continue its social and moral ascent at mid-century. It was not *Ulysses* that was being debated in the UN's Third Committee. It was as if modernism had never happened.

In fact, the 'after' modernism debates were happening elsewhere. Also in 1948 *Partisan Review* published *Why Do I Write?*, a three-way exchange of letters between Elizabeth Bowen, Graham Greene and V. S Pritchett (published as a book later the same year by Percival Marshall). A shadow of the 'international legal Robinsonade' going on in Paris, this discussion too was concerned with the role of the novel in the moral and political climate left by the war.[19] But while the UDHR drafters were keen to find in literature some unacknowledged way of legislating for the human personality, Bowen, Pritchett and Greene – all writers as indebted to their modernist predecessors as they were conscious of resuscitating forms of realism for the novel – are notably reluctant to take on the role of literary and cultural underwriters. Bowen, especially, finds something repulsive or 'frightening', as she puts it, about being obliged to give a public account of her work:

> the askers of that particular question ['Why do you write?'] are intelligent people, who are within their rights. At least I take it they are within their rights; I cannot say with authority what these are ... the intelligent people seem to be closing in on the artist like the rats on the selfish bishop who hoarded corn in famine time.[20]

Bowen's association between 'rights' and violent vengeance is all of a keeping with her political conservatism. It was more than what she once declared to be her youthful reading of the *Scarlet Pimpernel* that had made her leery of political radicalism; Bowen's ideology was firmly based in her conservative Anglo-Irish heritage.[21] Not only does she disdain the idea that the writer should give the world a new fiction of social life, but she also doubts whether he or she has the capacity to do so. 'At the moment', she writes to Pritchett, the writer is

> not simply being asked whether he is, feels himself to be, or should be, in relation to society; he's being asked implicitly, to create a society to be in

relation with. Or – in so far as society is a sensation as well as a form – to set up in people a sense of society. He seems from his book to know the secret: he ought to know how.[22]

The line in this passage between fiction (the writer being asked to 'create a society to be in relation with') and an already existing but invisible model on which this fiction might be based (which, like Maritain's 'mystery', the writer is assumed somehow mysteriously to divine) recalls 'the grammar' of the *Bildungsroman* being debated in Paris. Bowen, like her ideological ancestor, Burke, no doubt would have appreciated Franco Moretti's quip about the *Bildungsroman* narrating how the French Revolution might have been avoided.[23] But this is not an exact replay of the idea that the novel can safely legitimise tensions that might otherwise explode into violence, as Bowen's politely indignant irony suggests.

If Bowen seems surprised that she, of all people, should be asked to play literary social worker, this is because she had long been absorbed by the brittleness of the films by which the novel could create any sense of the world whatsoever. 'All my own discoveries about life have been capricious and inadvert. I should hesitate to lay down the law about anything,' she writes to Pritchett.[24] Bowen's sense that asking the novelist to invent a society to be in relation with is a bit *en retard*, is a pointedly late modernist response to the demand that the novel invent a new way of the world for the postwar age. For Bowen's generation, the idea that fiction could lay down the law about anything had already run aground by the First World War. Trauma, repetition and the capricious moment were the terms under which she served her literary apprenticeship. A life predicated on the advent of the inadvertent was one better captured by the short story; as Bowen's own prodigious production of the genre during the Second World War proved. As to the novel, any sense that the form could contain the excesses that once gave it its dynamism retreated in the face of the ascent of Fascism. 'Nothing I can break is law!' asserts Robert, the traitor, in *The Heat of the Day* (1948), a novel in which the 'sense or sensation' of society is of one too porous to contain not just the individual, but a sense of individuality itself.[25] Persons leak in Bowen's exemplary World War Two novel: into one another, in and out of nations. Treachery, disloyalty and trespass are the themes of the wartime social contract. If this results in a writing that sometimes shares the quality of an hallucination, as Jacqueline Rose has argued, this goes to show how close to the edge of its capacities Bowen was prepared to push the novel in the 1940s.[26]

Push, but not explode. 'We must have something to envisage, and we must act, and there must be law,' Stella says to Robert, in terms which echo directly Bowen's final words in the *Partisan Review* debate: 'We envisage, we are not passive, and we are not contributing to anarchy: that may be the most to be claimed for us.'[27] To envisage is not simply to imagine, as its prefix insists, it is also to imagine a possible future. More accurately for the late modernist writer at mid-century, it is to acknowledge the possibility of a future for literature even as – and this is Bowen's postwar dilemma – one cannot imagine a form for it. In a 1953 article for the *New Republic*, Bowen describes mid-century European literature and culture as 'still seeking their footing in actual time – both have the stigmata of an over-long drawn-out adolescence'. It is as though the youths who once fired the European *Bildungsroman* were now refusing to leave home, languishing in a literary form that, like the photographs still on the walls in Robert's creepy childhood bedroom in *The Heat of the Day*, reflect back images of an ideal passage through to maturity long since spent.[28]

One effect of joining up the literary debates of the drafters of the new judicial humanism with those happening in *Partisan Review* is to reveal a shared 'impossible time', as Bowen describes the space inhabited by the postwar generation in *A World of Love* (1955): a time when moving forward is also a pulling back, and where the 'new human beings' of the rights era are ghost-written by the fictional persons of a not quite dead literary tradition. It is also, however, to emphasise the discontinuities between these versions of what European literature can do at mid-century. While compelled to acknowledge a postwar future, late modernism is inflected by the meaninglessness of its more recent past. 'I can't help thinking – suppose the world was meant for human happiness after all?' asks a character in Bowen's short story, 'I Hear You Say So', first published in 1945. Her hopes are answered by the 'absolute' of the song of the Nightingale. 'It sang from a planet, beyond experience, drawing out longings, sending them back again frozen, piercing, not again to be borne.'[29] Jug, jug, it goes, again. 'Sending them back again' is also the theme of the first two novels Bowen produced after the war, *A World of Love* and *The Little Girls* (1964), in both of which the air-hungry past of the first part of the century sucks back the lives of those attempting to live in the second. So too, indeed, the arrested condition of the novel at mid-century, as Bowen argued in her 1950 essay, 'The Bend Back'. Like the war-traumatised population, she argued there, the novel can return to its past haunts, to history, childhood, nostalgia, only in a gentle parody of its former lives, stuck in a repetition compulsion with no exit. 'Are we to take it that our own time has been, from the point of view of its inhabitants, irreparably injured – that it shows some loss of vital deficiency?'[30]

When, with the British Council, Bowen visits newly Communist Hungary in the Autumn of 1948, and recommends that the import of 'attractive books' from the West 'would be ideal carriers of the Western idea', therefore, it is not at all clear that the novel she might have in mind embodies the qualities of the traditional *Bildungsroman* admired by the drafters of the UDHR.[31] Had the Hungarian reader been able to find such a fancy-catching novel, what she or he might have discovered is a kind of 'enforced return' of the sort of thing the novel used to be: a revenant of the ideal that was informing the new judicial humanism at almost exactly the same (impossible) time. To read Bowen as a late modernist shadow to the re-invention of the novel as a medium for the re-assertion of a universal humanity at mid-century, is to re-encounter the terms of that debate as a subtle, and frequently critical, form of repetition. Bowen's, we could say, is a late literary modernist rendering of the new rights era which runs not so much against its generic grain, as over it again, unpicking its threads, leaving the fabric of the novel – and the social contract implied within it – displaced.

But while the fabric of the novel might have been torn, the idea of some kind of society to be in a relation with is not, or at least not entirely. Back at the Paris Peace Conference in 1946, Bowen muses on the connection between the legislative and political work going on inside the Luxembourg Palace and the postwar atmosphere surrounding it: 'In my own mind, as the conference proceeded, I never ceased to feel a vital connection between the unconscious children playing around the green lawns, outdoors, and the intent men, indoors, seated around the green tables.'[32] Never ceasing to feel vital connections is also a pretty accurate description of the extraordinary visceral power of Bowen's own prose. The sheer sensuality of her writing puts a block on regarding it only in terms of socialisation. Even when she complains to Pritchett about being asked to imagine a new kind of social relation, she makes it clear that the only society she is prepared to imagine is one of 'a sensation as well as a form'. (There was never really going to be a sociology of the novel for Bowen.) It is precisely through such vital connections that the world is experienced at all in her writing. While she might demur at the prospect of literary social work, as Hepburn's publication of some of her most significant postwar journalism makes clear, it is as a recorder of sensation, of human feeling, that Bowen believes that the writer is better authorised (with the claims to moral legitimacy that word implies) to be 'let picture history in its actual making'. 'I may be pardoned for speaking intuitively, even sentimentally,' she writes of her impressions of Hungary in 1948.[33] 'How does it feel?' is the question – 'my own, personal, human, I suppose essentially feminine query' – she poses to postwar West German students in a 1954 article.[34]

Writing about Virginia Woolf in 1949, Bowen describes her predecessor as extending and deepening 'human susceptibility to sensation'. 'Ironically,' she adds, 'she was to do this at a time when, because of the pressure put on it by events, sensation could be an insupportable tax.'[35] Woolf's gift was to make sensation tell a truth about human experience at the very moment when sensation was traumatically decoupled from experience, and relocating itself in stupefying forms of mass cultural experience. Something very similar might be said of the emotional perspicacity of Bowen's own writing. 'You cannot depersonalize persons,' she wrote in the US postscript to her collection of wartime stories, *The Demon Lover* (1945); every writer during the war 'was aware of the passionate attachment of men and women to every object or image or place or love or fragment of memory'.[36] Passionate attachments are a guarantee of personhood: a form of resistance against uncontrolled absolutisms, to recall Wells's declaration. Yet Woolf's gift for feeling, Bowen also notes, already marks 'the extreme and final product of the English liberal mind'. If a feeling for the mystery of human personhood was also revived in the new judicial humanism (Althusser writes scathingly of a new 'international of decent feelings' in this period), this too is not so much a continuation of a literary tradition, as another example of the dislocating bend-back that characterises the effort to legislate for a concept of the human, as it were, beyond its historical term.[37]

Recognising the feeling of others, as Ian Watt was to argue, was another of the founding principles of the novel. At the beginning of the 'English liberal mind' was a writing that made sensation real in the social world. The distinctive thing about Richardson's novels was not so much the range of feelings on display, Watt wrote in *The Rise of the Novel*, even though it was much wider than your average sentimental novel, 'but the authenticity of its presentation: many writers of the period talked about "sympathetic tears"; even more deplorably Richardson talked about "pellucid fugitives", but he made them flow as no one else and as never before.'[38]

It was this sort of novelistic sympathy, historian Lynn Hunt has argued, that produced a cultural underpinning for the ascent of human rights in the eighteenth century.[39] But if Watt, in the mid-twentieth century, is uneasy about Richardson's ability to generate mass sympathy, this also speaks to a late-modernist suspicion of the manufacture of lived emotions by the culture industry. (Both Q. D. Leavis and Adorno are in the acknowledgements of *The Rise of the Novel*.)[40] If the new judicial humanism was accompanied by the performance of moral sentiments, it was so under the shadow of modernism, the 'extreme and final product of the liberal mind'.[41]

'Not to have read *L'Éducation sentimentale*', Bowen wrote in a 1941 review of a new translation of the novel she herself had begun to translate before the war, 'is, I believe, to be in a state of incomplete human experience.'[42] The quiet irony of that sentence echoes Flaubert's own: for the point about *Sentimental Education* (1869), one of the most extreme and final examples of the European *Bildungsroman*, is that complete human experience is only a promise from which we are kept by the seductive allure of the very forms through which experience is mediated. In Flaubert the association between human development and human feeling that had sustained the rise of the European novel is delicately picked apart; the best time one ever had (*'c'est là ce que nous avons eu de meilleur!'*) turns out to be the first time one's fantasies were more significant than a complete lived experience. Where Flaubert's novel was part of the crisis of the *Bildungsroman* that accompanied the beginnings of modernism, Bowen's late modernism reruns that crisis across the judicial humanism of the mid-century. Tears fall in her final writing, but they fall not from or for all humanity (as the rain still weeps in Woolf's final modernist classic, *Between the Acts* (1941)), but from the eyes of the monstrous, the extra-human, Eva Trout.[43] Pellucid fugitives might have been deplorable in Richardson; but they turn out to be perfect for the second age of human rights.

Changing scenes

> Since a man comes into this world through no fault of his own, since he is a joint inheritor of the accumulations of the past, and since those accumulations are more than sufficient to satisfy the claims that are here made on his behalf, it follows . . .
>
> H. G. Wells, 'Declaration of Rights'[44]

In so far as we come into this world through no fault of our own, and in so far as we are the inheritors of an accumulated past, H. G. Wells wrote in his 1941 Declaration, we are entitled to rights. It is a declaration that could also be made of the rights to a fictional existence of just about any central protagonist of the European *Bildungsroman*. Innocence and inheritance have always been important to Bowen's novels; read in sequence, *The Hotel* (1927), *A House in Paris* (1935) and *The Death of the Heart* (1938) track the accumulated damage done by the *rentier* class on its displaced children across the twentieth century. In Bowen's final novel, however, and her final *Bildungsroman*, both the innocence and the inheritance are outsize; Eva Trout's wealth, like her physical being in the world through no fault of her own, is colossal.

Everything about *Eva Trout* seems blown-up. Bored with people 'who say nostalgically to her, I did so love *The Death of the Heart*', Bowen seems to have written the novel as an exuberant kind of valedictory farewell to the form she had mastered so exquisitely.[45] Magnifying what she once kept in miniature, *Eva Trout* is at once a tribute to the power of fiction to confer persons with narrative rights – rights, for example, to moral development, to human personality – and a critique of the ethical limits of the novel in these terms. Coming as the book did at the end of her career, at a moment when she had thought a lot about fiction (this was the period during which Bowen would regularly travel to US campuses as a visiting professor) and was reading and admiring the new writing of Muriel Spark and Iris Murdoch, much recent criticism has seen in her final novel a subtle deconstruction of the novel form itself.[46] But to claim that Bowen is tacitly critical of the novel form in her final book is not necessarily to assert a postmodernism *avant la lettre* on her behalf. 'Freedom', Bowen wrote in the context of the 'revolution (it has been called so)' in 1960s writing 'is hard to envisage, though right in principle.'[47] There is a strong echo here of Burke's famous 'When I see the spirit of liberty in action, I see a strong principle at work; and this, for a while, is all I can possibly know of it.'[48] And as for Burke, for Bowen too the principle of liberty is best envisaged by tradition itself. 'Literary freedom can be chaotic if it shakes of the restraints of order and style; should it fail to do so it is not quite freedom, should it successfully do so, is it still literature?'[49]

Undoubtedly, *Eva Trout* is still literature, albeit historically qualified literature. Neither is the critic John Coates wrong in insisting on the novel's moral seriousness in his critique of some recent post-structuralist appropriations of the text. But the narrative of 'moral growth and development' (in his words) Coates wants to preserve in the novel, and thus its generic roots in the *Bildungsroman*, is also precisely that which Bowen, I think, is interested in capturing in its passing.[50] A further reason for situating Bowen's final novel in the context of mid-century judicial humanism is to catch the ethical import of the passing of a certain way of legitimating being in the novel.

Eva is a creature of the same impossible time that haunted the revival of judicial humanism in the postwar era. 'What *is* a person?' she wonders. 'Is it true, that there is no more than one of each? If so, is it this singular forcefulness, or forcefulness arising from being singular, which occasionally causes a person to bite on history?' Is it true being a person can cause one to bite on history rather than be bitten by it? The drafters of the UDHR certainly seemed to think so when they made the 'free and full development of the personality' a juridical category. 'All the more, in that case,' as Eva puts it, 'what *is* a person?'(*ET* 193). If this question was sidelined by the UDHR drafters in 1948, twenty years on Bowen gives her final answer to the demand that she rewrite the *Bildungsroman* for the postwar age. Eva Trout is both the last person of one literary tradition, and the new creature of another, half-seen, not quite visible, new way of being in the world.

Poised between two forms of judicial imagination, Bowen's final novel rehearses the paradox at the core of mid-century rights described by Arendt in *The Origins of Totalitarianism* (as we saw in the last chapter). The very moment that rights absolutely and categorically collapsed, she argued, coincided 'with the instant when a person becomes a human being in general' (*OT* 383). The acute vulnerability of the merely human came into view, that is, at the precise moment when the law was withdrawn, and when natural law was revealed for what it was: a fiction. In the final part of this chapter, I want to redraft this political paradox for the novel at mid-century; the point at which fiction ceased to make persons real by naturalising their 'moral growth and development' (ironically, the very model grafted into the UDHR) also coincided with the moment when such persons became merely human. In Bowen, this rip, or tear, in the fabric of the novel also marks a passage from the politics of rights and entitlements, to something like an ethics of love. And it is at this point, I also want to suggest, that the sensuality of her late writing becomes fully, and finally, poignant.

What kind of person is Eva Trout? Or perhaps we should ask instead in what kind of novel does she find herself? 'She was addressed by the Bench. "Is it *your* aim to fade from human memory?"' (*ET* 100). Constantine's 'judicial' question to his ward, one of many references to justice in the novel, is also a generic one; characters in fiction are supposed to materialise into memories, not fade out of them.[51] Eva, however, has by turns bothered and delighted readers by being fantastically 'implausible': '"But you, you see, change convulsively. Chaotically, without rhyme or reason – as no one else does, Eva; as no one else does"'(*ET* 102–3). Behaving irrationally, individualistically, in a novel is far from being a crime; indeed, it is the prerogative of the self-determining ingénue to flag up her difference from the rest. But convoluted change, change that curls itself up in loops, is a trespass against the sort of plot whereby plausible behaviour goes hand in hand with acquiring fictional rights and hence social and political legitimacy.

By contrast, Eva's late-modern person is almost too free: not growing incrementally into self-knowledge, but prowling in her Jaguar, galumphing rather than developing. Like Frédéric Moreau in *Sentimental Education*, Eva's inheritance licenses a capricious fiction-making. ('[S]he has a passion', complains her former teacher, Iseult Smith, 'for the fictitious for its own sake' (*ET* 242).) While her determination to forge a narrative out of her own life recalls the youths of an earlier modernist moment (Isobel Archer, Miriam Henderson, Stephen Dedalus), her peripatetic wandering belongs to the later modernism of Samuel Beckett's *Murphy* (1938), Jean Rhys's *Good Morning Midnight* (1939) and Djuna Barnes's *Nightwood*: the itinerant progeny of lumbering Leopold Bloom. Eva, a character inspired, so Bowen said, by a big girl at an airport.

Eva is too large, her dimensions too mythic, her wandering too extreme, for the *Bildungsroman* that at the same time ghosts the novel which she is in. But neither will Bowen let her protagonist outgrow the form entirely. So, on the one hand, she bends her writing back: back across itself in a series of echoes and repetitions, and back too, as many critics have noted, across the history of the novel – through 'James' territory', inside *Bleak House*, back indeed through the Bowen *Bildungsroman* itself, as though the accumulated inheritance of the novel form might ballast Eva's outrageous liberty with tradition. On the other hand, the novel bends out, or bulges, into pockets of mythic prose that bubble, seemingly inconsequentially, above an otherwise flamboyantly over-determined plot. This is not so much a misshapenness, as some readers have complained; the novel's episodic descents into mythic time make ethical sense of the historical dilemma at its heart.

'Coffee Shop', the chapter where Eva, in another of the novel's oversized coincidences, improbably re-encounters her school love, the preternaturally delicate Elisnore, in a cavernous, half-lit diner, is often read in terms of the novel's excavation of regressive or unconscious time.[52] As much as the scene with Elisnore catches Eva's dream-life, a desiring being for the most part submerged ('I am very heavy, however' (*ET* 64)), like the Hades episode in Joyce's *Ulysses*, it also stages a descent into the mythic origins of law and custom. It is not just Elisnore who Eva meets in the coffee shop, but her two friends, Joanne and Betti-Mae, making three, like the Furies, who take her downtown to an overheated apartment reeking of family cooking and floral air freshener to meet (who else?) an old Greek, Mr Anapoupolis (who had 'jacked up' the antique heating system so it 'sizzled and boiled'). At the very moment Eva inherits her father's wealth, the moment when she claims her entitlement, a trapdoor opens under one plot about legitimisation, and Eva finds herself in an altogether different judicial scenario. It was the Furies who took it upon themselves to guard the law, particularly blood law, when politics or the state failed to uphold it. Flanked by these three young matrons, guardians of the maternal line, Mr Anapoupolis, Nomos-like, lectures Eva both on the improprieties of her inheritance, her father's financial dealings that fair wrecked the market, and on the illegality of what she is about to do: buy a human baby.

> There's a black market in infants, unknowing babies: are you conscious they can be purchased, they can be traded? *Are* you aware, those who cannot by law adopt, due to ineligibility, become buyers? Are you aware that this is a market in which demand has come to exceed supply? (*ET* 139)

The scene might work as a moral lesson in the turpitude of wealth, and thus be rendered generically conventional in terms of the *Bildungsroman*, only if Eva could be somehow seen to change or develop in the light of it. But she does not. Impervious, Eva 'incurs' Jeremy, 'humanely speaking – by criminality', as Father Tony later puts it. And, while theirs is a love story, there is also a chilling instrumentality in the uses to which Jeremy is put – by both Eva and the novel (*ET* 187). This is not a story in which lost children become vehicles of moral enlightenment, as its fairy-tale beginning with a honeymoon that never happened foretells. *Eva Trout* is not so much Dickens neat as, to echo the title of the critical study Iseult is translating, Dickens *Le Grand Histrionique*. If the Hades scene is excessive, if Mr Anapoupolis seems to have wandered into the text from a Beckett novella ('left belly to downward-ripple, despondent, and thighs to spread' (*ET* 136)), this is because its ethical lesson requires a departure from novelistic good manners.

Eva and her adopted son, Jeremy, might share a kind of *ex nihilo* generative status – she an inarticulate orphan, he a deaf-mute adoptee – but their historical and generic origins are entirely different. Eva is one of the *Bildungsroman*'s final children, a radical outsider whose money, rather than granting her *entrée* to a world of plausible human persons, finances an existence strung together out of fictions in a shadow play of a former kind of novelistic life. Jeremy comes from a newer age. One of Arendt's 'new human beings', passed out of the law and out of the state, the trafficked baby joins the camp inmate, the refugee and the displaced person as one of those who have only the fact of their birth upon which to claim their 'humanity'.[53] It is, after all, another short step from eliminating 'the scum of the earth' to recycling them in a profitable economy. Jeremy comes from somewhere beyond a political language of rights and entitlements; that is why his nativity is announced in Hell and not in a vicarage.

One of the reasons for the disconcerting tenderness of Bowen's final novel comes from the effort to concatenate these two different kinds of lives: to create something meaningful from the debris of one tradition and the hell of the present. Thus, with his Christmas-time arrival and the 'miracle' of his second birth, Jeremy is the mute lamb whose innocence 'imposed on others a sense that *they* were, that it was *they* who were lacking in some faculty'(*ET* 158). The novel is scattered with Biblical allusions that do not so much give it a theological (still less a moral-theological) plot, as seed enigmatic portents in this manner, promising, but not quite delivering, redemptive time. It is to the Bible, specifically to Leviticus, that Eva turns when she returns to her hotel room to await the call that will take her to her child. 'From the under-shelf of the bed-table she took the Gideon Bible; she put her thumb in it. *"This is the law"*, she read, *"of the burnt offering, of the meat offering, and of the sin offering, and of the trespass offering, and of the consecrations of the peace offerings"* ' (*ET* 143). While the coming, or 'sacrifice', of Jeremy might well be a kind of peace offering, a Messianic moment, as Bowen would also have known, particularly from her time in the US, the burnt offering, *olah* in Hebrew, had recently acquired a new historical resonance as the Holocaust.[54]

This does not make *Eva Trout* a post-Holocaust novel, at least not straightforwardly so, but it does give a pointed inflection to Bowen's conspicuous attention to the question of persons in the novel: specifically to 'the human' as a category, on the one hand, to be attained or envisaged, and on the other, always just lost or missed. 'So these were humans, and this was what it was like being among them?' (*ET* 51). So Eva thinks when she first attends school. Going to school is often the making real, the educating, of freely developing persons in European fiction. Eva's first school, however, is 'experimental' (another timely word in the novel), and far from inculcating the social ego, is awash with desire.[55] It is here that Eva first encounters the 'passionately solicitous sense of' another's presence in the frail body of the half-dead Elisnore (*ET* 56); while the other children set 'Oedipus traps' for their teacher by placing an effigy of his mother in his bed. Less an education in becoming human, the sense of social self promised by the school turns out to be as elusive as the spring daffodils in the castle grounds that Eva never gets to see.

Eva's second school looks more promising in terms of giving her a more generically sound sentimental education; here at least love comes together with pedagogy, as so often in the female *Bildungsroman*, to conspire to give Eva something like human recognition. 'Till Iseult came, no human being had ever turned on Eva their full attention which could seem to be love' (*ET* 17). But as the convolution 'could seem to be' infers, this love is more conventional than real. '*You* not understand me?', Eva despairs, '– that cannot be possible. All that I know of me I have learned of you. What can you imagine that I would hide from you, *could* hide? What CAN you imagine?' (*ET* 66).

What – note not 'who' – you can imagine is a weighted question in *Eva Trout*. On the one hand, these forms of imagining, and hence legitimising, persons in the novel are narratives of the bend back, of the already read, ways of seeing that already deny a certain way of being human in their fiction-making. 'I am soiled by living more than a thousand lives,' writes Iseult; 'I have lived through books. I have lived internally' (*ET* 93). The 'harm' in Iseult (and Bowen is clear that she is a damaging type) was 'planted' by living through books, of already imagining the human in others too soon. In her eloquent self-recriminations, Iseult recalls the anti-hero of one of the new French novels she reads so avidly. Jean-Baptiste Clamence, the tortured narrator of Albert Camus's *La Chute* (1956), similarly damns the moral pretensions of the new judicial age, and himself, for failing to forge a commitment to others that is not soiled by a fictional imagination: 'I could only imagine the love of Iseult in a novel or on the stage . . . living among human beings without sharing their interests, I never managed to believe in the commitments I made.'[56] Bowen's Iseult shares Clamence's weakness: 'All had been nothing: life is an *anti*-novel,' she writes to Constantine, in homage to Camus's testimony to the impossibility of doing justice to damaged experience (*ET* 206).

Eva Trout, on the other hand, is not an anti-novel, or at least not quite. 'I wonder if anything human is *ever* over,' muses Mrs Dancey, who also wishes she had 'more imagination' in respect of Eva (*ET* 212, 75). The novel is pressed by the imperative to keep on imagining the human, even as it acknowledges that the sort of imagination required for the new world is yet to come. This is why it is also an 'experiment' in the possibilities of human love at mid-century.[57] Beyond the world of political rights, Arendt wrote, there is only the Augustinian injunction – 'I want you to be'– left to protect and nurture our lives together. This tacit imperative conditions the love between Eva and Jeremy. What is an illegality, a trespass of human rights, coincides with the becoming of a different kind of human existence; Eva begets Jeremy by simply wanting him to be. But it is a strange dreamlike world, this place the two call home. Sensual, cinematographic, Eva's and Jeremy's wordless union is a refuge for the politically, and generically, lawless. 'Society revolved at a distance from them like a ferris wheel dangling buckets of people. They were their own. Wasted, civilization extended round them as might acres of cannibalized cars' (*ET* 189). Bowen's writing does not so much describe this world as inhabit it from the inside. The bubbles in the novel expand to bursting point. Her trademark synaesthesia dilates. Persons become sensations: 'Stinging of their same faces by spray from cataracts too loud to be heard even by Eva' (*ET* 189). The *roman* is overtaken by a kind of outrageously sensual *Bild*.

The historical pathos of the novel, however, resides not so much in the otherworldly intimacy of its two fugitives, as in its inability, or perhaps refusal, to find a final home for this other way of being human. Even in an impossible time there has to be the sense of a future (Chapter 3 of the novel's second half is simply entitled 'Eva's Future'); narrative requires that there will be occurrence if not exactly development. When Eva finds her 'non-humanity' reflected back in the 'barely representational' large knot of clay Jeremy has made of her (like a Henry Moore mother), something shifts. The text begins to tug Jeremy and Eva, back into the plot, urging them forward into a world of recognition and legitimisation. So, Jeremy is 'made' in the novel in a way that Eva never quite was. What Iseult could not achieve in her seduction of Eva she repeats successfully in his abduction: an efficacious trauma, psychoanalytically speaking, that makes possible his gentle oedipalisation by the psychoanalyst couple, the Bonnards, and rebirth as a French speaker.

But what Bowen does not (cannot?) do is confer this psychoanalytic passage into personhood with fictional legitimacy; hence, for some readers at least, the novel's outrageous finale. Like other mid-century fictional no-exits (such as Henry Green's *Party Going* (1939) and Graham Greene's *The Ministry of Fear* (1943)), the novel ends on a London station with a train on which nobody is going to travel. Bowen's moment of arrested future, however, is made doubly poignant by the fact that, just before Eva's violent death, Henry's declaration of love turns her staged mimicry of a marriage – her final fictional extravagance – into a plausible reality. Finally, but tragically briefly, Eva is conferred with something like the fictional legitimacy promised by the *Bildungsroman*. Yet the parsing of that transformation owes nothing to the 'grammar' of the traditional novel. Instead, the moment that Eva, in one sense, becomes most real coincides with the most sensational passage in the entire novel:

> Something took place: a bewildering, brilliant, blurring filling up, swimming and brimming over; then, not a torrent from the eyes but one, two, three, four tears, each hesitating, surprised to be where it was, then wandering down. The speediest splashed on to the diamond brooch. 'Look what is *happening* to me!' exulted Eva. She had no handkerchief, not having expected to

require one – she blotted about on her face with a crunched-up glove. 'What a coronation day . . .'

    'Are you happy?' asked Henry, awed.

    'A coronation being living, today.' (*ET* 267)

'Pellucid fugitives' seems right for these opulent tears, which do not so much make the feelings of their host believable, as arrest the flow of fictional plausibility at the very moment it is being granted. As the tears move and feel their way on to Eva's brooch, the scene itself seems to freeze. Two of Bowen's most perspicacious critics have commented on the photographic qualities of this passage.[58] As in Walter Benjamin's famous definition of the photograph, the image of Eva's tears marks a moment in its vanishing. A version of naturalised human sovereignty is caught in Bowen's prose, paradoxically, just as it disappears: 'a coronation being living, today', and then, speedily, indecently, dead. When Jeremy, accidentally or not, shoots Eva, it is as if the model of human personality, enfranchised by the European novel and belatedly propagated by the UDHR, is finally assassinated by one of the twentieth-century's new legal and literary generic outlaws.

    Bowen's final ending outrages in the same way that Arendt's refugee style is indecent, in so far as it (literally in this case) fires a shot back across the judicial imagination of the European novel from the position of the radically stateless and rightless. Bowen's last fictional gesture, hence, is perhaps her most avant-garde. But it is also one of the most painfully affecting in her entire corpus. 'Corny as they are,' Maud Ellmann has written of Eva's tears, 'they elicit real emotion in the reader, just as the creakiest machinery of melodrama can move an audience more deeply than footage of the grisliest atrocities.'[59] I have argued in this chapter that that emotion is also a fragile opening-up to a domain of experience that could not be imagined within the rhetoric of the second age of human rights. The question that Bowen raises, but will not settle, is what form the novel of the future will have to take in order to do some kind of imaginative justice in the wake of the refugee. It is a question that Bowen's friend, Iris Murdoch, was to begin her career by addressing.

Notes

1. Elizabeth Bowen, *Eva Trout, or Changing Scenes* (1968; Harmondsworth: Penguin, 1982), p. 17. Hereafter abbreviated as *ET*.
2. Quoted in Gellhorn, 'They Talked of Peace' (1946), *The Face of War* (1959; London: Granta, 1999), p. 237.

3. Tony Judt, *Postwar: A History of Europe Since 1945* (2005; London: Pimlico, 2007), p. 29.

4. Elizabeth Bowen, 'Paris Peace Conference: 1946. An Impression', in *People, Places, Things*, ed. Allan Hepburn (Edinburgh: Edinburgh University Press, 2008), p. 66.

5. In a 1959 radio interview, quoted in Hepburn, *People, Places, Things*, p. 426.

6. Gellhorn is particularly good on the brutal disconnect between politics and justice at the conference: 'I have been told how the Ethiopians computed their desired reparations; with innocence and sadness and humility, they decided that a human life must be worth about five hundred dollars to Western peoples, so they multiplied their dead by five hundred dollars' (Gellhorn, 'They Talked of Peace', p. 236).

7. Bowen, 'Notes on Writing a Novel' (1945), in *The Mulberry Tree: Writings of Elizabeth Bowen*, ed. Hermione Lee (London: Virago, 1986), p. 39.

8. Bowen, 'The Bend Back' (1950), in *The Mulberry Tree*, p. 54.

9. Arendt, 'What is Existential Philosophy?', in *Essays in Understanding, 1930–1954*, ed. Jerome Kohn (New York: Schocken, 1994), p. 165.

10. Bowen, 'Why Do I Write? Part of a Correspondence with Graham Greene and V. S. Pritchett' (1948), in *The Mulberry Tree*, p. 223.

11. Where earlier critics were bothered by the novel's extravagances, more lately *Eva Trout* has re-emerged to take its place as Bowen's boldest fictional experiment in current criticism. This reclamation was begun in Andrew Bennett's and Nicholas Royle's important *Elizabeth Bowen and the Dissolution of the Novel*, Ch. 8 (Basingstoke: Macmillan, 1995) pp. 140–57.

12. Joseph R. Slaughter, *Human Rights, Inc: The World Novel, Narrative Form and International Law* (New York: Fordham University Press, 2007), pp. 45–55.

13. Slaughter, *Human Rights, Inc*, p. 48.

14. On the one hand, the refugees and displaced persons shuffling across the frontiers of Europe, India–Pakistan and, even as the delegates met, Palestine–Israel–Jordan seemed to provoke even more shrill assertions of the ineffability of rights in the face of their evident inefficacy. On the other, as delegates at the Third Committee well understood, in the postwar political context such assertions required the workings of positive law, which starts from the theoretical assumption that the human personality is a legal fiction because law is fundamentally about authority and power, not about imitating any extra-legal state of nature. Hence, for Slaughter, the fishy slipperiness of the UDHR's novelistic concept of a freely developing human personality provided a solution to a tension that went to the heart of its writing. See also Jacques Derrida, 'Declarations of Independence', in *Negotiations: Interventions and Interviews, 1971–2001*, ed. Elizabeth Rottenberg (Stanford: Stanford University Press, 2002), pp. 46–54. Costas Douzinas gives a thorough argument about the implications of this paradox for the politics of rights in *The End of Human Rights: Critical Legal Thought at the Turn of the Century* (Oxford: Hart, 2000).

15. Quoted in Slaughter, *Human Rights, Inc*, p. 55.
16. H. G. Wells, *The Rights of Man or What Are We Fighting For?* (Harmondsworth: Penguin, 1940), p. 78.
17. Ian Watt, *The Rise of the Novel* (1957; London: Pimlico, 2000), p. 11.
18. As Marina MacKay has argued, the extent to which Ian Watt's experience in Japanese prisoner-of-war camps frames his understanding of the rise of the novel, particularly in terms of the mediation of group violence, is striking. My thanks to MacKay for letting me read her unpublished draft, 'The Wartime Rise of *The Rise of the Novel*'.
19. Slaughter, *Human Rights Inc.*, p. 54.
20. Bowen, 'Why Do I Write?', p. 222.
21. See Maud Ellmann's discussion of Bowen's conservatism in *Elizabeth Bowen: The Shadow Across the Page* (Edinburgh: Edinburgh University Press, 2003), p. 116.
22. Bowen, 'Why Do I Write?', p. 225.
23. Franco Moretti, *The Way of the World: The Bildungsroman in European Culture*, trans. Albert Sbragia (1987; London: Verso, 2000), p. 64.
24. Bowen, 'Why Do I Write?', p. 225.
25. Bowen, *The Heat of the Day* (1948; Harmondsworth: Penguin, 1976), p. 269. *The Heat of the Day* is also a reckoning with postwar justice in its own right. See Allan Hepburn, 'Trials and Errors: *The Heat of the Day* and Postwar Culpability', in *Intermodernism: Literary Culture in Mid-Century Britain*, ed. Kirsten Bluemel (Edinburgh: Edinburgh University Press, 2009), pp. 46–54.
26. Jacqueline Rose, 'Bizarre Objects: Mary Butts and Elizabeth Bowen', *Critical Quarterly*, 42.1, 2000, pp. 75–85.
27. Bowen, 'Why Do I Write?', p. 229.
28. Bowen, 'English Fiction at Mid-Century' (1953), in *People, Places, Things*, p. 321.
29. Bowen, 'I Hear You Say So', in *The Collected Stories of Elizabeth Bowen*, ed. Angus Wilson (1945; Harmondsworth: Penguin, 1983), p. 753.
30. Bowen, 'The Bend Back', p. 55.
31. Bowen, 'Hungary' (1948), in *People, Places, Things*, p. 91.
32. Bowen, 'Paris Peace Conference – Some Impressions 1', in *People, Places, Things*, p. 74.
33. Bowen, 'Hungary', p. 88.
34. Bowen, 'Without Coffee, Cigarettes, or Feeling' (1955), in *People, Places, Things*, p. 93.
35. Bowen, 'The Achievement of Virginia Woolf', in *Collected Impressions* (1949; London: Longmans Green, 1950), p. 79.
36. Bowen, '*The Demon Lover*: Postscript to the first U.S. edition', in *The Mulberry Tree*, p. 97.
37. Louis Althusser, 'The International of Decent Feelings', in *The Spectre of Hegel*, ed. François Matheron, trans. G. M. Goshgarian (London: Verso, 1997), pp. 21–35.
38. Ian Watt, *The Rise of the Novel*, p. 74.
39. Lynn Hunt, 'Torrents of Emotion: Reading Novels and Imagining Equality', in *The Invention of Human Rights* (New York: W.W. Norton, 2007), pp. 35–69.

40. Marina MacKay discusses Watt's unease with *Pamela*'s ability to generate a mass market in human feeling in 'The Wartime Rise of the Novel'.

41. The fact that feelings could indeed have a meaningful judicial life for Bowen is beautifully expressed in the two recommendations that she made in her report for the Royal Commission on Capital Punishment to which she was appointed in 1949. In her personal contribution, she argued that verbal as well as physical provocation should be capable of turning a murder charge into one of manslaughter because, in effect, words can be felt as violence. Second, she argued that the clemency currently granted to a man provoked by his wife's adultery should be extended to a man whose mistress 'distresses him in the same way', with the impeccable logic that 'in an irregular relationship passion and sexual feeling is nearer the surface' (Victoria Glendinning, *Elizabeth Bowen: A Biography* (1977; New York: Anchor, 2005), p. 222). That Bowen was appointed to the Commission in the first place is another example of the extent to which literature was drafted into the new legal humanism.

42. Bowen, 'Flaubert's *Sentimental Education*' (1941), in *The Mulberry Tree*, p. 156.

43. 'Down it poured like all people in the world weeping. Tears tears . . . they were the people's tears, weeping for all people . . . the rain was sudden and universal' (Virginia Woolf, *Between the Acts* (1941; Harmondsworth: Penguin, 1992), p. 107).

44. H. G. Wells, 'Declaration of Human Rights', in *The Rights of Man*, p. 14.

45. Charles Ritchie, *Undiplomatic Diaries 1937–1971* (Toronto: McClelland & Stewart, 2008), p. 513.

46. Andrew Bennett and Nicholas Royle, for example, demonstrate how the novel undermines the epistemological assumptions of the novel form (*Elizabeth Bowen and the Dissolution of the Novel*, pp. 140–57). Both Neil Corcoran and Maud Ellmann draw attention to the ethical dimensions of Bowen's fictional convolutions. Corcoran traces the 'sometimes peculiar or disconcerting ethics' that emerges out of the novel's focus on maternity, while Ellmann reads *Eva* as asking a question of how far fiction can go without ethics (Neil Corcoran, *Elizabeth Bowen: The Enforced Return* (Oxford: Oxford University Press, 2004), pp. 126–44; Maud Ellmann, *Elizabeth Bowen: The Shadow Across the Page*, p. 204).

47. Bowen, '*Preface* to Critics Who Have Influenced Taste' (1965), in *People, Places, Things*, p. 333.

48. Edmund Burke, *Reflections on the Revolution in France*, ed. Conor Cruise O'Brien (1790; Harmondsworth: Penguin, 2004), p. 90.

49. Bowen, '*Preface* to Critics Who Have Influenced Taste', p. 333.

50. John Coates, 'The Misfortunes of Eva Trout', *Essays in Criticism*, 47.1, 1999, p. 72.

51. Chapter 8 of Part II of the novel, for instance, is simply called 'Indictment', although it is not entirely clear who (or what) is being indicted. Just as pointedly, Reverend Dancey is writing a book on justice entitled *The Faulty Scales*. Issues of familial and national (and familial as national) legitimacy also run right through the novel: from Eva's inheritance and begetting of Jeremy, to the mother of Eric's children, a Norwegian who will be deported if their union is not legitimised. Iseult is particularly good on the

self-recriminations of the existential hero in the new judicial age. 'I murdered my life, and I defy anybody to defend me. I should hang for it' (*ET* 91), she types. But when Iseult confesses to Father Tony with the words, 'I have no right to your time,' he responds, 'My good lady, nobody has any "right" to anything. We subsist on mercy' (*ET* 241).

52. Bowen's incorporation of desire into the plotting of the female *Bildungsroman* has been the focus of much critical discussion. See Renée C. Hoogland, *Elizabeth Bowen: A Reputation in Writing* (New York: New York University Press, 1994) and Petra-Utta Rau, *Moving Dangerously: Desire and Narrative Structure in the Fiction of Elizabeth Bowen, Rosamond Lehmann and Sylvia Townsend Warner*, PhD thesis, University of East Anglia, 2000.

53. Agamben has argued, after Arendt, that refugees (to whom we might add trafficked people) cause such disquiet for concepts of the state because 'by breaking the continuity by man and citizen, *nativity* and *nationality*, they put the originary fiction of modern sovereignty into crisis'; that is, they expose the fact that simply being born human is no guarantee of legitimacy (*Homo Sacer: Sovereign Power and Bare Life*, trans. Daniel Heller-Roazen (1995; Stanford: Stanford University Press, 1998), p. 131). That Jeremy's birth cannot be sustained by the fiction of modern sovereignty embodied by the *Bildungsroman* is his tragedy.

54. Arendt was one of the first to use the term 'Holocaust' in popular print in her reports on the Eichmann trial. See Esther Benbassa, *Suffering as Identity: The Jewish Paradigm*, trans. G. M. Goshgarian (2007; London: Verso, 2010), pp. 118–23, for an account of the development of the term, and Anna-Vera Calimani Sullman, 'A Name for Extermination', *Modern Language Review*, 94, 1999, pp. 978–99.

55. Intentionally or not, Bowen dates the opening of the school at the castle to the Autumn of 1948, thus making it contemporary with other experiments in nurturing the freely developing personality within progressive institutions, such as the United Nations' UDHR.

56. Albert Camus, *The Fall*, trans. Robin Buss (1956; Harmondsworth: Penguin, 2006), p. 55.

57. Frequently in *Eva*, moments that usually have a conventional significance in fiction become 'experiments'. For instance, Eric's shaking of Eva (in a strange mimicry of some kind of narrative congress) is described as a 'crisis' that becomes 'an experiment' (*ET* 88). Not only does experiment have a timely period flavour, but Bowen is also experimenting with the weight that a novel can bear.

58. Corcoran discusses the 'distorted-mirror anamorphosis' of the passage in terms of André Kertész's nudes (*Elizabeth Bowen: The Enforced Return*, p. 130), while Ellmann evokes Man Ray's famous 'Glass Tear' (*The Shadow Across the Page*, p. 222).

59. Ellmann, *The Shadow Across the Page*, p. 222.

Chapter 6

The 'Dark Background of Difference': Love and the Refugee in Iris Murdoch

Love is the only justice. Forgiveness, reconciliation, not law.
Iris Murdoch, *The Nice and the Good*[1]

This mere existence, that is, all that is mysteriously given us by birth and which includes the shape of our bodies and the talents of our minds, can be adequately dealt with only by the unpredictable hazards of friendship and sympathy, or by the great and incalculable grace of love, which says with Augustine, '*Volo ust sis* [I want you to be],' without being able to give any particular reason for such supreme and unsurpassable affirmation.
Hannah Arendt, *The Origins of Totalitarianism* (382)

A note I made, in memory of the UNRRA camps. Branislav Djekic, Radovan . . ., Dragomir Pardanjac. Handsome Serbs. Also: Boris Leontic . . . (Draga and Djekic, with help from me and Mrs Lewis, came to England, I saw something of Draga. Then lost touch.) March 14. Thinking of Branislav Djekic and Dragomir Pardanjac – should they have gone home? Draga cd have had hopes for his boy. What happened to Draga?
Iris Murdoch, *UNRAA Notes*[2]

I want to start with two experiences that came out of working in the United Nations Relief and Rehabilitation Administration (UNRRA) camps in the aftermath of the war.[3] The first is from Gitta Sereny's account of the trauma of repatriating children who had been stolen by the Nazis as part of the 'Germanisation' programme. Sereny had discovered Polish twins living with a German farming family. She later runs into them in a transit camp, awaiting their return to Poland. The boy flies at Sereny in a rage: 'Du, Du, Du,' he cries and hits out at her. The girl is limp, listless, dead to her strange new world. Later that evening, Sereny gives the girl her bottle:

> she lay there, eyes shut, her body apparently boneless, the only movement the sucking of her lips and the swallowing of her small thin throat. I held her until she was asleep. It helped me, but not, I fear, her. What are we doing, I asked myself. What in God's name were we doing?[4]

Nothing could seem more right than returning the stolen children to their natural parents. And yet holding the still body of the infant in transit, a child only just existing at the limits of race, nation and life, Sereny experiences a kind of moral horror: what are we doing? This is not a child made alive again by the prospect of return, but one who carries the burden of her times in her frail, listless body. Limp on Sereny's lap, Marie is reduced to what both Nazi racism and the UN repatriation projects have made her: a body in transit. And yet, it is out of this extreme vulnerability that Sereny encounters something in Marie that exists beyond her legal status as a child package. And it is at that moment, too, that Sereny recognises that her care, her surrogate mothering, is more important to her than it is a comfort to the child on her lap: a child who once ran into the arms of her adoptive German mother and who was now, once again, homeless.

The second scene comes from Iris Murdoch's novel, *The Flight from the Enchanter* (1956). Like Sereny, Murdoch worked in the UNRRA camps, and her early novels, in particular, are crowded with exiles, refugees and displaced persons. Two of the most disturbing of these are the Polish boys, the Lusiewicz brothers, from Murdoch's second published novel. Like Sereny's twins, the Lusiewicz brothers are otherworldly and awaken in their protector, and then mistress, Rosa, a feeling Murdoch describes as 'some profound seam of vulnerability and grief'.[5] But where in Sereny's writing that vulnerability pulls open the veil between the refugee and the life that pulses so precariously within that category (hence its moral shock), Rosa's encounter with the brothers is a story of mutual, and dangerous, enchantment. 'In their presence', writes Murdoch, Rosa 'was always breathless, as one in a new beautiful country, full of an inexplicable rapture and never very far from tears' (*FE* 51). Wrapped in an exquisite gauze of unnameable grief, this is a love that cancels out moral thought. As she enters – in what must be one of the strangest narrative fantasies in postwar British fiction – into a *ménage à trois* with the brothers, it is not moral revelation that Rosa experiences, but 'a numb paralysis which is the deliberate dulling of thought by itself' (*FE* 53). By the end of the novel, the enchantment that drew Rosa to the brothers, and they to her, turns into a dark and brutal power play – an enchantment that must be fled.

The fact that the figure of the stateless person is at the centre of both scenes is not coincidental; neither Sereny nor Murdoch is writing about limit encounters with others in general, but with a particular category of others. For Sereny, Marie becomes something other than a displaced person at the moment when the juridical and political apparatus intended to restore her national rights reveals its awful commensurability with the logic that deprived her of them in the first place. Murdoch's early writings, I suggest in this chapter, are also an attempt to grasp the elusive figure that appears in between the withdrawal and the granting of rights: the refugee or displaced person, or as Murdoch would probably put it, the human individual. For Murdoch, only an ethical love can make the refugee appear. The moral scandal of Rosa's enchantment with the brothers is not only to do with sexual passion, but with the way that desire prevents her from attending to the suffering of statelessness – from loving differently. Love, as both Sereny and Murdoch recognise, can be inadequate; frequently self-interested and capricious, love alone cannot grant rights where there are none. But as Murdoch never ceased believing, perhaps only love can occupy the ethical void left by the operation of the law.

If much of this book has been about the attempt to imagine the law in the postwar period, in this final chapter I turn to the question of imagining an experience that exists, by dint of the law itself, beyond it. Writing out of the chaos of the transit camps that sprung up in the immediate postwar period, often on the sites of former concentration camps, Sereny and Murdoch remind us that the world of the refugee did not end with the liberation of the camps. Efforts to legislate for a post-Holocaust world, to put it to rights, as Sereny's story so painfully reveals, were hamstrung not only by the Cold War's normalisation of a politics that continued to trade in population transfers (as if the reduction of life to the nation state had nothing to do with the Nazi horrors on trial at Nuremberg), but also by the paradox revealed by these bodies in transit that Hannah Arendt had began to explore in her writing of the 1940s (the subject of Chapter 4). 'The paradox involved in the loss of human rights', Arendt wrote in *The Origins of Totalitarianism*, 'is that such a loss coincides with the instant when a person becomes a human being in general' (*OT* 383). We can read this paradox in the Sereny passage as a moment of pathos; hence the calling up of a loving, but morally inadequate, pity. In Marie's case, the paradox is all the more brutal for there being a double removal of her rights, once as a victim of

Nazi totalitarianism and again at the precise moment when her so-called national rights are being restored.

The sense of a mourning for a category of life lost to a world of cold politics and legal reason runs across postwar writing. 'In the practical world there may be only mourning and the final acceptance of the incomplete,' writes Murdoch in her 1959 essay 'The Sublime and the Good'.[6] Much of Murdoch's early writing is an attempt to accept this incompletion without the consolations of form, to get through enchantment, we could say, to the refugee. 'Form', she writes in the same essay, 'is the greatest consolation of love, but it is also its greatest temptation.'[7] Such scrupulous and loving attention to the particularities of a life almost lost reminds us that Murdoch is a writer of moral philosophy, as well as of fiction. It is also, however, a kind of loving that has perhaps contributed, especially in the years following her death, to the cultivation of Murdoch's image as a kind of unworldly enchantress, a Platonic lover of the Good, or just too much of a lover in more prurient accounts: like Kant, as she herself once described him, mildly resentful of the hold that history has on ethics. More than one reader of *The Flight from the Enchanter* has thought to point out that, despite Murdoch's fantastically surreal scenarios in the novel, 'real' refugees do actually exist and suffer.[8]

Murdoch, of course, knew this all too well. In fact, as I argue here, the suffering of real refugees is at the core of her fraught engagement with the enchantments of novel-writing right from the beginning. Murdoch began her career surrounded by refugees: people such as the Jančars, friends she made in Graz, a camp on the Austrian border, along with the desperate, beautiful youths who awaited deportation back to a bullet in the head in Tito's Yugoslavia. In 1947 Murdoch met Wasfi Hijab, a Palestinian refugee, and Alexandrian Pierre Riches, Jewish, both at Cambridge where she first went on her return from the camps in 1947. A year later, at Oxford, she became friends with the Italian Jew, Arnaldo Momigliano, and, most incisively for Murdoch's writing and life, fell in love with Franz Baermann Steiner. Steiner was a Prague Jew, anthropologist, poet, aphorist, Zionist and author of 'Orientpolitik' (1936), in which he claimed that a radical Jewish alliance with the Middle and Far East was a stronger, and more natural, defence against European anti-Semitism than founding a state on European, imperialist and orientalist values.[9] Arguably, it was Steiner, as much as the larger-than-life Elias Canetti (another Jewish exile and to whom Murdoch dedicated the novel), who was to leave his biographical and moral mark on *The Flight from the Enchanter*, as well as, later, *The Nice and the Good* (1968), *A Fairly Honourable Defeat* (1970) and, finally, *The Message to the Planet* (1989).

Asked about the prevalence of refugees in her writing in a 1982 interview with Susan Hill, Murdoch replied: 'These are images of human suffering, kinds of people that one has met. Such persons are windows through which one looks into terrible worlds.'[10] Images and metaphors, Murdoch was to insist, are part of the play through which we make moral sense of the world.[11] The slippage between 'images of suffering' and the 'kinds of people that one has met' in her reply to Hill, between the glassiness of the imagination and our real-life encounters with persons, repeats itself throughout her writing, fictional and philosophical, as a tension, sometimes a paradox, through which she articulates her moral vision. To look through these 'windows' into 'terrible worlds' is not just to meditate on suffering, but to encounter the limits of how, by conjuring up images or making metaphors, we can imagine that world. What is also so terrible about the world of the refugee, apart from its evident awfulness, for Murdoch at least, is the extent to which it disturbs our capacity to make images that are adequate to it. The sublime, she argues elsewhere, is the mere existence of other people.[12] The love in which Murdoch invests so much is a love that frequently finds itself in the entanglements of image and metaphor as we move to and from these others.

Such enchantments do not necessarily take us from the world of law and politics – not, at any rate, without a struggle – and however much Murdoch eventually makes metaphysics a guide to morals, and morals the guiding principle of her increasingly liberal politics. Although she began her life on the left, later Murdoch did not so much veer right as upwards, beyond politics.[13] By the end of the twentieth century, she would argue that only a loving morality could ground political justice. Rights, in this liberal interpretation, are neither foundational nor political in themselves, but necessary and mobile axioms for the working of moral good in the political world. 'Rights', she wrote in *Metaphysics as a Guide to Morals* (1992), 'are political flags representing moral ideas in a public political scene.'[14] In this chapter, however, I want to resist the ascendancy of liberal morals in Murdoch, at least for a moment, by dwelling instead, as indeed, I think, she did in the forties, fifties and early sixties, on the 'terrible world' of the refugee as a place that challenges our ability to envision the good.

Murdoch's 'terrible' postwar world, as I want to think about it here, occupies the same dark region that Arendt, writing at the same time, both acknowledged as a source of ethics and, not without good reason, also feared in political and historical terms. The 'human being in general', who paradoxically emerges out of the failure of human rights in Arendt's account, is often evoked in terms of pathos in human rights literature, as the pitiful human wretch whose naked vulnerability is exposed by the withdrawal of rights, for instance. Less well quoted, however, are the lines which follow, where Arendt makes it clear that there is no political redemption to be wrought from this newly revealed human form:

> The paradox involved in the loss of human rights is that such loss coincides with the instant a person becomes a human being in general – without a profession, without a citizenship, without an opinion, without a deed by which to identify and specify himself – *and* different in general, representing nothing but his own absolutely unique individuality which, deprived of expression within and action upon a common world, loses all significance. (*OT* 383)

The human being in general is a person with absolutely no political or juridical status. It is not, in other words, the positive workings of the law that make us human, and not the case that better human rights law would produce better people; on the contrary, the critical and ethical force of Arendt's 'human being in general' kicks in as the law's negative trace. This is not a world in which inequalities can be dealt with through axioms, or politics through better morals, but one of absolute and unique difference. While such a world effectively closes the door on the kind of political morality that Murdoch later advocates, the 'absolutely unique individuality' that Arendt writes of as left behind in the trail of the failure of rights is arguably what a younger Murdoch, secondary witness to the camps, strives towards in her early writing. Indeed, it is the imperative to recognise the 'unique individuality' of other persons, to some extent at least, that lies behind the very large claims that Murdoch makes for the ethical superiority of the novel in the postwar period. 'In the case of the novel', she writes, 'the most important thing to be [. . .] revealed, not necessarily the only thing, but incomparably the most important thing, is that other people exist.'[15]

Like Murdoch, Arendt is aware of the ethics that has to work in what she calls 'the dark background of difference' or 'mere givenness'. Here only the grace of love, Augustine's 'I want you to be' (the subject of her 1929 Heidelberg dissertation), or the 'unpredictable hazards of friendship and sympathy' prevail against oblivion. What, however, for one reading might be the prompt for ethical care is, by the same logic, also a source of political danger. For Arendt, such an extra-juridical, extra-political insignificance exercises a two-fold check on the political world, the world of rights, laws and of the nation state. On the one hand, the very presence of persons without political significance marks the limits of our activity as political agents. Arendt describes the 'dark background of mere givenness' as 'breaking into the political scene as the alien', reminding us that we are only the masters, not the creators of worldly life. On the other hand, she argues, the 'ever-increasing numbers' of such people are a 'threat' – these are not friendly ghosts; they intrude, 'break in', as aliens – to political life that, in another grim paradox, is created from within the judicial and political world itself. 'The danger is', Arendt concludes her section on imperialism in *Origins*, is 'that a global, universal interrelated civilisation may produce barbarians from its own midst by forcing people into conditions which, despite all appearances, are the conditions of savages' (*OT* 384).

The refugee and her world, then, are at once an ethical check on the limitations of political life and, by the same logic, a living menace to that life. It is at this uncomfortable juncture (one that also well describes the shuttling between liberal sentiment and phobia that characterises much recent political discourse on contemporary refugees) that I next want to place Murdoch's early writing, and in particular her 1956 novel, *The Flight from the Enchanter*. The wager of this writing, I hazard, is in daring to imagine a world without politics or law. What has frequently been described as a moral turn inward to a new humanism in Murdoch (a characterisation sometimes followed by accusations of moral mysticism) is something far more risky than a notion of a historical retreat to the good might imply. Indeed, it is because of this tension between ethics and menace that the idea of an enchanted encounter with the refugee is not, as some of her more critical readers have assumed, a well-intentioned but in the end politically insidious downgrading of historical suffering. Far from it. The powerful artifice of fiction for Murdoch, like the artifice of the political world for Arendt, is precisely that through which the ethical charge of the figure of the refugee can be encountered. When Murdoch, famously, writes of the imperative for the postwar novel to be 'a house for free characters to live in' she is not simply sloganeering for a new liberal fiction (and, in any case, Murdoch's demands on liberalism are far from trivial); she is also asking how the novel might bear the weight, not of a wished-for freedom (as in the cliché of the emancipatory 1960s novel which still hangs around her work), but the far more dangerous, because lawless, freedom which exists in the world of mere givenness.[16] If Murdoch's writing succeeds only partially in incorporating this profound, perhaps even extravagant, moral vision, this is because in the end she encounters the same threat as Arendt did: that of a human existence that imperils the artifice of worldly life at its very core. The refugee in Murdoch's writing, hence, becomes not only (as in Arendt) a limit concept of political, juridical and speaking life, but of fiction too, and of the very possibility of a moral novel-writing.

Missing persons

> 'We are offered things or truths. What we have lost is persons.'
> Iris Murdoch, 'The Sublime and the Good Revisited'[17]

Like the transit camps she had worked in, for Murdoch the novel was a place for attending to lost persons. It was because she thought that fiction could rehabilitate the displaced that she would claim that it was better equipped, in moral terms, than philosophy to administer to the postwar world. This was the argument she made in a series of early essays published in the late 1950s and early 1960s, and also more (and sometimes less) implicitly in her early novels, peopled not only with refugees and exiles, but philosopher-drifters, failed scholars and, most conspicuously, the magic men and women of theatre and film. Murdoch's argument for the morality of art in this period went something like this. Locked in its logic of words and their truth claims, empiricism has turned moral agency into a language game: offering us mere things, and a man who exists solely by what he 'observably does'. Similarly left shuddering in the cold of the human condition is the Hegelian subject, re-invented for the postwar period by Sartre's existentialism, for whom other people are, chillingly, true only in so far as they are 'organised menacing extensions of the consciousness of the human subject'.[18] Neither view is capable of attending to human life in its messy, infinite particularity. Only in the novel can the displaced persons of modern times find just care. In the last chapter, we saw how the pre-modernist novel was re-invented for a new postwar judicial humanism. Murdoch too bends back in order to rediscover the contours of a lost liberal ethics in an older tradition. With an unfashionable emphasis on its 'un-Hegelian nature' (Murdoch must be one of the tiny minority who did not think the novel was Hegelian in this period), what, she argues, is disclosed in the nineteenth-century novel is what is missing in contemporary philosophy: 'a real apprehension of persons other than the author having a right to exist'.[19] Rights, in this formulation, then, come with the recognition of the absolute singularity of persons. Nowhere more so can this morality be seen, she argues, than in the novel where persons are coaxed out of the dark background of difference and re-entitled, morally at least, if not (conspicuously) politically, through a kind of attentive loving.

These are bold and purposefully valorising claims. At her most extravagant, Murdoch erects a new liberalism upon what is perhaps rather frail ethical ground. The person who emerges out the attentions of prose, she argues in her famous 1961 essay 'Against Dryness', is the same 'substantial, impenetrable, individual and valuable' person who 'is

perhaps problem, is how far it is possible to make this unseen experience live, to attend to it without betraying it. The enchantment to be flown, in this context, is first of all an enchantment that destroys the very experience it calls up.

The dilemma, as so often in Murdoch's prose, is how a writing so enamoured of the magical properties of fiction can lift the embroidered nets of its own making. If some of her readers seem to think that Murdoch makes light of the plight of refugees and exiles in *Flight*, this is because of its exuberant literariness, the colour and light that, especially in her first novels, she cannot seem to help herself from conjuring up. Thus the novel's memorable opening with the 'cosmopolitan ragamuffin's', Annette's, exultant exit from her finishing school – swinging from a chandelier which 'began to ring, not with a deafening peal but with a very high and sweet tinkling sound', with 'the sort of sound, after all, which you would expect a wave of the sea to make if it had been immobilized and turned into glass: a tiny internal rippling, a mixture of sound and light' (*FE* 10–11). But in Murdoch's world, to be lured by this enchanting writing, called by the song of the glass sea, is to risk the same kind of ethical dereliction as Annette herself, whose enchantment with the world is of a dozy, self-interested kind, 'like being at the pictures' (*FE* 283). Like Bowen's Eva Trout, Annette is another of postwar fiction's slippery fish-like cosmopolitan heiresses. But where, as we saw in the last chapter, Bowen's Eva eludes the identity-making capacities of fiction, Murdoch's Annette is a pure pastiche of the statelessness that haunts the novel. 'I have no home. I'm a refugee!' Annette cries just before her faux overdose on milk of magnesia (*FE* 249). In truth, that is, in Murdoch's moral truth, Annette is too rich to need a home, and is a refugee only from her own vanity.

There is a kind of disavowal, then, involved in Murdoch's fiction-making, as she calls up the powers of her art only at the same time to repudiate them in moral terms. The stakes of that double movement towards and away from enchantment are far more difficult – both for the novel and for Murdoch's moral vision – in the case of Rosa's extraordinary love of the Lusiewicz brothers with which I opened this chapter. In their L-shaped Pimlico bedsit, dominated by the distorting presence of a huge old iron bed-frame, an aged mother on a mattress in the corner (one can almost hear Murphy's rocking chair creaking on the floor above), the magic conjured up by the brothers is a source of both incantatory pleasure and revulsion. Here, as elsewhere when the novel veers towards Eastern Europe, Murdoch departs from the task of re-inventing the nineteenth-century novel, for the didactic possibilities of modernist anthropology. In one of a series of bizarre scenes between the three, for example, the mother on the mattress becomes something like a 'native god':

> 'She is earth, earth,' Stefan would say in solemn tones to Rosa. 'She is our own earth. She is our land,' said Jan. 'Sometimes we dance on top of her, we do the dance of land. Eh, old woman!' he shouted suddenly, prodding her with his foot.

Venerated for her connection with a land that is, as the boys say, no more because of 'Hitler', the mother is also mere matter to be kicked and killed.

> 'You old rubbish! You old sack' cried Jan. 'We soon kill you, we put you under floorboard, you not stink there worse than here! We kill you! We kill you!' And he would make as if to jump on to her stomach. (*FE* 49)

Readings of the novel that cast the menace of the Lusiewicz brothers purely in terms of aggressive male sexual power miss the point that, in Murdoch's world, they are coming from a place quite apart from the commonplaces of psychological realism. Sacred and yet able to be killed, Murdoch's old woman recalls the syntax of Agamben's *homo sacer*: the form of life that, for him, is the political corollary of exceptional sovereign power; the 'bare humanity' that reveals its political authenticity in the camps.[25] Closer, though, to Murdoch's early thinking in this period would have been the thought of her lover, the refugee anthropologist Franz Baermann Steiner, who, she would claim, proposed to her the night before his death from heart failure in 1952: another victim, she said, of Hitler. (Steiner's family perished in Treblinka; he was the sole survivor.) Taboo, Steiner once wrote, and from a position of one who lived his own taboo status as well as studied it, is foremost concerned with the 'sociology of danger', 'with the protection of individuals who are in danger, and [. . .] with the projection of society from those endangered – and therefore dangerous – persons'.[26] Endangered 'and therefore dangerous': the point is very similar to Arendt's fear of the political 'menace' of those who live only in the dark background of mere givenness (and neither will this be the only time Steiner will create a link between Murdoch and Arendt in this chapter).

The refugee, and particularly the Jewish refugee in Murdoch's fiction, often carries with him or her an aura of magic and menace. Honor Klein, for example, the Jewish anthropologist and enchantress in *The Severed Head* (1961), is given a similar occult power to the objects of her expertise; hence both her attractiveness and her menace. According to Peter J. Conradi, in an early draft all the characters in *Flight* were

Jewish.[27] In the end Murdoch did not follow through this ambitious act of what, in her terms, would be moral imagination – others might call it enthusiastic naivety. This decision, perhaps, was due not to moral rectitude (what can I claim to know about these lives?) but more to the fact that the kind of novel to which Murdoch aspired could not bear the weight of so much otherworldliness. (How many severed heads can one novel bear?) The point here is not simply about orientalist exoticisation or a rather tightly sprung philo-Semitism, although both are present in her writing. Murdoch's moral concern, rather, is with the capacity of contemporary taboos to disappear under the magic which at the same time conjures them into the world. Her challenge to herself in this period, I think, is to write the kind of fiction that can demonstrate this without performing a similar disappearing act. Rosa, once alarmed by the brothers' behaviour, pretty soon gets used to it and treats the mother 'as if she had been another quaint piece of furniture' (*FE* 48). What kind of magic, we could ask at this point, stops making taboo persons part of the furniture of fiction? Put slightly differently, how can we resist normalising the 'new kind of human beings' (to recall Arendt's powerful phrase once more) without exploding the terms of thought or, in this instance, prose itself?

Murdoch's solution, which is also perhaps a resistance to the enchantments of her own fiction, is to borrow from the nineteenth-century novel the trick of sublimating her writing's own dilemmas into the moral choices of her characters, a technique that she will perfect in her later novels.[28] Not attending adequately, or loving indifferently, thus, is the moral yardstick by which characters are judged and damned. Enchanted by the brothers' story of their first double-seduction, motivated by revenge for a slap on the face by their village schoolteacher, Rosa not only fails to recognise that the story is an allegory of her own; she also fails, morally speaking, to attend to it at all.

> 'Was she Jewish?' asked Rosa.
>   Stefan shrugged his shoulders. 'Perhaps was Jewish, perhaps was Jewish, perhaps Socialist. I don't know.'
>   'I think she was gipsy,' said Jan. 'Hitler not like gipsies either, he kill gipsies too, so they say in Poland.' (*FE* 72)

Steiner, who had made a study of the Roma before leaving Prague for good in 1938, had in all likelihood discussed with Murdoch his theory that it was the cultural identities between Eastern peoples that proved that anti-Semitism was not just local European politics, but intrinsic to the imperialist construction of the European nation state itself – an argument that echoes Arendt's famous connection between imperialism and totalitarianism in *Origins*.[29] Rosa embodies what Patricia Duncker has aptly described as the 'ghost of political commitment' in the novel; she works in a factory out of a Weil-like commitment to the truth of labour, is responsible for saving the feminist journal *The Artemis*, and is named after Rosa Luxemburg – 'she never stood a chance,' quips Murdoch (*FE* 15). She knows, then, to ask the right political question of the brothers – was she Jewish, this suicide in the enchanted village of which you speak?[30] What she cannot do, and hence, for Murdoch, her moral failure, is attend to their answer in her being. Worse still, it is the effort not to attend to the horror at the heart of enchantment that grants Rosa the kind of triumph of life denied to those unseen presences that pulse, faintly, in and out of the novel:

> Rosa sat down on the mattress and closed her eyes. She stiffened her body and crushed down out of her consciousness something that was crying out in horror. It was nearly gone, it was gone; and now as she sat rigid, like a stone goddess, and as she felt herself to be there, empty of thoughts and feelings, she experienced a kind of triumph. (*FE* 73)

Achtung, we might well say here, as what is repressed at the heart of enchantment.

Rosa's failure to attend to the lives of others is the reason why the sinister Calvin Blick can finally blackmail her. It is not so much, he implies, the compromising photographs he has taken of her with the Lusiewicz brothers that make her morally unfit as a lover for Mischa Fox, the novel's famously enigmatic enchanter, but the fact that wrapped in her own desire she twice betrays Nina, the dressmaker refugee, who upon learning she was about to be deported, has thrown herself out of her window rather than face another refusal at yet another frontier. But if inattention, or loving the refugee badly, is the moral yardstick of the novel, what does it mean that it is Mischa, perhaps the most radically displaced person in the entire novel, who is set up as judge? To whom, or perhaps what, in other words, are Murdoch's characters answerable? In part, it means that judgement is enigmatic. (Murdoch might later say mystical.) Mischa's haunting absent presence is why Calvin Blick can refer to him as an obscure moral authority, a subject-supposed-to-know, with one blue and one brown eye and an undetermined national origin: 'Where was he born? What blood is in his veins? No one knows. And if you try to imagine you are paralysed' (*FE* 35). The novel's sublime centre, Mischa is a source of magic and awe, love and terror. He is also, however (and here there is an echo of Gitta Sereny's moral trauma in the transit camps), a figure of pathos. Readings which identify Mischa's power with his male sexuality tend to miss the part that vulnerability can play in allure. Haunted by a suffering which the novel invokes but does not, perhaps even cannot, describe, Mischa more often than not reduces his companions to tears of pity rather than rapturous surrender. 'The hair of his head, darkened by the water, streamed down each side of his face and water-drops stood upon his cheeks like tears. When Annette saw this she began to cry' (*FE* 203).

This is the same profound seam of grief which I evoked at the beginning of this chapter: the grief that comes with the recognition of the life quivering within the historical, political and juridical category of statelessness. One line of thought in *The Flight from the Enchanter* equates vulnerability – an opening out to the grief of the other – with violence; hence Rosa's quiet triumph, and hence too Mischa's own 'intolerable compassion'. Why do we not see the dead?, Mischa wonders. He is talking about the small animals, chicks, kittens, moths that dart across the text, often associated with the precious vulnerability of the refugee; but the conspicuous invisibility of the camp dead is clearly implied in the magnitude of absent corpses: 'Yet one hardly ever sees one dead. Where do they go to? The surface of the world ought to be covered with dead animals. When I thought about this [. . .] I used sometimes to [. . .] kill animals' (*FE* 208). The cruelty of pity: violence as a defence against grief. The 'key to the nature of all power', Murdoch wrote in her 1962 review of Elias Canetti's classic study of the enchantments of totalitarianism, 'is the passion to survive.'[31] Murdoch comes close, dangerously so perhaps, to suggesting that suffering breeds violence, and that to survive is to triumph over suffering. At any rate, we seem to have wandered, once more, into that region that Arendt feared in political terms: the darkness at the centre of a world of population transfers, which forces people into conditions 'which, despite all appearances, are the conditions' of moral monsters. In this world, we could say, echoing Hobbes who is surely not too far away here either, man is fox to man.

What kind of love is possible in such a place is, I have been suggesting, the question Murdoch's novel raises but, finally, struggles to answer. Writing about Sartre's *Les Chemins de la liberté* in 1953, Murdoch complains that the novels, as in so many of his philosophical fictions, present only the beginning of the problem of postwar life as she sees it: 'Human life *begins*. But the complexity of the moral virtues, which must return, more deeply perhaps, with the task of "going on from there", this we are not shown.'[32] In *The Flight from the Enchanter* we might reverse this formulation and say that the complexity of moral virtues is well demonstrated, but the status of 'human life', a life that has a political as well as moral determination, this we are not shown. Or perhaps it is more accurate to say that we are only half-shown in Murdoch's depiction of the caprices of the law which are also, and problematically, those of her own fiction.

When the law works at all in *Flight* it does, at least in part, to arrest a sense of moral vertigo through the authority of plot. The absurd Farthest Point East (FPE), the line on the map of Europe that determines whose entry into Britain is within the law and whose remains outside it, is the tragicomic mark in the novel that turns natality into destiny. ' "It would be a sad thing for a man," said Hunter, "to have his fate decided by where he was born. He didn't choose where he was born." ' (Annette thinks Dante cruel for similarly making a monster out of the Minotaur – hunters, in this novel, are always partial innocents.) Amid the delicate play of moral virtues, the FPE is a quietly stupid reminder that the sovereign power of the nation state trumps all other political and moral axioms when it comes to the fate of human life. But if Murdoch verges on turning this grim political and juridical fact into farce (SELIB, the Special European Labour Immigration Board, based on the real-life agencies that administered the flow of skilled labour ('European Volunteer Workers'), is presented as a typically British institutional comedy of gender and manners), this might not be because she thinks it trivial; it is rather because the terms of the novel can find no way of legislating, no fictional making sense of or rationalising the lawlessness that it, at the same time, inscribes at the centre of political governance.

This is why there is a second sense of enchantment in the novel, one more dangerous than the ethical dereliction of love gone astray, precisely because it so closely approximates the capricious dark magic of the law itself. What the novel brings us to the brink of, but cannot quite show, is that the 'terrible world' of the refugee, the world born, as Arendt would say, from the centre of political and juridical life, has moved from the periphery (from the dark background) to the centre. When the refugee moves in too close, in the novel quite literally when Stefan installs himself in Rosa's home in an intimacy too far, it is not to the common law that she turns, nor to the world of practical reason, but to the twilight world of Mischa Fox. 'Stefan had come from a place far outside the world of rules and reciprocal concerns and considerations in which Rosa mostly lived,' Murdoch writes; he 'did not belong to human society [. . .] Only some spirit which came out of the same region beyond the docility of the social world could do this work for her. She knew she must go and see Mischa Fox' (*FE* 235). To read this as evidence of Mischa's absolute power, a reading that Murdoch to an extent encourages, is to miss the darker point – and one far more intractable for her liberal politics – that his machinations are made possible not despite, but because of the law itself – 'only darkness could cast out darkness,' Murdoch writes (*FE* 235). The moral tragedy behind this farce is not only the tragedy, as Murdoch puts it in 'The Sublime and the Good', that 'we all have an indefinitely extended capacity to imagine the being of others,' and on which we invariably, achingly, default. The tragedy is that, however capacious that imagination, whatever the strength of love, the being of others comes to light only as the brutality of the law is forced into the open.[33] Thus the real tragedy in *The Flight from the Enchanter* belongs to Nina, the dressmaker who stitches up others into the clothes of a social life she observes but cannot belong to, and is haunted by dreams of swirling fabric, wrapping itself 'round and round her limbs like a winding-sheet. Before it enveloped her she saw its pattern clearly at last; it was a map of all the countries of the world' (*FE* 139).

It is Nina who finally, if fleetingly, shows the geopolitical pattern – and the category of life lost within that pattern – against which complexity of the moral virtues is played out in the novel.

> She stared at her passport, and it seemed to her suddenly like a death warrant. It filled her with shame and horror [. . .] Here was her very soul upon record, stamped and filed: a soul without a nationality, a soul without a home. She turned the faded pages. The earlier ones carried the names of the frontiers of her childhood, frontiers which no longer existed in the world. The later pages were covered with the continually renewed permits from the Ministry of Labour. The Foreign Office which had issued this document had disappeared from the face of the earth. Now nothing could make it new. It remained like the Book of Judgement, the record of her sins, the final and irrevocable sentence of society upon her. She was without identity in a world where to be without identity is the first and most universal of crimes, the crime which, whatever else it may overlook, every State punishes. She had no official existence. (*FE* 263–4)

The 'first and most universal of crimes': Nina's is a trespass that defines all others, not because it transgresses the law but, rather, because it reveals that the universality of the law is based upon an original exclusion. It is no coincidence, in this context, that this is the only scene in the entire novel where the enmeshments of the imagination are not on show, as if we have finally arrived at a 'unique individuality', a point at which the literary imagination can go no further. No profound seams of grief are opened up by Nina's suffering; there are no witnesses to her death. Only the reader is left to catch the pathos of this wraith of life as she slips out of the window of fiction into oblivion. With echoes of the negative liberty of the refugee in Arendt's 1943 essay on stateless life, Nina is the only character in *The Flight from the Enchanter* who succeeds in taking flight. 'Only one frontier remained, the frontier where no papers are asked for, which can be crossed without an identity into the land which remains, for the persecuted, always open' (*FE* 265).

Statelessness, suffering and the judicial imagination: conclusion

Some states claim their sacred right to parts of the earth's surface so emphatically that it is hard to believe that human beings have a home at all.

Franz Baermann Steiner[34]

As Nina weeps, unseen, she begins to sing: 'a low and regular wailing sound [...] came from her lips, without her will, in a rhythmical cadence. It rose and fell like a song.' This chanting is different from the incantatory spells of dream and desire that hum through the rest of the novel. Nina's is not an en-chantment, but a song of lamentation:

> She had heard lamentation like this in childhood, but she had never understood it. Now she knew how it was possible to sing in the presence of death. People whom she had known long ago, came to her now, not clearly seen but present in multitude, in a great community. She held out her hands to them across the recent past. (*FE* 265)

One way to read *The Flight from the Enchanter* is as a novel that tries to move, but does not quite succeed, from enchantment, the conjuring up of another, to lamentation, the mourning of the other. If that mourning is blocked or unseen, this perhaps is because there is no collective, Arendt might say, no politics, before which mourning can take place in the novel. Only Nina is capable of reaching out to a lost community that legitimates her suffering within its collective of grief. But no one else can see that community or hear its song. The rest of the novel is lost to a dangerous freedom in which only the unpredictable hazards of love and imagination can underwrite the existence of others. This is a place beyond the law – a dark background of difference – produced by the law itself. 'I'm lost in a forest,' cries Rosa. In Murdoch's world, we are all in a dark place where only the grace of love can offer redemption (*FE* 240).

In the novel's final scene Rosa asks Peter Saward to marry her – a final bid, maybe, for the enchantments of love. This scene is widely thought to be based on Murdoch's own transitory and quite possibly entirely fictional engagement to Franz Baermann Steiner the evening before his death. It is less the missed opportunities of human love that give the moment its piquancy, however, than the very final paragraph of the novel in which Peter hands Rosa an album of photographs to 'distract her' from her grief. These are photographs Mischa has commissioned to be taken of his birthplace: 'here is the old market square and here is the famous bronze fountain, and here is the medieval bridge across the river' (*FE* 287). Here, recognisably, is Prague as it once was. Steiner too coveted photographs of postwar Prague, wanting proof of the continued existence of the place, even if its communal past had been completely blown away. Rosa sees 'the pictures through gathering haze of tears' (*FE* 287).

If one line of thinking in Murdoch's novel runs the survival of suffering into power (à la Canetti), I want to conclude with the suggestion that there is another that hints towards a different ethics of justice and survival, which has its origin, I think, in the thought and life of Steiner, whose death, it is probably true to say, Murdoch never ceased to lament and, in some senses, perform in her writing. 'How Iris is endlessly surprised about me, as if I were the sole example of a species, a little dog with feathers, or a bird with six legs instead of wings,' Steiner wrote in his diary during their romance. All the refugees in *Flight* are compared to small animals at some point (examples of a new species, Arendt might say). 'I probably am,' he continues, 'but I never thought of such a creature as loveable before now.'[35] Whatever the power of the grace of love, however, this does not alter the fact that it is not just persons who are lost in the postwar period, but also the sense of a just law.

In a sense, that loss is what this study has been about. Mourning cannot take place before the law, if it is the law itself, or a sense of it that can be imagined as collectively meaningful, that is being mourned. That was what Rebecca West discovered at Nuremberg and replayed in the extravagances of melodrama. The suffering testified to in the Eichmann trial crafted a powerful ethics of remembrance and grief in response to that lack, but whether the very real necessity to insist repeatedly on the reality of that suffering is in itself a form of justice is open to question. That question is what I hear in Muriel Spark's restless refusal of pathos and in Arendt's bitingly precise irony. If both thus distance themselves from suffering, this is not to rise above it through rhetorical loftiness, but is part of a refusal to concede justice to suffering alone. Irony, to this extent, is not so much opposed to traumatic testimony as its necessary political echo. In the doubling of voice, its way of being inside and outside the context it describes, irony insists that a justice adequate to this suffering is not yet, not here and not now, perfect.

It is because Arendt keeps faith with political redemption that somewhere too in that irony is a lament for a law capable of universalism. But before we are too quick to condemn Arendt and her contemporaries for nostalgically evoking a cosmopolitanism that never was, we need to

recognise that their dissatisfaction with the law was also a bold indictment of the world's failure to recognise its on-going complicity with
the lawlessness unleashed in the last century. Nazi contempt of the law
was not just barbarism; it demonstrated a fundamental repudiation of
the idea of the rights of any living being beyond the frontiers of the
nation state. It was because it could not acknowledge this, that despite
its brilliant legal and political audacity, Nuremberg could never entirely
eradicate the limp charge of 'victor's justice' (a charge heard again, in
an even more historically twisted moral form, ahead of the Eichmann
trial). If the law and art are always struggling to catch up with history
(as Rebecca West once wrote), nowhere is this perhaps clearer than in
our continued inability to grasp the extent to which statelessness is the
defining misery of our age.

Martha Gellhorn's journalist alter ego, Mary Douglas, turned out
to be right when, in *A Stricken Field*, she predicted that she would 'be
reporting disaster and defeat her whole life'. The justice she yearned for
in the refugee fields of Czechoslovakia remained for her contemporaries,
as for us today, a justice 'yet to come', in Jacques Derrida's provocative
formulation.[36] As I have been arguing throughout this book, however,
that 'yet' is very far from being a defeatist acceptance of the impossibility of delivering worldly justice. It is, rather, to be heard as a call
back to politics. 'That justice exceeds the law and calculation', Derrida
stresses, 'cannot and should not serve as an alibi for staying out of
juridico-political battles.' Arendt would have agreed that, left stranded
from the law and politics, justice alone, even one premised on an ethics
of incalculability, 'can always be reappropriated by the most perverse
calculation.'[37]

In Murdoch's writing, by contrast, the absence of a just law is
mourned through the over-compensations of love. This is why, I think,
despite (or perhaps even because of) her fascination with the love of
the good, she takes us into the dark background of difference, only to
leave us there. In the end, love is not enough in the world of the stateless, as Sereny, with the limp Marie on her lap, perhaps knew better. I
want, however, to give the last word of this chapter, and of this book,
to Murdoch's real-life refugee lover. To say that Steiner was no stranger
to the suffering of statelessness is to state the obviousness of the appeal
of his vulnerability to a moral lover such as Murdoch. Less well known,
however, are his own writings on suffering. As his biographers have
argued, to an extent Steiner survived the war by making suffering his
own.[38] In an extraordinary letter written to his friend and the publisher
of his poems, Georg Rapp, right in the middle of the war and just as the
fate of Europe's Jews was becoming clear (at least to the community in

exile), he argues that while life without suffering is valueless, it absolutely does not and must not follow that suffering should be a value in itself. Rather, suffering gives life meaning because it gives us common cause. What the symbolic systems of the world's religions provide, Steiner argues, is 'nothing other than the ground upon which, and the language in which, people can communicate about the possibility of ending their various sufferings and our own, common age of suffering'.[39] Steiner says the 'world's religions', but it is clear that the idea of a ritual language giving form to suffering belongs primarily to Judaism and, for Steiner at least, also to Buddhism and other Eastern religions. Attempting to make a value out of suffering itself, as he thinks the Christian misinterpretation of Christ's sacrifice does, is to fail to grasp the full weight of suffering (to put death at a half-remove from oneself, to suffer only vicariously).

While the language is theological, the context of Steiner's letter is thoroughly historical. (This alone, perhaps, should qualify his letter for a place in current thinking on testimony and trauma.) Steiner is angry with his young friend, principally for his failure to take the suffering of his people with the real seriousness it demands, and we can read in his affirmation an insistence that suffering should not be trivialised. And not trivialising suffering for Steiner, as for Arendt and Spark after her, means a fierce repudiation of the language of victims and villains. This is why, indeed, Steiner refuses to testify to suffering. If, he writes (as Rapp and others have accused), he has been conspicuously silent about the genocide of his people, if he has failed to make his horror and lamentation public, refused the pathos of the victim, this is because, Steiner says, it is foremost the 'common age of suffering' to which he is answerable, not to suffering itself and certainly not to a group identity premised on suffering alone. 'Don't think that I have discovered some special comfort which enables me to keep silent when others complain,' he writes, in a passage which it is incredible to think was written in 1943:

> It is much rather the case that, for me, every horror which people perpetuate (against whomsoever) defines the nature of man. That man am I. If I refused to recognise that every, but really every abomination which so-called Germans, so-called English, Romanians, Poles perpetrate is simply the precise extension of obscure thoughts and feelings which I have had at one time or another, then everything that I believe about man, about creation, about sin, would become meaningless. Nothing is made easier for me by it. I am not permitted any accusation of that which 'takes place outside myself,' of a sin, 'which has nothing to do with me'. Nor am I permitted that which Christians apparently love so much: forgiveness. For me it is not a question of accusing or forgiving so-called 'other' people. What does that mean: other? Here, humanity as a single whole is committing a crime, and the longer that

continues the less can be seen how you, YOU, WE can be forgiven. The fact
that the greater part of the Jewish people is undergoing destruction can only
intensify our suffering into boundlessness.[40]

Here, perhaps, is another version of the unesoteric mysticism that
Murdoch once invoked. Where Murdoch's love, however, ultimately
depends on the unpredictable hazards of the liberal self, Steiner's ethics
are those of the ritual and taboo that were his subjects of study and
his grounds for belief. In this world there is neither space for the consolations of pity, nor justification for further cruelty. What is instead
ritualised is a bond both with suffering and, importantly, with 'humanity as a single whole'. The suffering Steiner evokes here is not, then, as
it so often is in contemporary rights culture, made in the context of a
seemingly endless appeal to an ever more allusive justice (and hence
vulnerable to the most calculated of perversions). Nor is it dependent
on the caprices of the moral axioms that Murdoch thought capable of
giving rights political authority. If ritual obligations are important for
Steiner it is because it is through them that 'people can communicate
about the possibility of ending their various sufferings'. It is at this
point, perhaps, that it is finally possible to affirm a common humanity,
and a future political hope, from within – quite literally so, Steiner, like
Arendt, writes as a refugee – the dark background of mere givenness. 'If
we seriously consider whatever could be called "value",' Steiner writes,
it cannot possibly be by making suffering itself into a value; that would
be a moral and, by implication, a political obscenity. Value will not be
discovered in suffering itself, says Steiner, but rather in something that
Arendt would also have recognised as a kind of political action. Value
'must be: everything that contributes to the alleviation of suffering,
everything which gives us the strength to overcome suffering, everything
which can make suffering cease'.[41] I cannot think of a better description of the commitment to a profoundly worldly justice that unites the
writers discussed in this book.

Notes

1. Iris Murdoch, *The Nice and the Good* (London: Chatto & Windus, 1968),
   p. 305.
2. Quoted in Peter J. Conradi, *Iris Murdoch: A Life* (London: HarperCollins,
   2001), p. 236.
3. UNRRA was founded in 1943 in anticipation of the end of the war. It
   played a vital role in feeding, housing and repatriating huge numbers of displaced persons in postwar Europe. At its peak in 1945 it is estimated that

6,795,000 people were in the care of the UNRRA (Tony Judt, *Postwar: A History of Europe Since 1945* (2005; London: Pimlico, 2007), p. 29). See Michael R. Marrus, *The Unwanted: European Refugees in the Twentieth Century* (Oxford: Oxford University Press, 1985) and Ben Shephard, *The Long Road Home: The Aftermath of the Second World War* (London: Bodley Head, 2010).

4. Gitta Sereny, 'Stolen Children', in *The German Trauma: Experiences and Reflections* (Harmondsworth: Penguin, 2000), p. 49.
5. Murdoch, *The Flight from the Enchanter* (1956; London: Vintage, 2000), p. 51. Hereafter abbreviated as *FE*.
6. Murdoch, 'The Sublime and the Good', in *Existentialists and Mystics*, ed. Peter Conradi (1959; Harmondsworth: Penguin, 1997), p. 220.
7. Ibid., p. 220.
8. In her introduction to Vintage's 2000 edition of the novel, Patricia Duncker protests that because of the 'unreality' of Murdoch's fiction there is no political or moral space to consider those 'murdered , deported and mistreated' in England ('they are now, and even in Murdoch's fictional England, they were then') ('Introduction', p. xii). In an earlier critique, Olga McDonald Meidner made a similar criticism: 'it is apparent that the real feelings of homeless people, D.P's, are not fully explored in this book' ('Reviewers' Bane, *Flight from the Enchanter*', *Essays in Criticism*, II, October 1961, p. 443).
9. Franz Baermann Steiner, 'Orientpolitik', in *Orientpolitik, Value, and Civilisation, Selected Writings, Vol. 2*, ed. Jeremy Adler and Richard Fardon (Oxford: Berghahn, 1999), pp. 107–11.
10. Quoted in Conradi, *Iris Murdoch*, p. 239.
11. Murdoch, *The Sovereignty of Good* (1970; London: Routledge, 2001), p. 75.
12. Murdoch, 'The Sublime and the Good Revisited' (1959), in *Existentialists and Mystics*, p. 282.
13. The famous story about Murdoch declaring her past Communist Party membership on her US visa declaration, thus missing out on a postgraduate career at Vassar and making her visits problematic for the rest of her life, captures her political innocence in this period.
14. Murdoch, *Metaphysics as a Guide to Morals* (London: Chatto & Windus, 1992), p. 355. This belief in axiomatic moral reasoning is also why, in an interview shortly before her death, Murdoch could talk of human rights as being effective as fictional oughts: 'We should hold a view of the individual which treats him as worthy of respect and someone who needs freedom and someone who is supposed to be compassionate and just and so on' ('An Interview with Iris Murdoch', S. B. Sagare, *Modern Fiction Studies*, 47.3, Fall 2001, p. 712). The gap between the views we think we ought to hold about persons and putting those views into political legislation is where many recent critiques of human rights begin.
15. Murdoch, 'The Sublime and the Good Revisited', p. 282.
16. Ibid., p. 289.
17. Ibid., p. 278.
18. Ibid., p. 269.
19. Ibid., p. 271.

20. Murdoch, 'Against Dryness', in *Existentialists and Mystics*, p. 294.
21. Murdoch, 'The Sublime and the Good', p. 212. A little later, Murdoch's writings on love and illusion shift as she begins her life-long and sustained rereading of Plato in the late 1960s and 1970s. Martha Nussbaum has explored the workings of Platonic love in Murdoch's fiction and phil-osophy writing in two powerful essays, 'Love and Vision: Iris Murdoch on Eros and the Individual', in *Iris Murdoch and the Search for Human Goodness*, ed. Maria Antonaccio and William Schweiker (Chicago: University of Chicago Press, 1996), pp. 29–53, and ' "Faint with Secret Knowledge": Love and Vision in Murdoch's The Black Prince', *Poetics Today*, 25.4, Winter 2004, pp. 659–710.
22. Murdoch, *The Sovereignty of Good*, p. 93.
23. There is a similar moment of ethical jarring in Murdoch's 1968 novel, *The Nice and the Good*. Willy, another of Murdoch's melancholic refugees, confesses to his friend Theo that he betrayed two people in Dachau because he was afraid. 'They were gassed. My life wasn't even threatened' (p. 342). More alarming here than what could be read as a somewhat opportunist rendering of survivor guilt, is Theo's response. Listening, but pointedly not hearing Willy's story, Theo thinks:

> What can I say to him. That one must soon forget one's sins in the claims of others. But how to forget. The point is that nothing matters except loving what is good. Not to look at evil but to look at good. Only this contemplation breaks the tyranny of the past, breaks the adherence of evil to the personality, breaks, in the end, the personality. In the light of the good, evil can be seen in its place, not owned, just existing, in its place. (p. 344)

There is no irony in Theo's decision to contemplate the good rather than attend to Willy's testimony. Murdoch clearly means for Willy's suffer-ing to be answered by a call to goodness. As much as it wants to move towards the other, the sovereignty of good can also be a rather cloth-eared repudiation of the particularity of the experience of the camp inmate.
24. Shelley is a quietly persistent touchstone for Murdoch in this period. 'Fantasy', she writes in 'The Sublime and the Good', 'is the enemy of art, is the enemy of true imagination: Love, an exercise of the imagination. This was what Shelley meant when he said that egotism was the great enemy of poetry' (p. 216).
25. Giorgio Agamben, *Homo Sacer: Sovereign Power and Bare Life*, trans. Daniel Heller-Roazen (1995; Stanford: Stanford University Press, 1998), pp. 71–118.
26. Franz Baermann Steiner, *Taboo, Truth, and Religion, Selected Writings, vol. 1*, ed. Jeremy Adler and Richard Fardon (Oxford: Berghahn, 1999), p. 108.
27. Conradi, *Iris Murdoch*, p. 389.
28. For example, in the perfect Chinese boxes of illusion and delusion that Murdoch calibrates around her obsessive-destructive narrator, theatre director Charles Arrowby, in the Booker Prize-winning *The Sea, the Sea* (1978).

29. Steiner, 'Gypsies in Carpathian Russia' (1938), in *Orientpolitik*, pp. 112–14.
30. Duncker, 'Introduction', p. xiii.
31. Murdoch, 'Mass, Might and Myth' (1962), in *Existentialists and Mystics*, p. 188.
32. Murdoch, *Sartre, Romantic Rationalist* (1953; London: Vintage, 1999), p. 60.
33. Murdoch, 'The Sublime and the Good', p. 216.
34. Steiner, 'On the Margins of Social Sciences', in *Orientpolitik*, p. 231.
35. Quoted in Jeremy Adler and Richard Fardon, 'An Oriental in the West: The Life of Franz Baermann Steiner', *Taboo, Truth, and Religion*, p. 97.
36. Derrida, 'Force of Law': The "Mystical Foundation of Authority"', trans. Mary Quaintance, *Cardozo Law Review*, 11, 5/6, 1990, p. 969.
37. Ibid., p. 971.
38. Jeremy Adler and Richard Fardon, 'An Oriental in the West', p. 84.
39. Steiner, 'Letter to Georg Rapp', in *Orientpolitik*, p. 116.
40. Ibid., p. 119.
41. Ibid., p. 116.

Bibliography

Agamben, Giorgio, *Homo Sacer: Sovereign Power and Bare Life*, trans. Daniel Heller-Roazen (1995; Stanford: Stanford University Press, 1998).
— *Means without End: Notes on Politics*, trans. Vincenzo Binette and Cesare Casarino (Minneapolis: University of Minnesota Press, 2000).
Althusser, Louis, 'The International of Decent Feelings', in *The Spectre of Hegel*, ed. François Matheron, trans. G. M. Goshgarian (London: Verso, 1997), pp. 21–35.
Arendt, Hannah, *Eichmann in Jerusalem: A Report on the Banality of Evil* (1963; Harmondsworth: Penguin, 1994).
— ' "Eichmann in Jerusalem": Exchange of Letters Between Gershom Scholem and Hannah Arendt' (January 1964), in *The Jew as Pariah: Jewish Identity and Politics in the Modern Age*, ed. Ron H. Feldman (New York: Grove, 1978).
— *Essays in Understanding, 1930–1954: Formation, Exile, and Totalitarianism*, ed. Jerome Kohn (New York: Schocken, 1994).
— *The Human Condition* (1958; Chicago: Chicago University Press, 1998).
— *Lectures on Kant's Political Philosophy*, ed. Ronald Beiner (Chicago: University of Chicago Press, 1992).
— 'Letter to Gershom Scholem', in *The Jewish Writings*, ed. Jerome Kohn and Ron H. Feldman (New York: Schocken, 2007).
— *Life of the Mind* (1971; New York: Harcourt Brace Jovanovich, 1978).
— *The Origins of Totalitarianism* (1951; New York: Schocken, 2004).
— *The Portable Hannah Arendt*, ed. Peter Baehr (Harmondsworth: Penguin, 2000).
— *Rahel Varnhagen: Life of a Jewess*, trans. Richard and Clara Winston (1957; Baltimore: Johns Hopkins University Press, 1997).
— *Responsibility and Judgment*, ed. Jerome Kohn (New York: Schocken, 2003).
— ' "The Rights of Man": What are They?', *Modern Review*, 3.1, Summer 1949, pp. 467–83.
— 'Understanding and Politics', *Partisan Review*, 20, 1953, pp. 377–92.
— 'We Refugees', in *The Jew as Pariah: Jewish Identity and Politics in the Modern Age*, ed. Ron H. Feldman (1943; New York: Grove, 1978).
— 'What is Existential Philosophy?', in *Essays in Understanding, 1930–1954*, ed. Jerome Kohn (New York: Schocken, 1994), pp. 163–87.

— and Karl Jaspers, *Hannah Arendt, Karl Jaspers Correspondence 1926–1969*, ed. Lotte Kohler and Hans Saner (New York: Harcourt Brace, 1992).

— and Mary McCarthy, *Between Friends: The Correspondence of Hannah Arendt and Mary McCarthy 1949–1975*, ed. Carol Brightman (London: Secker & Warburg, 1995).

Barnouw, Dagmar, *Visible Spaces: Hannah Arendt and the German-Jewish Experience* (Baltimore: Johns Hopkins University Press, 1990).

Bartov, Omer, *Mirrors of Destruction: War, Genocide, and Modern Identity* (Oxford: Oxford University Press, 2000).

Bedford, Sybille, 'Frontier Regions', *Spectator*, 29 October 1965.

Bellow, Saul, *Mr Sammler's Planet* (London: Weidenfeld & Nicolson, 1969).

Benbassa, Esther, *Suffering as Identity: The Jewish Paradigm*, trans. G. M. Goshgarian (2007; London: Verso, 2010).

Benhabib, Seyla, 'Judgement and the Moral Foundations of Politics in Hannah Arendt's Thought', *Political Theory*, 16.1, 1988, pp. 29–51.

— *The Reluctant Modernism of Hannah Arendt* (2000; Lanham: Rowman & Littlefield, 2003).

Benjamin, Walter, *Illuminations*, ed. Harry Zohn (New York: Schocken, 1970).

Bennett, Andrew and Nicholas Royle, *Elizabeth Bowen and the Dissolution of the Novel* (Basingstoke: Macmillan, 1995).

Bernstein, Richard, *Hannah Arendt and the Jewish Question* (Cambridge, MA: MIT Press, 1997).

— 'Hannah Arendt on the Stateless', *Parallax*, 11.1, 2005, pp. 46–60.

Bilsky, Leora, 'Between Justice and Politics: The Competition of Storytellers in the Eichmann Trial', in *Hannah Arendt in Jerusalem*, ed. Steven E. Ascheim (Berkeley: University of California Press, 2001), pp. 232–52.

Bloxham, Donald, 'Defeat, Due Process, and Denial: War Crimes Trials and Nationalist Revisionism in Comparative Perspective', in *Defeat and Memory: Cultural Histories of Military Defeat in the Modern Era*, ed. Jenny Macleod (Basingstoke: Palgrave, 2008).

— *Genocide on Trial: War Crime Trials and the Formation of Holocaust History and Memory* (Oxford: Oxford University Press, 2001).

Bowen, Elizabeth, *Collected Impressions* (London: Longmans Green, 1950).

— *The Collected Stories of Elizabeth Bowen*, ed. Angus Wilson (Harmondsworth: Penguin, 1983).

— *Eva Trout, or Changing Scenes* (1968; Harmondsworth: Penguin, 1982).

— *The Heat of the Day* (1948; Harmondsworth: Penguin, 1976).

— *The Mulberry Tree: Writings of Elizabeth Bowen*, ed. Hermione Lee (London: Virago, 1986).

— *People, Places, Things*, ed. Allan Hepburn (Edinburgh: Edinburgh University Press, 2008).

Boym, Svetlana, 'Poetics and Politics of Estrangement: Victor Shklovsky and Hannah Arendt', *Poetics Today*, 26.4, Winter 2005, pp. 581–611.

Brooks, Peter, *The Melodramatic Imagination: Balzac, Henry James, Melodrama, and the Mode of Excess* (1976; New Haven, CT: Yale University Press, 1995).

Burke, Edmund, *Reflections on the Revolution in France*, ed. Conor Cruise O'Brien (1790; Harmondsworth: Penguin, 2004).

Calimani Sullman, Anna-Vera, 'A Name for Extermination', *Modern Language Review*, 94, 1999, pp. 978–99.

Camus, Albert, *The Fall*, trans. Robin Buss (1956; Harmondsworth: Penguin, 2006).

Caruth, Cathy, 'Parting Words: Trauma, Silence and Survival', in *Between the Psyche and the Polis: Refiguring History in Literature and Theory*, ed. Michael Rossington and Anne Whitehead (Aldershot: Ashgate, 2000), pp. 77–96.

— *Unclaimed Experience: Trauma, Narrative and History* (Baltimore: Johns Hopkins University Press, 1996).

Cesarani, David, *Eichmann: His Life and Crimes* (London: Heinemann, 2004).

Cheyette, Bryan, 'Writing against Conversion: Muriel Spark and the Gentile Jewess', in *Theorising Muriel Spark: Gender, Deconstruction, and Psychoanalysis*, ed. Martin McQuillan (Basingstoke: Palgrave, 2002), pp. 95–112.

Coates, John, 'The Misfortunes of Eva Trout', *Essays in Criticism*, 47.1, 1999, pp. 59–79.

Cohen, Debra Rae, 'Rebecca West's Palimpsestic Praxis: Crafting the Intermodern Voice of Witness', in *Intermodernism: Literary Culture in Mid-Twentieth Century Britain*, ed. Kirsten Bluemel (Edinburgh: Edinburgh University Press, 2009), pp. 150–69.

Cohen, Richard I., 'A Generation's Response to *Eichmann in Jerusalem*', in *Hannah Arendt in Jerusalem*, ed. Steven E. Ascheim (Berkeley: University of California Press, 2001), pp. 253–80.

Conradi, Peter J., *Iris Murdoch: A Life* (London: HarperCollins, 2001).

Corcoran, Neil, *Elizabeth Bowen: The Enforced Return* (Oxford: Oxford University Press, 2004).

Cover, Robert M., 'Violence and the Word', in *On Violence*, ed. Bruce B. Lawrence and Aisha Karim (Durham, NC: Duke University Press, 2007), pp. 292–313.

de Vabres, Henri Donnedieu, 'The Nuremberg Trial and the Modern Principles of International Criminal Law', in *Perspectives on the Nuremberg Trial*, ed. Guénaël Mettraux (Oxford: Oxford University Press, 2008), pp. 213–73.

Dean, Carolyn J., *The Fragility of Empathy after the Holocaust* (Ithaca, NY: Cornell University Press, 2004).

Derrida, Jacques, 'Force of Law': The "Mystical Foundation of Authority"', trans. Mary Quaintance, *Cardozo Law Review*, 11, 5/6, 1990, pp. 919–1046.

— 'Declarations of Independence', *Negotiations: Interventions and Interviews, 1971–2001*, ed. Elizabeth Rottenberg (Stanford: Stanford University Press, 2002), pp. 46–54.

Dietz, Mary, 'Arendt and the Holocaust', in *The Cambridge Companion to Hannah Arendt*, ed. Dana Villa (Cambridge: Cambridge University Press, 2000), pp. 86–112.

Douglas, Lawrence, *The Memory of Judgment: Making Law and History in the Trials of the Holocaust* (New Haven, CT: Yale University Press, 2001).

Douzinas, Costas, *The End of Human Rights: Critical Legal Thought at the Turn of the Century* (Oxford: Hart, 2000).

Ellmann, Maud, *Elizabeth Bowen: The Shadow Across the Page* (Edinburgh: Edinburgh University Press, 2003).

Enright, D. J., 'Public Doctrine and Private Judging', *New Statesman*, 15 October 1965.

Esty, Jed, *A Shrinking Island: Modernism and National Culture in England* (Princeton: Princeton University Press, 2004).

Felman, Shoshana, *The Juridical Unconscious: Trials and Traumas in the Twentieth Century* (Cambridge, MA: Harvard University Press, 2002).

— with Dori Laub, *Testimony: Crises of Witnessing in Literature, Psychoanalysis, and History* (New York: Routledge, 1992).

Flanner, Janet, *Janet Flanner's World: Uncollected Writings, 1932–1975*, ed. Irving Drutman (New York: Harcourt Brace Jovanovich, 1979).

Fried, Lewis, 'Creating Hebraism, Confronting Hellenism: The *Menorah Journal* and its Struggle for the Jewish Imagination', *American Jewish Archives Journal*, LIII, 1–2, 2000, pp. 147–74.

Freud, Sigmund, 'Thoughts for the Times on War and Death', *The Pelican Freud Library*, vol. 12 (1915; Harmondsworth: Penguin, 1985).

— 'Zeitgasses über Krieg und Tod', *Gesammelte Werke 1913–1917* (1915; Frankfurt: Fischer, 1967).

Gellhorn, Martha, 'The Arabs of Palestine', *Atlantic Monthly*, October 1961, pp. 45–65.

— 'Eichmann and the Private Conscience', *Atlantic Monthly*, February 1962.

— *The Face of War* (1959; London: Granta, 1999).

— *A Stricken Field* (1940; London: Virago, 1986).

Gilbert, G. M., *Nuremberg Diary* (1947; New York: Da Capa, 1995).

Glendinning, Victoria, *Elizabeth Bowen: A Biography* (1977; New York: Anchor, 2005).

Goldberg, Amos, 'The Victim's Voice and Melodramatic Aesthetics in History', *History and Theory*, 48, October 2009, pp. 220–37.

Halbwachs, Maurice, *On Collective Memory*, ed. and trans. Lewis A. Coser (Chicago: University of Chicago Press, 1992).

Hamacher, Werner, 'The Right to Have Rights (Four-and-a-Half-Remarks)', *South Atlantic Quarterly*, 103, 2/3, 2004, pp. 343–56.

Hamburger, Michael, 'In a Cold Season', in *Ownerless Earth: New Selected Poems* (New York: Dutton, 1973).

Hartman, Geoffrey, *The Longest Shadow: In the Aftermath of the Holocaust* (Basingstoke: Palgrave, 2002).

Heuer, Wolfgang, 'Europe and its Refugees: Arendt on the Politicization of Minorities', *Social Research*, 74.4, 2007, pp. 1159–72.

Hoogland, Renée C., *Elizabeth Bowen: A Reputation in Writing* (New York: New York University Press, 1994).

Hunt, Lynn, *The Invention of Human Rights* (New York: W. W. Norton, 2007).

Hyndman, Jennifer, *Managing Displacement: Refugees and the Politics of Humanitarianism* (Minneapolis: University of Minnesota Press, 2000).

Hynes, Joseph (ed.), *Critical Essays on Muriel Spark* (New York: G. K. Hall, 1992).

Jones, Elwyn, 'Miss West – Beware! We Cannot Stop Fascism by Stopping our Ears', *Evening Standard*, 8 October 1947, p. 6.

Judt, Tony, *Postwar: A History of Europe Since 1945* (2005; London: Pimlico, 2007).

Kazin, Alfred, 'Dispassionate Pilgrimage', *Book Week*, 17 October 1965.

Kermode, Frank, 'The Novel as Jerusalem', *Atlantic Monthly*, 216, October 1965, pp. 92–8.

Koestler, Arthur, *The Scum of the Earth* (New York: Macmillan, 1941).

Kristeva, Julia, *Hannah Arendt*, trans. Ross Buberman (New York: Columbia University Press, 2001).

Lewis, Pericles, *Modernism, Nationalism and the Novel* (Cambridge: Cambridge University Press, 2000).

McCarthy, Mary, *The Seventeenth Degree* (London: Weidenfeld & Nicolson, 1974).

McQuillan, Martin (ed.), *Theorizing Muriel Spark: Gender, Race, Deconstruction* (Basingstoke: Palgrave, 2002).

Marrus, Michael R., *The Unwanted: European Refugees in the Twentieth Century* (Oxford: Oxford University Press, 1985).

Marx, Karl, 'On the Jewish Question', *Early Texts*, ed. D. McLellan (Oxford: Blackwell, 1971), pp. 115–29.

Meidner, Olga McDonald, 'Reviewers' Bane, *Flight from the Enchanter*', *Essays in Criticism II*, October 1961, pp. 435–47.

Moretti, Franco, *The Way of the World: The Bildungsroman in European Culture*, trans. Albert Sbragia (1987; London: Verso, 2000).

Mulisch, Harry, *Criminal Case 40.61, The Trial of Adolf Eichmann*, trans. Robert Naborn (1961; Philadelphia: University of Philadelphia Press, 2005).

Murdoch, Iris, *Existentialists and Mystics*, ed. Peter Conradi (Harmondsworth: Penguin, 1997).

— *The Flight from the Enchanter* (1956; London: Vintage, 2000).

— *Metaphysics as a Guide to Morals* (London: Chatto & Windus, 1992).

— *The Nice and the Good* (London: Chatto & Windus, 1968).

— *Sartre, Romantic Rationalist* (1953; London: Vintage, 1999).

— *The Sovereignty of Good* (1970; London: Routledge, 2001).

— with S. B. Sagare, 'An Interview with Iris Murdoch', *Modern Fiction Studies*, 47.3, Fall, 2001, pp. 696–714.

Nelson, Deborah, 'Suffering and Thinking: The Scandal of Tone in *Eichmann in Jerusalem*', in *Compassion: The Culture and Politics of an Emotion*, ed. Lauren Berlant (London: Routledge, 2004), pp. 219–44.

Nussbaum, Martha, ' "Faint with Secret Knowledge": Love and Vision in Murdoch's The Black Prince', *Poetics Today*, 25.4, Winter 2004, pp. 659–710.

— 'Love and Vision: Iris Murdoch on Eros and the Individual', in *Iris Murdoch and the Search for Human Goodness*, ed. Maria Antonaccio and William Schweiker (Chicago: University of Chicago Press, 1996), pp. 29–53.

Owens, Patricia, *Between War and Politics: International Relations and the Thought of Hannah Arendt* (Oxford: Oxford University Press, 2007).

— 'The Ethic of Reality in Hannah Arendt', in *Political Thought and International Relations: Variations on a Realist Theme*, ed. Duncan Bell (Oxford: Oxford University Press, 2008), pp. 105–21.

— 'Reclaiming "Bare Life"?: Against Agamben on Refugees', *International Relations*, 23.4, 2009, pp. 567–82.

Rancière, Jacques, 'Who is the Subject of the Rights of Man?', *South Atlantic Quarterly*, 103, 2.3, 2004, pp. 297–310.

Rau, Petra-Utta, *Moving Dangerously: Desire and Narrative Structure in the Fiction of Elizabeth Bowen, Rosamond Lehmann and Sylvia Townsend Warner*, PhD thesis, University of East Anglia, 2000.

Reichman, Ravit, *The Affective Life of Law: Legal Modernism and the Literary Imagination* (Stanford: Stanford University Press, 2009).

Reznikoff, Charles, *Holocaust* (New York: Black Sparrow, 2007).

Ricœur, Paul, *The Just*, trans. David Pellauer (Chicago: Chicago University Press, 2000).

Riley, Denise, *The Words of Selves: Identification, Solidarity, Irony* (Stanford: Stanford University Press, 2000).

Ritchie, Charles, *Undiplomatic Diaries 1937–1971* (Toronto: McClelland & Stewart, 2008).

Robinson, Richard, *Narratives of the European Border: A History of Nowhere* (Basingstoke: Palgrave, 2007).

Rose, Gillian, *The Broken Middle: Out of our Ancient Society* (Oxford: Blackwell, 1992).

— *Mourning Becomes the Law* (Cambridge: Cambridge University Press, 1996).

Rose, Jacqueline, 'Bizarre Objects: Mary Butts and Elizabeth Bowen', *Critical Quarterly*, 42.1, 2000, pp. 75–85.

Rosen, Norma, *Touching Evil* (New York: Harcourt Brace, 1969).

Rothberg, Michael, *Multidirectional Memory: Remembering the Holocaust in the Age of Decolonization* (Stanford: Stanford University Press, 2009).

Sebald, W. G., *On the Natural History of Destruction*, trans. Anthea Bell (London: Hamish Hamilton, 2003).

Sereny, Gitta, *The German Trauma: Experiences and Reflections* (Harmondsworth: Penguin, 2000).

Shephard, Ben, *The Long Road Home: The Aftermath of the Second World War* (London: Bodley Head, 2010).

Slaughter, Joseph R., *Human Rights, Inc: The World Novel, Narrative Form and International Law* (New York: Fordham University Press, 2007).

Sontag, Susan, 'Reflections on *The Deputy*', in *The Storm Over The Deputy*, ed. Eric Bentley (New York: Grove, 1964).

Spark, Muriel, *The Complete Short Stories* (Harmondsworth: Penguin, 2001).

— Letter to John Smith, 3 July 1961, pp. 1–3, Box Folder 1/10, Washington University in St Louis Library.

— *The Mandelbaum Gate* (1965; Harmondsworth: Penguin, 1967).

— 'The Mystery of Job's Suffering: Jung's New Interpretation Examined', *Church of England Newspaper*, 15 April 1955, p. 7.

— Notebook 39.5, Muriel Spark Archive, McFarlin Library, Special Collections, University of Tulsa.

— Notebook 39.6, Muriel Spark Archive, McFarlin Library, Special Collections, University of Tulsa.

— 'When Israel Went to the Vatican', *Tablet*, 24 March 1973, pp. 277–8.

— with James Brooker and Margarita Estévez Saá, 'Interview with Dame Muriel Spark', *Women's Studies*, 33.8, December 2004, pp. 1035–46.

— with Sarah Frankel, 'An Interview with Muriel Spark', *Partisan Review*, 54, Summer 1987, pp. 443–57.

Stannard, Martin, *Muriel Spark: The Biography* (London: Weidenfeld & Nicholson, 2009).

Steiner, Franz Baermann, *Orientpolitik, Value, and Civilisation, Selected Writings, Vol. 2*, ed. Jeremy Adler and Richard Fardon (Oxford: Berghahn, 1999).

— *Taboo, Truth, and Religion, Selected Writings, Vol. 1*, ed. Jeremy Adler and Richard Fardon (Oxford: Berghahn, 1999).

Stetz, Margaret, 'Rebecca West and the Nuremberg Trials', *Peace Review*, 13.2, 2001, pp. 223–4.

Stone, Dan, *Constructing the Holocaust: A Study in Historiography* (London: Valentine Mitchell, 2003).

Terada, Rei, 'Thinking for Oneself: Realism and Defiance in Arendt', *ELH*, 71.4, Winter 2004, pp. 839–66.

Thompson, Dorothy, *Refugees: Anarchy or Organization?* (New York: Random House, 1938).

Trilling, Lionel, 'Treason in the Modern World', *Nation*, 10 January 1948, pp. 46–7.

Villa, Dana, *Arendt and Heidegger: The Fate of the Political* (Princeton: Princeton University Press, 1996).

— (ed.), *The Cambridge Companion to Hannah Arendt* (Cambridge: Cambridge University Press, 2000).

Walkowitz, Rebecca L., *Cosmopolitan Style: Modernism Beyond the Nation* (New York: Columbia University Press, 2006).

Watt, Ian, *The Rise of the Novel* (1957; London: Pimlico, 2000).

Wells, H. G., *The Rights of Man or What Are We Fighting For?* (Harmondsworth: Penguin, 1940).

West, Rebecca, 'The Birch Leaves Falling', *New Yorker*, 22 October 1946, pp. 94–103.

— *Black Lamb, Grey Falcon* (1941; Harmondsworth: Penguin, 1994).

— *The Court and the Castle: Some Treatments of a Recurrent Theme* (New Haven, CT: Yale University Press, 1957).

— 'Extraordinary Exile', *New Yorker*, 23 August 1946, pp. 34–46.

— 'Heil Hamm! – II', *New Yorker*, 14 August 1948, pp. 26–47.

— *The Meaning of Treason* (1949; London: Phoenix, 2000).

— 'The Necessity and Grandeur of the International Ideal', in *Woman as Artist and Thinker* (1935; Lincoln: iUniverse: 2006), pp. 42–55.

— *The Strange Necessity, Essays and Reviews* (1928; London: Virago, 1987).

— *A Train of Powder: Six Reports on the Problem of Guilt and Punishment in Our Time* (Chicago: Ivan R. Dee, 1955).

Whittaker, Ruth, *The Faith and Fiction of Muriel Spark* (Basingstoke: Macmillan, 1982).

Wiesel, Elie, 'Eichmann's Victims and the Unheard Testimony', *Commentary*, 32.6, December 1961, pp. 510–16.

Wiviorka, Annette, *The Era of the Witness* (Ithaca, NY: Cornell University Press, 2006).

Woolf, Virginia, *Between the Acts* (1941; Harmondsworth: Penguin, 1992).

— *Three Guineas*, in *A Room of One's Own and Three Guineas* (1938; Vintage: London: Vintage, 2001).

Young-Bruehl, Elisabeth, *Hannah Arendt: For Love of the World* (New Haven, CT: Yale University Press, 1982).

Zertal, Idith, *Israel's Holocaust and the Politics of Nationhood* (Cambridge: Cambridge University Press, 2005).

Index

Agamben, Giorgio, 10, 37, 102, 107,
    140n
Althusser, Louis, 127
Améry, Jean, 66
Arendt, Hannah, 2–3, 8–9, 12–13, 30,
    31, 47–72, 81, 82, 101–15, 130,
    132, 140n
  banality of evil, 30
  Walter Benjamin, 63–4, 102
  Adolf Eichmann, 47, 50–2, 60, 62
  Eichmann in Jerusalem, 7, 48–61,
    63–8, 73, 74, 106–7, 108
  Martin Heidegger, 7, 8, 61, 71n,
    116n
  The Human Condition, 19n, 49,
    110
  Edmund Husserl, 119
  'The Image of Hell', 6–7, 9
  irony, 47–9, 57, 65–8, 104–6, 107,
    110–11, 113–14, 159
  Karl Jaspers, 2–3, 31, 48, 58, 59
  judgement, 3, 7, 40, 48–51, 54, 58–9,
    62–4, 66–8, 69n
  Lectures on Kant, 63
  The Life of the Mind, 58
  Origins of Totalitarianism, 11, 36–7,
    39, 40, 58, 60, 102–3, 104, 109,
    111–13, 130
  public and private, 19n, 109–10
  Gershom Scholem, 30, 65, 73
  Muriel Spark, 73, 82
  statelessness, 10–13, 36–7, 39,
    101–15, 119–20, 130, 132, 145–7,
    152, 157
  thinking, 7, 49, 51, 59–63, 65
  'Thinking and Moral
    Considerations', 60–1, 65
  'Truth and Politics', 63–4
  'We Refugees', 103–11, 136, 157
  Rebecca West, 13, 45n
Auerbach, Erich, *Mimesis*, 122

Barnes, Djuna, *Nightwood*, 28, 131
Barnouw, Dagmar, 18n
Bartov, Omer, 56
Beckett, Samuel, 132
  Murphy, 131
Bedford, Sybille, 76
Bellow, Saul, *Mr Sammler's Planet*, 97n
Ben Gurion, David, 50, 68
Benbassa, Esther, *Suffering as Identity*,
    86, 140n
Benhabib, Seyla, *The Reluctant
    Modernism of Hannah Arendt*,
    6–7, 8, 71n, 116n
Benjamin, Walter, 63–4, 102, 136
Bennett, Andrew and Andrew
    Royle, *Elizabeth Bowen and the
    Dissolution of the Novel*, 137,
    139n
Bernstein, Richard, 7
Bildungsroman, 12, 121–3, 124–7, 128,
    129–34, 135
Bilsky, Leora, 70n
Bloxham, Donald, 25, 38, 45n
Bowen, Elizabeth, 2, 12, 13, 118–40
  'The Bend Back', 125
  The Demon Lover, 127
  Eva Trout, 12, 120, 129–36
  The Heat of the Day, 124

Bowen, Elizabeth (*cont.*)
  'I Hear You Say', 125
  The Little Girls, 125
  Paris Peace Conference, 118–19, 126
  recommendations to the Royal
    Commission on Capital
    Punishment, 138n
  'Why Do I Write?', 123–5
  A World of Love, 125
Boym, Svetlana, 18n
Brauman, Rony, 47, 49
Brooks, Peter, 29, 90
Burke, Edmund, 13, 40–1, 124, 129
Bush, George, 16

Canetti, Elias, 144, 155
Camus, Albert, *La Chute*, 134
Caruth, Cathy, 70n
Cesarani, David, 50–1, 70n
Cheyette, Bryan, 80
Coates, John, 129
Cohen, Debra Rae, 45n
Conradi, Peter J., 152
Corcoran, Neil, 139n, 140n
cosmopolitanism, 13, 42, 101–2, 104,
  115, 159
  turned nightmare, 112
Cover, Robert, 58
crimes against humanity, 25, 26, 36,
  37, 39, 48, 50, 53, 67–8, 103

De Vabres, Henri Donnedieu, 25
Dean, Carolyn, 97n
Derrida, Jacques, 137n, 160
Dickens, Charles, 32, 132
Dietz, Mary, 7
Douglas, Lawrence, 28, 45n
Douzinas, Costas, 137n
Duncker, Patricia, 154, 163n

Eichmann Trial, Jerusalem, 3–4, 9, 10,
  13, 47–72, 73–6, 73–82, 84, 85–6,
  88–91, 96n, 103, 104, 149, 159
Ellmann, Maud, 136, 139n, 140n
Enright, D.J., 83

Felman, Shoshana, *The Juridical
  Unconscious*, 4, 6, 16, 55–8, 59,
  64

Flanner, Janet, 27, 37
Flaubert, Gustav, 128, 131
Freud, Sigmund, 'Thoughts for the
  Times on War and Death',
  113–15

Gellhorn, Martha
  'The Arabs of Palestine', 5, 10
  'Dachau', 17n
  'Eichmann and the Private
    Conscience', 4, 84
  Nuremberg Trial, 27, 31
  Paris Peace Conference, 119,
    137n
  A Stricken Field, 1–3, 12, 160
  support for Israel, 17n
Gilbert, G.M., 28–9
Goldberg, Amos, 30, 31
gothic, 27–8, 29
Green, Henry, *Party Going*, 135
Greene, Graham, 123
  The Ministry of Fear, 135

Halbwachs, Maurice, 82, 83
Hamacher, Werner, 116n
Hamburger, Michael, 80
Hartman, Geoffrey, 49
Hausner, Gideon, 48, 53, 66, 67, 78
Heidegger, Martin, Hannah Arendt, 7,
  8, 61, 71n, 116n
Hepburn, Allan, 119, 138n
Hobbes, Thomas, 155
Holocaust, the, 26, 33, 35, 41, 53–4,
  75, 77–8, 81, 85–6, 86, 89, 117n,
  123, 133, 140n, 143, 152
  Hannah Arendt, 6, 7, 31
  Auschwitz, 15
  Dachau, 17n, 164n
  Eva Trout, 133
  naming, 140n
  Nazi Concentration Camps, 28, 47,
    45
  Nazi crime, 2–3, 6, 7–8, 9–10, 31,
    38–9, 42, 48
  sidelined at Nuremberg, 24–6, 34,
    35, 37, 45n, 55
  Franz Steiner, 152, 160–2
  testimony to, 3–4, 6, 30, 31, 49,
    54–8, 63–5, 48–9

see also crimes against humanity;
Eichmann Trial; human rights;
justice; Nuremberg Trial;
testimony; suffering
Hoogland, Reneé C., 140n
human rights, 2, 11, 12, 38–41, 58–9,
108, 118, 120–2, 130, 132, 137n,
143, 145–6, 162, 163n
Hunt, Lynn, 127
Husserl, Edmund, 119

irony, 47–9, 57, 59, 65–8, 103, 104,
105–7, 159
Israel, 13, 40, 48, 53–4, 55, 68, 72n,
73–6, 77–9, 82, 87, 93–5, 96n,
144

James, Henry, 43n, 131
Jaspers, Karl, 2–3, 31, 48, 58, 59
Job, 85–9
Jones, Elwyn, 32
Joyce, James, *Ulysses*, 123, 131
judgement, 3, 5, 7, 8, 9, 48–51, 54,
58–9, 62–4, 66–8, 69n, 78, 82–3,
86, 91–2, 154–5
Judt, Tony, 118
justice, 1–3, 4, 5, 7, 14–15, 16, 48, 74,
86, 91, 159–60, 162
calculable, 4, 24, 160
failure at Nuremberg, 25, 35
incalculable, 5, 9, 24, 68, 160
political, 13, 14, 16, 40, 95
postwar blame game, 38
worldly, 162

Kant, Emanuel, 61, 63, 68, 84, 91
Ka-Zetnik, 8, 12, 34, 56–8, 64
*Salamandra: A Chronicle of a Jewish
Family in the Twentieth Century*,
56
Kazin, Alfred, 74, 75, 76
Kermode, Frank, 82, 87
Knight, Laura, 15–16
Koestler, Arthur, *The Scum of the
Earth*, 101–2
Kristeva, Julia, 63

Landau, Moshe, 51, 56–7
Laor, Yitzshak, 32

Laub, Dori, 70
law, the, 2–5, 8, 10, 14–17, 19n, 24–6,
29–30, 35, 37, 39, 41–2, 54, 57–8,
70n, 74, 102–4, 107, 109, 121–2,
123, 124–5, 130, 131–2, 138–9n,
143, 149, 156–7, 159–60
exploded by Nazi crime, 2–3, 48,
50
international, 24, 41, 48
Nazis and Nazi Collaborators
(Punishment) Law, 1950, 72n
and trauma, 3–5, 16, 55–9
see also human rights
Lemkin, Raphael, 25
love, 59, 110, 112, 134–5, 143, 145,
146, 148, 149, 150–1, 159
Lukács, Georg, 122
Luxemburg, Rosa, 15, 154

MacCarthy, Mary, 16, 45n, 69n,
71–2n
Macdonald Meidner, Olga, 163n
MacKay, Marina, 138n,
Maritan, Jacques, 122
Marx, Karl, 108
Meir, Golda, 94–5
melodrama, 9, 29–33, 43n, 90–2, 159
modernism, 119, 123, 128, 131
cosmopolitanism, 42, 101–2, 104
late, 12, 24, 28, 123, 128, 131
and the nation state, 10, 18n
Moretti, Franco, 124
Mulisch, Harry, 53
Murdoch, Iris, 12–13, 129, 136,
141–65
Elias Canetti, 144, 155
'Against Dryness', 148–9
The Flight from the Enchanter,
142–3, 144, 147, 150–9
Metaphysics as a Guide to Morals,
145
The Nice and the Good, 164n
J.P. Sartre, 148, 155
The Sea, the Sea, 164n
The Severed Head, 152
Sovereignty of the Good, 149
Franz Steiner, 144, 152, 153, 158–9
'The Sublime and the Good', 144,
157, 164n

Nakba, the, 75
Nelson, Deborah, 69n
Nuremberg Trial, 2–3, 15–16, 24–42, 48, 53, 91, 118, 123, 159, 160
Nussbaum, Martha, 164n

Owens, Patricia, 7, 18n, 70n

Palestine, 5, 10, 37, 38
Paris Peace Conference, 2, 118–19, 126
Pritchett, V.S., 123
psychoanalysis, 59, 112, 113–15, 135

Rancière, Jacques, 116n
Rau, Petra Utta, 140n
refugees, 11–12, 36–9, 101–15, 118–20, 132, 140n, 150–62; *see also* statelessness
Reichman, Ravit, *The Affective Life of Law*, 14, 30n, 44n, 44–5n
Rhys, Jean, *Good Morning Midnight*, 131
Ricoeur, Paul, 116n
Riley, Denise, 65–6, 105
Robinson Crusoe, 121
Rose, Gillian, 14–16
Rose, Jacqueline, 124
Rosen, Norma, *Touching Evil*, 97n
Rothberg, Michael, 18n, 117n
Royle, Nicholas and Andrew Bennett, *Elizabeth Bowen and the Dissolution of the Novel*, 137, 139n

Schlegel, Friedrich, *Lucinde*, 67
Scholem, Gershom, 30, 65, 73
Sebald, W.G., 66
Sentimental Education, 128, 131
Sereny, Gitta, 141–2, 143, 154, 160
Shawcross, Hartley Sir, 31
Shelley, P.B., 150, 164n
Sivan, Eyal, 47, 49
Slaughter, Joseph, 12, 121–2, 137n
Sontag, Susan, 49
The Specialist, 47, 49
speech
    Eichmann's efforts at, 51–3, 60, 62
    ironic, 9, 65–6, 105–6, 159

Jewish, 108
Nazi, 51–3, 62
political, 7, 8, 11, 109, 110, 113, 115, 159
refugee, 11–12, 104, 107, 110–11, 119
Spark, Muriel, 13, 73–95, 129
    Hannah Arendt, 73, 82
    The Comforters, 87
    'The Desegregation of Art', 88
    The Driver's Seat, 80, 88
    'The Gentile Jewess', 74, 78, 92–3
    Job, 86–9
    Kant, 84, 91
    The Mandelbaum Gate, 9, 30, 73–95, 96n
    melodrama, 9, 90–2
    The Only Problem, 87
    'When Israel Went to the Vatican', 93–5
Stannard, Martin, 74
statelessness, 9–13, 36–8, 101–15, 118–20, 141–9, 150–62; *see also* refugees
Steiner, Franz Baermann, 13, 144, 152, 158–9
    Holocaust, the, 152, 160–2
    Iris Murdoch, 144, 152, 153–2, 158–9
    suffering, 158–62
Stetz, Margaret, 44n
suffering, 7, 49, 69n, 85–9, 93, 145, 155–6, 158–62

Terada, Rei, 70n
testimony, 3–7, 15, 48
    Eichmann Trial, 3–7, 48–9, 54–8, 64, 78
    Zindel Grynzspan's, 64–5
    Ka-Zetnik's, 8, 12, 34, 56–8, 64
    Nuremberg Trial, 25, 31–2, 49
    traumatic, 3–7, 8, 9, 31, 55, 57–8, 159
thinking, 7, 49, 51, 59–63, 65
Thompson, Dorothy, *Refugees: Anarchy or Organization?*, 37
trauma theory, 5, 33, 150
Trilling, Lionel, 13, 26, 42

United Nations Relief and
Rehabilitation Administration
(UNRRA), 38, 141, 142, 162–3
Universal Declaration of Human Rights
(UDHR), 2, 12, 84, 121–3, 130,
136, 140n

Valliant-Couturier, Marie Claude, 25
Varnhagen, Rahel, 15, 106
Vietnam, 17
Villa, Dana, 7, 71n

Walkovitz, Rebecca, 105
Watt, Alan, 121
Watt, Ian, *The Rise of the Novel*, 121,
122, 127
Weber, Max, 149
Weil, Simone, 149
Weizmann, Chaim, 37
Wells, H.G., *The Rights of Man*, 122,
128
West, Rebecca, 10, 13
Hannah Arendt, 13, 45n
'The Birch Leaves Falling', 24
The Birds Fall Down, 43n
Black Lamb, Grey Falcon, 24, 26,
28, 34, 36, 40–1, 42
The Court and the Castle, 44n

'Extraordinary Exile', 26–8
The Fountain Overflows, 43n
'The Grandeur and Necessity of the
International Ideal', 42
'Greenhouse with Cyclamens I', 34–6
'Greenhouse with Cyclamens II',
38–9
'Greenhouse with Cyclamens III', 42
'Heil Hamm – II', 32
The Meaning of Treason, 29, 41
melodrama, 9, 29–33, 159
Nuremberg Trial, 9, 23–46, 159
'Opera in Greenville', 40
The Return of the Soldier, 43n
The Strange Necessity, 29, 42
The Train of Powder, 33
Whittaker, Ruth, 83
Wiesel, Eli, 85–6
witnessing, 4, 5, 24, 31, 45n, 48–9,
54–8, 78, 159; *see also* testimony
Woolf, Virginia, 101, 104, 116n, 127
Between the Acts, 128, 139n
Woomera refugees, 11–12

Yewdall Jermings, R., 102

Zertal, Idith, *Israel's Holocaust and the
Politics of Nationhood*, 66, 69n